THE
ANIMAL RIGHTS
MOVEMENT IN AMERICA

From Compassion to Respect

SOCIAL MOVEMENTS PAST AND PRESENT

Irwin T. Sanders, Editor

Abolitionism: A Revolutionary Movement
by Herbert Aptheker

The American Communist Movement: Storming Heaven Itself
by Harvey Klehr and John Earl Haynes

The American Peace Movement: Ideals and Activism
by Charles Chatfield

American Temperance Movements: Cycles of Reform
by Jack S. Blocker Jr.

*The Anti-Abortion Movement and the Rise of the Religious Right:
From Polite to Fiery Protest*
by Dallas A. Blanchard

The Antinuclear Movement, Updated Edition
by Jerome Price

The Charismatic Movement: Is There a New Pentecost?
by Margaret Poloma

The Children's Rights Movement: A History of Advocacy and Protection
by Joseph M. Hawes

Civil Rights: The 1960s Freedom Struggle
by Rhoda Lois Blumberg

The Conservative Movement, Revised Edition
by Paul Gottfried

The Consumer Movement: Guardians of the Marketplace
by Robert N. Mayer

Controversy and Coalition: The New Feminist Movement
by Myra Marx Ferree and Beth B. Hess

The Creationist Movement in Modern America
by Raymond A. Eve and Francis B. Harrold

*Family Planning and Population Control: The Challenges
of a Successful Movement*
by Kurt W. Back

The Health Movement: Promoting Fitness in America
by Michael S. Goldstein

THE
ANIMAL RIGHTS
MOVEMENT
IN AMERICA

From Compassion to Respect

Lawrence Finsen and Susan Finsen

Twayne Publishers • New York
Maxwell Macmillan Canada • Toronto
Maxwell Macmillan International • New York Oxford Singapore Sydney

179.3
F516
cop.1

The Animal Rights Movement in America: From Compassion to Respect
Lawrence Finsen and Susan Finsen

Twayne Publishers
Macmillan Publishing Company
866 Third Avenue
New York, New York 10022

Maxwell Macmillan Canada, Inc.
1200 Eglinton Avenue East
Suite 200
Don Mills, Ontario M3C 3N1

Library of Congress Cataloging-in-Publication Data

Finsen, Lawrence.
The animal rights movement in America / Lawrence Finsen and Susan Finsen.
    p.   cm.—(Social Movements Past and Present)
    Includes bibliographical references and index.
    ISBN 0–8057–3883–5   —   ISBN 0–8057–3884–3 (pbk.)
    1. Animal rights movement—United States—History.   I. Finsen.
    Susan. II. Title. III. Series.
HV4764.F57   1994
179'.3'0973—dc20   93–41223
                                                                          CIP

The paper used in this publication meets the minimum requirements of American
National Standard for Information Sciences—Permanence of Paper for Printed Library
Materials, ANSI Z39.48-1984. ∞™

10 9 8 7 6 5 4 3 2   (alk. paper)
10 9 8 7 6 5 4 3 2   (pbk.: alk. paper)

Printed and bound in the United States of America.

15.95
8/26/94
DS

To our favorite animal activist of all—our daughter, Thalia—who had to put up with the writing of this book, and then threw confetti when it was finished.

Contents

Illustrations

Preface

In the last decade animal rights has become a familiar concept to Americans, largely through media accounts of activists' efforts. Though the events most typically reported—demonstrations, raids on laboratories, civil disobedience—are dramatic, the historical and philosophical context from which this movement to liberate animals from human oppression emerged is not as well known to the general public. Our aim in this book is to supply that context by making clear the major ideas of the movement, the kinds of activism and organizations that have emerged, the response of those threatened by these ideas, and the challenges that the young movement faces in its second decade. In this book, we hope to provide basic information about the movement's ideas and history sufficient to enable unfamiliar readers to understand what motivates activists. At the same time, we hope that our analysis of philosophies and challenges facing the movement will be of use to those already familiar with the animal rights movement in furthering discussion of these important issues.

In order to set the stage for understanding the movement, one needs some background information. One may be tempted to think that the ideas of the animal rights movement are simply the old ideas of humaneness and compassion dressed up in new clothing. While compassionate concern for animals is clearly important in the new movement, there is a significant shift in thinking that must be understood in order to recognize the animal rights movement properly. In the first chapter, we outline this shift in the most general terms.

It is also very important that the reader be familiar with the most basic facts concerning contemporary uses of animals by our society. One of the characteristics of contemporary institutional uses of animals that should not pass unnoticed is that most of it is hidden from public view, though it is not such a secret any longer, thanks primarily to the pioneering efforts of a number of writers (Ruth Harrison, Jim Mason and Peter Singer, John Vyvyan and Richard Ryder, to name just a few). In the second part of the first chapter, we provide some background information for those who have not been exposed to these accounts. A full account would be subject for an entire book, however, so all we hope to do here is detail some examples of the major forms of animal use, especially as these relate to campaigns we discuss in later chapters.

After this initial introductory chapter, the book is divided into two major sections. The early chapters (2–5) tell the story of the animal rights movement—its history, the organizations, campaigns, and the activities of those who have opposed animal rights. In the second section (chapters 6–8) we discuss the ideas that have played an important role in developing an intellectual foundation for the movement—the philosophies, the ideas of other related movements, and the challenges that face this young movement as it comes of age.

It would be difficult to write about such a heated issue as animal rights with an entirely neutral stance, and we do not attempt to do so. We have not endeavored in this book to hide our position as advocates of animal rights, nor do we think that would be particularly intellectually honest or desirable. Nonetheless, we have strived for objectivity in our account of the movement and the philosophical ideas that ground it. After all, objectivity and even-handedness do not mean that an author must remain neutral on the subject, just as keeping an open mind does not mean leaving one's head empty of all ideas, hypotheses, or assumptions.

A note about terminology may be useful at the outset. The movement about which we write in this book is most widely known as the "animal rights movement." There are many, however, who refer to the goal of "animal liberation," and one could equally well speak of the "animal liberation movement." Throughout this book, we generally use the term *animal rights movement* for two reasons. For one, the term *animal liberation* may occasionally cause confusion, because of its association with the activities of the Animal Liberation Front (such as breaking into laboratories and literally "liberating" animals). Second, this is the term that has gained widest acceptance and recognition. Still, as we will see in later chapters, there are a variety of philosophical stances that emphasize the value of individual animals but do not consider moral rights central. Some even object to theories that place rights in this privileged position. Where the term would not distort, we use *animal rights*; in other contexts (e.g., Chapter 7, where we speak of ecofeminist views), we speak of animal liberation. Of course, as we use the expression in such contexts, it does not refer to any specific kind of activity (such as raiding laboratories), legal or otherwise, but to the goal of emancipating animals from speciesism.

We have many people to thank for their contributions to our ability to write this book, though, of course they might not all agree with what we have written. A number of people connected to the animal rights movement were kind enough to allow us to interview them for this book: Alex Pacheco, Chris DeRose, Alex Hershaft, Peter Link, Michael W. Fox, Cres Vellucci, and Henry Hutto. Though not all of the interviews are explicitly mentioned in the chapters that follow, all helped us form a picture of the diversity of approaches within the movement. The staff at the University of Redlands Armacost Library, especially Sandy Richie and Bill Kennedy, were enormously helpful in obtaining materials we needed, however obscure. Carol Chin, senior editor at Twayne, made a number of perceptive comments that helped us in the revision process; and Irwin Sanders, editor of the Social Movements: Past and Present series, was supportive and helpful throughout the writing process. His careful reading of our early drafts and insightful suggestions were of great value to us.

On a more personal level, we wish to thank a number of special people in our lives: our parents—Bill and Edna Mills and Irving and Gita Finsen—for all the support they have given us in our academic careers. Without that support, we could not have gotten here. Our daughter, Thalia, has been enormously patient through the years we worked on the manuscript. We cannot count the number of times we begged off going on some adventure "because we have to work on the book." And, finally, we owe a special thanks to Tom and Nancy Regan, who made our co-authoring anything at all possible by introducing us to each other.

Chapter One

Why Animal Rights?

In 1865, shortly after the end of the Civil War, the *New York Times* published an editorial pointing out that readers concerned with cruelty need not look to the reports of barbarity abroad but could find plenty to trouble themselves with right here in the United States. The editorial listed a number of concerns, all relating to the treatment of animals before slaughter, and concluded that "the manner in which . . . live cattle are dragged or driven to the shambles [slaughterhouse] is an outrage upon the natural feelings of anyone not utterly hardened by familiarity with cruelty in its most barbarous forms."[1]

One hundred and twenty-four years later a lone woman in St. Paul, Minnesota, began to visit a nearby stockyard early each morning, even though she worked late nights as a cocktail waitress. Becky Sanstedt had bought a video camera on credit so that she could video the "downers" at the United Stockyards in south St. Paul. "Downers" are animals who arrive at the stockyard too weak or injured to walk. The footage she made showed scenes amazingly similar to those complained of in that editorial of 1865: downed animals lying in holding pens for days, unable to reach food and water troughs; heavy chains dragging cows by hind legs, tearing them from sockets and breaking bones; others are being scooped off the ground with tractors. She also reported witnessing four hogs go for six days with no food or water in temperatures as low as –22° F and a live cow frozen to the ground.

After collecting over 40 hours of video documentation, Sanstedt publicized her findings. By May of 1991, United Stockyards had been

1

Downed cow dying slowly at OK stockyard as calf looks on. *Courtesy Farm Sanctuary*

forced to announce a new policy regarding downed animals: livestock producers would no longer receive money for them but would be charged a rendering fee, since the animals were to be immediately euthanized. The policy applied not only to the south St. Paul stockyard but to the company's other six stockyards as well.[2]

Though some conditions at stockyards had not changed in over 100 years, 1989 was quite different from 1865. At the time of that *New York Times* editorial, no organized movement to protect animals existed; the first American organization, the American Society for the Prevention of Cruelty to Animals (ASPCA) was not founded until the next year, and very few voices were raised before that to defend animals (especially those destined to be eaten) against harsh treatment. By the time Becky Sanstedt visited the stockyard, a movement to defend animals had taken form, activists had learned how to gain access to mass media and had made "animal rights" a familiar concept, if not yet a fact for animals. Indeed, Sanstedt's first trip to the stockyard was prompted by an animal rights pamphlet about downed cattle and a television show about stockyard practices. And after she revealed her videotapes, a New York animal rights organization, Farm Sanctuary, paid off her camera loan and hired her as a staff investigator. Though she had begun alone, she was soon working with an organization dedicated to eliminating just the sort of thing Becky had witnessed.

In the 120 years between the founding of the ASPCA and Becky Sanstedt's videotapings much had happened. A movement to protect animals against cruelty emerged in the late nineteenth century, the "humane movement." By the late 1970s a newly revitalized movement—the animal rights movement—was emerging, in some ways continuous with the earlier humane movement but also differing sharply from it. New organizations, philosophies, campaigns, and tactics were in evidence as the animal rights movement arose.

In this chapter we discuss the forces that gave rise to a newly shaped mass movement to defend animals in the 1970s and 1980s. In doing so, we introduce the reader to the ideas of the modern movement in the most general sense and discuss these in more detail in later chapters. We also provide a brief look at the treatment of animals in our society, for the awareness of the ways in which animals are treated today has been a crucial element in the transformation of humane concern to animal rights activism. Without this background information, it is impossible to understand why activists have been willing to take the ideas of the movement so seriously.

The Idea of Animal Rights

Prior to the emergence of the current animal rights movement, the aims of eliminating cruelty and encouraging a more compassionate attitude toward animals dominated the thinking of those who gave any thought at all to the treatment of animals in America. While at first blush the animal liberationist may seem to be advocating the same things (albeit more loudly than ever before), there are significant differences between the humane movement and the animal rights movement. The humane movement promoted kindness and the elimination of cruelty without challenging the assumption of human superiority or the institutions that reflect that assumption. The animal rights movement, on the other hand, does not seek humane reforms but challenges the assumption of human superiority and demands abolition of institutions it considers exploitive. Rather than asking for a greater (and optional) charity toward animals, the animal rights movement demands justice, equality, fairness, and rights.

It would be a mistake to conclude, however, that the sentiments of kindness and compassion for animals have simply been replaced by rational theorizing. The call for justice and rights, for respecting the dignity of animals, engages the moral imagination and sentiments of people just as much as does a call for kindness. If it did not, it would be hard to understand the fact that many people have been stimulated to act to change the world in light of these theories—a point emphasized by David Hume over 200 years ago.[3] Rather than replace activists' sentiments, the role of the new theories of animal rights and liberation has been to provide an intellectual justification for what activists are doing and to clarify the goals of that activism.

It is no longer so easy to dismiss pro-animal sentiment as simply personal, misplaced passion in today's social climate, which sees issues about animals as serious, significant moral questions. Animal liberation has earned a place both in the scholarship of moral philosophers and in the university ethics curriculum itself (thanks in large part to the work of Tom Regan and Peter Singer), and this fact represents a major difference between the older humane and the animal rights movement. Prior to the mid-1970s there were few scholarly discussions of the ethics of our treatment of animals, and university-level classes touching on ethics included little if any discussion of such issues as vivisection, consumption of animals for food, hunting and trapping, or use of animals in various forms of entertainment (rodeos, bullfights, racing, etc.).

A partial explanation of this tendency might be found in the fact that American ethicists were only emerging in the 1960s from the influential view that what philosophers could contribute to the study of ethics was not at the normative level, only at the level of metaethics. According to this view, the central questions for philosophical ethics were not the concrete questions of what is right or wrong, good or evil, but rather questions such as those about the meaning of ethical terms and the possibility of ethical knowledge. In the 1960s philosophical ethicists emerged from this positivistic freeze to concern themselves with what they might say more concretely about such issues as the destruction of the environment, peace, nuclear arms, racism, sexism, abortion and euthanasia. While such a thaw might help explain the emergence of concern for animals as a philosophical issue, this cannot be the whole story, for this concern emerged later than many other issues. Even specialized classes in such areas as medical ethics in the early 1970s would standardly touch on the use of human subjects in medical research but ignore the question of using animals. The issues were simply invisible to philosophers, as they had been to the general public. But they could not long remain invisible, for a number of reasons.

For one thing, the extent of animal usage has increased tremendously in this century. With the victory of proponents of vivisection over the nineteenth century antivivisectionist movement, animals became an ever more important part of the research paradigm in many areas of science. The growing importance of animal experimentation to the institution of science is reflected in the increasing numbers of animals used since the nineteenth century. Currently, the number of animals used in the U.S. has increased to upwards of 60 million per year.

Farming methods have also changed drastically in the period following World War II, from small diverse farms in which animals roamed outdoors to current intensive farming operations. The transformation in scale has vastly changed the very institution of animal agriculture, as well as increased the numbers of animals consumed each year. At the same time, animal agriculture has come to be conducted behind closed doors, removed from the public eye. Today, billions of farm animals are raised indoors in conditions largely unknown to the general public.

As animal usage has grown in scale, it has been transformed in significant ways (some examples of which we provide later in this chapter). In the most general terms, practices that have come in for criticism today seem to have become part of the ordinary way of doing business—they have become accepted methods within the institution. Whereas cruel treatment by farmers in the past might have been viewed reasonably as exceptional behavior having little to do with proper farming practices, today's intensive farming methods, encouraged by government and agricultural researchers, have led to "normal" practices critics find objectionable.

Ironically, this expanding animal usage during the postwar years was accompanied by serious challenges to its philosophical underpinnings, though the challenges emerged from sources quite independent of concern for animals. The idea that humans are fundamentally different from and superior to animals does not square well with modern evolutionary theory, which posits no such hierarchies or categorical differences. Dualism, which supposes that the mind and body are fundamentally distinct and separate substances, had been historically influential in separating humans from animals, for, according to most proponents of this view, it is only humans who have an immaterial mind or soul, and it is this that accounts for human superiority. But both philosophers and scientists have discredited this view as philosophically indefensible and unscientific. As the dualistic worldview has appeared less and less tenable, the assumed superiority of the human species also had to come into question, for dualism lies at the foundation of the belief in human superiority. Once dualism came into question, it was not long before thinkers realized that differences between humans and animals can no longer be described as resting on our unique possession of immortal souls but rather amount at most to differences of degree. The rejection of dualism has thus undermined one central justification for using animals as people do today.

The loss of confidence in homocentric ethics together with the vast and institutionalized usages of animals created a climate in which philosophers such as Peter Singer and Tom Regan could forcefully raise the question of what place animals should have in an enlightened morality. Aware of the extensive usage of animals, they and others raised challenges from a variety of intellectual footings to what they came to see as exploitation of animals. While the activists who now largely make up the movement are no more or less intellectuals than those in any other movement, the animal rights movement seems somewhat distinct in being initially animated by serious consideration of ideas by scholars.

Animal Industries Today: An Overview

Animal Agriculture.   Agricultural uses of animals constitute the most extensive uses of animals in this country today. Over 5 billion animals are consumed by Americans each year. While the mere fact of slaughtering animals—depriving them prematurely of their lives—is objectionable according to animal rights philosophies, many other objections have been raised to modern animal farming that do not depend on recognizing that any animal has a right to life. Most of the animal foods eaten today in this country are the products of agricultural systems developed earlier this century, known as "intensive farming systems"—or, more pejoratively, "factory farming." The key to intensive farming is to increase the density and number of animals housed together, to mechanize as many processes as possible (feeding, watering, climate control), and thereby to decrease labor costs. One person may literally care for tens of thousands of animals in an intensive system. Such "intensification" means that farmers cannot attend to the health of individual animals—individual animals are dispensable if a large enough number survive—and animals are exposed to less and less natural conditions, greater amounts of stress, and a variety of problems imposed by the intensive conditions, which farmers deal with by further manipulation of the animals. Critics of intensive farming have pointed to battery cages, veal crates, and sow farrowing systems as examples of what they find most objectionable.[4]

Veal is the tender, pale flesh of young calves, typically the male offspring of dairy cows. Though the veal industry is not very large compared with beef, poultry, or pork production, it has been at the forefront of discussions of the ethics of farming practices. In the nineteenth century calves were sometimes bled a number of times before slaughter in the belief that this produced paler meat. More typically, however, up until the introduction of modern veal systems in the 1950s in Holland, veal calves were slaughtered before they were weaned. But as calves are weaned at just a few weeks, the weight at slaughter was only about 90 pounds, not a sufficient weight to make much profit. Dutch vealers discovered that calves could be fattened for as much as 20 weeks (weighing close to 400 pounds) without losing the tenderness and paleness of the flesh if certain sacrifices were made.

In modern veal production calves are taken from their mothers when they are about one day of age, placed in highly restricted conditions, and not allowed to graze or have physical contact with other cows. As the tenderness of veal is produced by lack of muscular development, calves are restricted from any exercise that would toughen their muscles, including walking and grazing. Thus, calves are taken shortly after birth and placed in "veal crates"—wooden stalls not much larger than the calf will grow to be in its four to five months. While calves are still small enough to turn, they are kept tethered to prevent even this much exercise. A typical veal crate in the United States measures 22 inches by 52 inches.

The restricted environment in which veal calves are placed has been a source of much criticism. A scientific group headed by Professor John Webster of the animal husbandry unit of the University of Bristol said in their report of British practices:

Veal calves in crates 750 mm [30 in] wide cannot, of course, lie flat with their legs extended. . . . Calves may lie like this when they feel warm and wish to lose heat. . . . Well-grown veal calves at air temperatures above 20 degrees C

Veal calves spend their lives confined in small (22 by 54 in.) crates, which are designed to prevent movement. *Photo by Dale Smith*

[68°F] may be uncomfortably hot. Denying them the opportunity to adopt a position designed to maximise heat loss only makes things worse. . . . Veal calves in boxes over the age of 10 weeks were unable to adopt a normal sleeping position with their heads tucked into their sides. We conclude that denying veal calves the opportunity to adopt a normal sleeping posture is a significant insult to welfare. To overcome this, the crates would need to be at least 900 mm [36 in.] wide. (Quoted in Singer 1990, 131)

In addition, critics point out that the narrow stalls prevent calves from grooming themselves, which they have a strong urge to do because they shed their coats and suffer from parasites. The hard floors without bedding are rough on their knees, and the slats (for ease of washing away manure) are difficult and uncomfortable for animals with hooves.

The consumer's preference for pale flesh has led to another criticism of veal systems. The paleness of veal does not contribute to its nutritional value as human food, but in fact results from the calf being anemic. To achieve this effect, calves are not allowed access to any source of iron—grass, straw bedding, even iron fittings in the stall that they might lick. They live entirely on an iron-deficient liquid diet based on milk powder, vitamins, minerals and growth-promoting drugs.

Calves kept in veal crates are said to live an exceedingly boring and frustrating life—beyond drinking their liquid food, there is nothing that they are able to do except stand or lie, and they cannot do either of these things very comfortably. Veal producers often respond to the restlessness of bored calves by keeping the calves in the dark as much as 22 hours per day. In such extreme conditions, a mortality rate of between 10 percent and 15 percent before 15 weeks is not uncommon (Singer 1990, 135).

In modern egg farms the egg layers are housed in cages known as battery cages because they constitute a series of connected units, or a "battery." The cages allow greater numbers of birds to be housed, fed, watered and kept warm within one building. Cages are typically arranged in tiers, with food and water troughs fed from a central source. The cages have sloping wire floors: sloping so that eggs will roll toward the front for easy removal, wire so that excrement will fall through eliminating the need to clean individual cages. At the same time, the sloping wire floor is difficult for birds to stand on comfortably—often damaging hens' feet, which without solid ground to wear down their claws may even grow so long as to become enmeshed in the wire.

Laying hens spend their lives crushed together in small cages. *Courtesy People for the Ethical Treatment of Animals*

A standard size for a cage holding up to five chickens is 12 by 20 inches, which means an individual hen will have somewhere between 48 and 240 square inches, depending on how many birds are kept to a cage. The higher figure is less than the 250 square inches that one study showed a typical hen requires to remain at rest. Easily turning around requires 662 square inches. Chickens kept in conditions this crowded cannot walk around, scratch the ground, dustbathe, build nests, or stretch their wings. In some facilities, chickens are crushed against each other and immobilized, unable to do anything other than eat and lay eggs.

Defenders of battery cages sometimes maintain that laying chickens have had these instincts bred out of them. Studies show, however, that hens revert to behavior typical of uncaged chickens very rapidly. One study showed that hens will work as hard to get to nests as they do to reach food after being deprived of it for 24 hours. In another study, hens who had been kept in cages for the first six months of their lives were released: within the first 10 minutes, half had already flapped their wings, and they also took quickly to dustbathing (which helps maintain feather quality).

In the old-fashioned farmyard, chickens establish a "pecking order," which enables them to know which chickens to defer to and which must defer to them. By this hierarchical social interaction, more serious harm to chickens is avoided. But animals kept in such crowded conditions as the battery cages frequently become more aggressive than they would be otherwise. At the same time, those who are the victims of their attacks have no escape: they are imprisoned together in a small cage for their entire lives. Such aggression can hurt farmers' profits, so they must prevent it. Two innovations are used for this purpose: low lighting levels (chickens are less active in lower light) and "debeaking." Debeaking is widely used today—it is common for egg-laying hens to go through this process twice in their lives. The end of the chick's beak is cut off with a hot blade. Defenders of the practice point out that the cutting occurs quite quickly (an experienced worker can debeak about 15 birds per minute), and the birds recover quickly. Critics, however, point out that with such quick work, mistakes are made. Blades can be too hot or too cool, and technicians can miss and cut too much off. But even when the procedure is done properly, it is painful, as the British government committee headed by the zoologist F. W. Rogers Brambell found in the mid-1960s: "Between the horn and the bone is a thin layer of highly sensitive soft tissue, resembling the 'quick' of the human nail. The hot knife used in debeaking cuts through this complex of horn, bone and sensitive tissue, causing severe pain" (quoted in Singer 1990, 101–102).

Another source of criticism of battery operations concerns the fate of male chicks. Newly hatched chicks are sorted, and males—which have no commercial value—are discarded. They are either gassed, stuffed into plastic bags where they suffocate under the weight of other chicks, or simply ground up (still alive) and turned into feed for the female chicks. Approximately 160 million chicks die in these ways each year in the United States.

Chickens have a natural lifespan of upwards of seven years. In egg operations they are only allowed to live for one to two years, as they lay fewer eggs after this. But even within that short span, the conditions under which battery hens are raised make mortality rates very high: "It is commonplace for an egg farm to lose between 10 and 15 percent of its hens in one year, many of them clearly dying of stress from overcrowding and related problems" (Singer 1990, 117).

Methods of pig farming have also undergone significant intensification in recent decades, leading to confinement systems that make it impossible for them to perform much of their natural behavior. When given the opportunity, pigs form stable social groups, build communal nests, use dunging areas at a distance from their nests, and lead an active life rooting in woodlands. When ready to give birth, sows build their own separate nests, which they line with grass and twigs. They live there for a little more than a week, then return to the communal nest with their newborn piglets.

In intensive farms, however, most of these activities are impossible. Pigs are confined without bedding materials (which would complicate cleaning) and without much in the way of stimulation. For animals as intelligent as pigs, a highly restricted environment can clearly cause boredom. Even pig farmers occasionally call attention to this—as did one who wrote to a farming magazine when he discovered how much his pigs played when given a novel and highly stimulating environment (a deserted farmhouse in which they ran up and down the stairs): "Our stock need variety of surroundings. . . . Gadgets of different make, shape and size should be provided. . . . Like human beings, they dislike monotony and boredom" (quoted in Singer 1990, 120).

A number of studies have confirmed that pigs can suffer from stress when bored. One study cited by Singer found that pigs kept in barren environments become so bored that when given a choice

12

Pregnant sows repeatedly gnaw at the bars of the stalls in which they are confined. *Courtesy People for the Ethical Treatment of Animals*

between food and an earth-filled trough, they will root around in the trough before eating (Singer 1990, 120–21). But farmers have known this all along, because pigs—like other animals—when overcrowded and understimulated are likely to engage in certain "vices," such as fighting and tail-biting. The U.S. Department of Agriculture (USDA) recommends to farmers the standard solution of "tail docking"—cutting off the pigs' tails "1/4 to 1/2 in from the body with side-cutting pliers or another blunt instrument," though they make no mention of using anesthesia or trying to eliminate the causes of these vices (Singer 1990, 121). Stress can even kill pigs, and apparently does so more often in confinement systems. "Porcine stress syndrome," as it is called, is a condition in which animals experience "extreme stress . . . rigidity, blotchy skin, panting, anxiety, and often—sudden death" (from *Farm Journal*, as quoted in Singer 1990, 122).

But the most extreme aspect of pig farming is the confinement of sows, which live the most restricted lives of all pigs. For 10 months of every year a pregnant or nursing sow cannot turn around. While pregnant, she will be placed in a stall just larger than she is, where she will be confined—possibly also tethered—for two or three months. Then she will be moved to a "farrowing pen" to give birth and nurse the piglets. The farrowing pen is designed to confine her but allow the piglets to escape under bars to a connected chamber, thus preventing her from rolling onto them. When first placed in farrowing stalls, the pregnant sows often spend hours in violent attempts to escape. In 1988 a government advisory body in Great Britain, the Farm Animal Welfare Council, saw the problem of sow confinement as so serious that they recommended urgent legislation to prevent further installation of stall and tether systems. It was also revealed by a study published in 1988 that sows and boars kept for breeding (rather than being fattened for slaughter) were persistently underfed. After feeding they showed as much readiness to press levers to receive additional food as before feeding, and the reason wasn't hard to find: pigs fed the amounts recommended by the Agricultural Research Council in Great Britain get only 60 percent of what they would eat if food were freely available to them (Singer 1990, 128–29).

Furs: Trapping and Ranching.   Furs are the skins of animals obtained in one of two ways. Either the animals are trapped in the wild, or they are raised on "fur ranches." Ultimately, advocates of animal rights find both equally objectionable in imposing immense suffering and depriving animals of their lives, but there are some issues that pertain only to one or the other of these methods. In addition, the public has been alerted to the issues surrounding trapping to a greater extent than to ranching, so it is useful to speak about each in turn.

The objections to trapping, especially the notorious "steel-jaw leghold traps," are probably best known to the public. There are a number of different kinds of traps—leghold, snare, connibear, box, and cage traps are some of the main kinds. Banned in some 75 countries, the leghold traps are most commonly used in this country, though their use seems to be declining in response to the negative press they have received. Leghold traps comprised 71 percent of the traps used in the United States in 1987, as opposed to 89 percent in 1974. Leghold traps slam closed on an animal's limb (or possibly the neck) with a powerful grip—the force supplied by a strong spring released when the animal steps on a trigger. The snares and connibear traps are supposedly more humane, because they are designed to kill the animal quickly, but critics point out that they are only more humane if the animal enters the trap in just the right way—otherwise they may grip the animal in the midsection and cause slow suffocation, or grab a limb and function as a leghold trap. Trappers are also using leghold traps that are presumably more humane because they have a hard rubber lining added—these appear to cut into flesh less, and also to damage pelts less than the older steel-jaw legholds. But tests by Woodstream, a major trap manufacturer, showed that animals caught in the padded traps still suffer bone fractures, dislocated joints and severed muscles.[5]

Defenders of trapping maintain that animals caught in such traps do not suffer, but animal advocates charge that this is mere propaganda. Animals caught in traps may die of shock, exposure, starvation, thirst, predation, or drowning (in water-set traps), and they will sometimes even gnaw or twist off their own limb in their attempt to escape. If still alive when the trapper returns to inspect the trap, they are likely to meet their death by being clubbed or stomped to death, since these are the methods of killing that will not damage the pelt, and are recommended by industry and the Fish and Game departments. Traps are also indiscriminate—there is no guarantee that only the targeted species will be caught. Trappers refer to the many animals inadvertently trapped as "trash" animals, since they have no economic value. Such animals comprise over half those caught in traps, and include dogs, cats, birds, and endangered species such as eagles.[6]

Defenders of trapping maintain that trapping contributes to sound wildlife conservation, by helping to regulate populations that would otherwise grow out of control, resulting in death by disease or starvation for the animals. Opponents respond that natural mechanisms such as disease and starvation, while unfortunate, help keep a population strong, because healthy animals that survive these challenges are the ones that go on to reproduce. Trapping, they maintain, does not promote genuine conservation because it is utterly indiscriminate, failing to target the weaker animals or overpopulated species. It is therefore disruptive of the species' overall ability to survive.

Though there are some limitations in law concerning trapping, they are very difficult to enforce, and critics maintain that little effort or resources go into doing so. About a dozen states have banned traps that have teeth, as these clearly add to the pain suffered while an animal is struggling in a trap. The laws of states that do regulate trapping presuppose trapping is acceptable and aim only to minimize the suffering of trapped animals. They do this primarily by setting maximum allowable periods during which traps may be left unchecked. The strongest requirement is 12 hours (Montana); 25 states require traps be checked every 24 hours, three call for a 36-hour maximum, three set a 48-hour maximum, and another three only require traps be checked every 72 hours. Ten states have no limit on how long a trap may remain unchecked.[7]

Many fur coats today carry labels such as "ranch raised" or "ranch mink," referring to the fact that they come from animals raised on fur ranches rather than trapped in the wild. Clearly, marketers believe that consumers who might object to trapping will not find ranch-raised furs objectionable, and to the extent that Americans are much less aware of conditions on fur ranches, this belief appears to be correct. Consequently, a growing number of fur animals are raised on ranches, where conditions are typically much like those on "factory farms." As Wim J. De Kok of the World Society for the Protection of Animals put it, "Fur ranches look the same everywhere in the world. They can be described as long rows of wire mesh cages under a shed. . . . The standard measures for mink cages are 28"x10"x16". . . made of wire netting, which makes it difficult for the animals to walk on, especially the younger ones.[8] De Kok points out that since fur-bearing animals have only been bred in captivity for about 100 years, they are not truly domesticated, leading them to suffer even more intensely under the conditions of restrictive confinement typical of these farms:

Mink live along the wooded banks of small streams, rivers, marshes and lakes. They are excellent swimmers and spend a large part of their life in the water. Since they are nocturnal animals, they are rarely visible, often only footprints indicate their presence. They cover enormous distances. The 4 to 6 pups are born in spring and stay with their mother until fall comes around, after which they go their own way. Minks are very agile creatures. They love running, swimming, playing, climbing on things, and they are very inquisitive. But the 40 million mink on the world's fur ranches can only dream of a life like that. (De Kok 1989, 21–22)

Stress leads to self-mutilating behavior (e.g., tail- and skin-biting, gnawing at themselves) as well as stereotyped behavior (pacing endlessly and other purposeless, repetitive activity). In the heat of summer, the animals try to cool themselves by repeatedly dipping their paws in their small watering bowls.

Ranch-raised animals are not protected by the laws that protect intensive-farmed animals in this country: no federal laws regulate the treatment of animals on fur farms, no inspections are mandated, and the killing of fur-bearing animals is not regulated under the federal Humane Slaughter Act (which does regulate the killing of food animals).[9]

As is the case with trapped animals, animals ranched for their furs are killed in ways that will not harm the value of the pelt. Typical methods include gas, poison, anal electrocution, neck snapping, and decompression. All of these methods are painful—none employ anesthesia, and most are forbidden by law for other animals (e.g., under the Humane Slaughter Act and various state laws covering methods dogs and cats in shelters may be "euthanized").[10]

Experimentation.   Clearly, one of the most hotly contested uses to which animals are put is in scientific research and related kinds of laboratory procedures. People unfamiliar with the details of the history and law here sometimes assume that our government oversees research to ensure that it is conducted humanely. As we discuss in the next chapter, the federal law that relates to laboratory animals was never intended to restrict the conduct of animal research. The Federal Animal Welfare Act regulates purchase, handling, shipping, housing, killing, and disposal of laboratory animals but does not regulate what may be done to animals during the course of experimentation.

Estimates of the number of animals used each year in the United States are at best approximations, since no government agency has reliable figures, and for many uses of animals no report is required. Congress's Office of Technology Assessment (OTA) notes that estimates from different sources range from 10 to 100 million.[11] Peter Singer argues that 60 million is a conservative guess, given the sales of animals from suppliers. One of the major laboratory animal breeders, Charles River Breeding labs, alone produces over 22 million animals annually (Singer 1990, 37). Andrew Rowan estimated use at 71 million per year in 1984.[12] After considering the various estimates, the OTA settled on a much lower range between 17 and 22 million (OTA 1988, 43, 64). Typically, the higher estimates are offered by critics of research, while supporters tend to find less animal use. But, more significantly, the variability in estimates of numbers of animals used is a symptom of the overall lack of regulation of the industry of animal research. Until recently, rats, mice, and farm animals were exempt from regulation under the Federal Animal Welfare Act, and funds for enforcement of the act are notoriously lacking. As the OTA analysis points out, the very forms used to report uses of animals to the appropriate government agency are unreliable because they are confusing and may include redundancies and omissions. One can safely conclude that animal experimentation in the United States annually consumes many millions of animals. Compared with other uses of animals (except agriculture, which numbers in the billions consumed each year), this is a significant figure.

A tremendous variety of things happen to the animals used in U.S. laboratories each year, and it is impossible to quantify accurately the types and frequency with which various procedures are performed. The uses to which animals are put in the broad category of research or vivisection can be subdivided into several categories, only some of which qualify as scientific experimentation. Animals are used in household product and cosmetic testing, classroom dissection and as teaching aids, in various kinds of military research, in psychological research, in various kinds of "basic" research and medical research. Only the latter three categories can be accurately classified as scientific research.

There are different kinds of product tests that use animals. Perhaps the best known are the "Draize" and the "LD50." In the Draize (in use since 1944, and named after its inventor) a product is tested for irritancy by placing it in the eyes of rabbits (who have usually been immobilized) and then charting the progressive deterioration of the eyes over three to four days. The irritancy of a prospective product is shown by comparing the degree of deterioration of the eye after a certain number of hours with the known degree of deterioration (as shown in slides provided by the U.S. Consumer Products Safety Commission) for such substances as lye, ammonia, and oven cleaner.

The LD50 is a test of "acute toxicity"—it is used to identify substances that have a dramatic poisonous effect in a short time. In use since 1927, the test is conducted by forcing a group of animals—dogs, cats, rodents, and occasionally even primates—to ingest the substance in question in increasingly large doses until the dosage at which 50 percent of the test animals die is determined ("LD50" stands for "lethal dose 50 percent"). Under such circumstances, animals do not simply die but suffer enormously beforehand.[13] In product safety testing it is

18

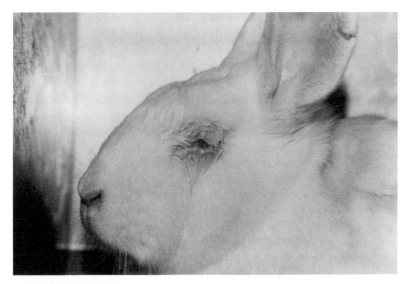

A Draize eye test for a Benetton product. After People for the Ethical Treatment of Animals exposed Biosearch Lab, Benetton stopped all tests on animals. *Courtesy People for the Ethical Treatment of Animals*

standard practice to withhold analgesics or anesthesia, in case these might interfere with the effects one is attempting to observe.

Both of these tests have been widely regarded for years as essentially worthless in protecting consumers. In the case of the LD50, the test gives no insight into the mechanisms or sites of toxicity, and thus no indication of appropriate treatments should the substance be improperly ingested. As Rollin has put it, "the LD50 typically tells mice what dose of a chemical they need in order to commit suicide."[14] Companies continue to perform the tests in the hopes that this will protect them in cases where consumers are injured by a product and sue the company. In the case of the Draize test, the eye of the rabbit is significantly different from the human eye, making extrapolation of results questionable. Neither of the tests provides information about long-range effects or interactive effects of substances with other products or substances.

It is common in classes in psychology, neurophysiology, and biology for students to be given "hands-on" experience.[15] In some cases of classroom dissection, the animals are already dead when they reach the student, and it might be thought that they were thus supplied to schools without suffering. Recent revelations and USDA indictments of the major supply houses (Carolina Biological Supply and Wards Biological) furnishing these carcasses reveal that this is not true. Animals at Carolina Biological are often stolen pets who are transported in tiny cages and kept in substandard living conditions in extremes of heat, according to People for the Ethical Treatment of Animals. They have charged that animals are sometimes still living when they are stapled to boards and embalmed, a highly painful procedure.[16]

Classroom experiments with live animals sometimes involve surgery, such as the implantation of electrodes in the hypothalamic region of the brains of rats, exposure to painful stimuli (e.g., experimentation with electric shock), or food deprivation. Lack of skill on the part of students compounds the suffering of animals in such classroom contexts.

Animals have been used to test military weapons since before World War I, and tests of explosives, chemical weapons, and radiation studies continue to be conducted on tens of thousands of animals annually. Six months after the bombing of Hiroshima and Nagasaki, a Navy assault ship was converted into a nuclear "ark" in which 4,000 animals were transported to Bikini atoll and subjected at close range to radiation from an atomic bomb blast equivalent to 20,000 tons of dynamite. Nearly a quarter of them were killed outright, and two months later, the half remaining alive were returned to Washington for studies of radiation poisoning. Military spokespersons claimed they suffered "no real pain," and most went untreated.[17]

In 1967 the Atomic Energy Commission acknowledged the use of 5 million animals annually in research on "radiation originating from peaceful uses of atomic energy." This research included whole body radiation, injection of plutonium into the skin of miniature swine, and inhalation of radioactive dust by rats (*Agenda*, June 1987, 48). To estimate performance levels of irradiated troops, the Armed Forces Radiobiology Research Institute radiated monkeys to "determine levels at which they could no longer work and at which they would die."

The popular film *Project X* (1987) made many Americans aware that radiation research on animals is an ongoing military activity. The film is a dramatization of actual research on chimpanzees, who are trained to operate a flight simulator using extensive aversive conditioning (i.e., electric shock) and are then irradiated. They are observed to determine for how long and at what doses of radiation they can continue to perform their tasks. Former military researcher Donald Barnes resigned in protest of the pointlessness of this research, which had been conducted for years on hundreds of chimpanzees. He has subsequently become an outspoken supporter of the animal rights movement (Singer 1990, 28).

Thousands of goats and pigs are shot yearly in Department of Defense "wound laboratories" around the country. The animals are restrained and shot with high powered military weapons, so that military physicians can study their wounds and learn how to treat them. When People for the Ethical Treatment of Animals (PETA) learned in 1982 that such a wound laboratory about to open in Bethesda, Maryland, planned to shoot dogs, they mounted a campaign of protest that succeeded in preventing the lab's opening. But public support for pigs and goats is not as strong, and PETA was not able to prevent the wounding of these less popular animals.

A vast range of psychological research is conducted on animals, much of it highly aversive. Infant rhesus monkeys have been removed from their mothers and raised in isolation to study the effects of maternal deprivation.[18] Millions of rats, dogs, cats, and other species have been shocked and deprived of food, water, sleep, and normal amounts of stimulation; others have been given inescapable shocks to study "learned helplessness," have been drowned in water chambers, immobilized in stereotaxic devices and restraining chairs, pitted in fights against each other in studies of aggression, and taught to shock each other to avoid receiving shock themselves.[19]

As with psychological research, there is such a vast range of research conducted that it is impossible to describe it in any detail. Basic research simply means any research meant to examine a scientific hypothesis without regard to practical applications. Thus, such research could involve anything from neural mapping to ethological observation.

To induce the injuries and illnesses that medical researchers wish to study, animals are burned; exposed to carcinogens; forced to smoke, drink alcohol, and take various drugs; injected with various diseases; and have various of their organs removed, their bones broken, and their spinal chords severed. They have electrodes implanted in their brains; they are blinded and subjected to high-impact head injuries. They even have had their heads transplanted (by Dr. Robert White of Case Western Reserve University in Cleveland). In recent years they have been genetically altered to carry debilitating diseases, such as diabetes and arthritis.

A few salient features of invasive medical research with animals should be noted. First, while animals have served as subjects in pain research for decades, attention to animal pain has, paradoxically, only a recent history, as Bernard Rollin has detailed.[20] The administration of postoperative analgesics to diminish pain was, until quite recently, virtually unheard of, and anesthesia during surgery has been regarded as a form of chemical restraint, rather than as relief for pain (117). Postoperative animals may be left without veterinary attention over weekends, and many cases of animals who have bled to death in their cages postoperatively have been documented, from the time of the first investigations by humane societies to the present (Rowan 1984, 54). Animals may be kept for months or even years in small cages in social isolation if they are part of long-term studies. Dogs in long-term studies are surgically debarked so that they cannot howl and create a disturbance, and the National Institutes of Health (which funds and provides guidelines for most animal research in the United States) has resisted attempts to strengthen the Federal Animal Welfare Act to require exercise for dogs and an enriched environment for primates.

Of course, not all research on animals involves pain, since some of it is noninvasive, and some involves killing the animal before it recovers from anesthesia. Given the lack of regulation and the massive amount of research done in the United States, it is impossible to determine the percentage of research involving acute or prolonged discomfort. Use of curare (a paralytic that does not block pain) as a surgical restraint is no longer accepted, and researchers are not allowed to pass animals along after invasive experiments to be used in further invasive research; they must be destroyed. Thus, in some ways the conditions of laboratory animals have improved in recent years. In the wake of revelations and incriminating videotapes researchers are more vigilant about keeping cages cleaned and vivariums in decent condition. A decade ago prominent researchers could maintain that use of animals posed no moral problems (Singer 1990, 75); in light of the attention the animal rights movement has brought to the issue, such a statement would be unthinkable in 1993.

Why has an animal rights movement emerged in the past decade? No doubt there are many social forces at work here, but surely prominent among them is simply the relevation of the facts of animal suffering on such a massive scale. That such suffering is endorsed as normal practice by a variety of industries and institutions is also a significant factor, leading to the necessity of a more powerful critique than the traditional categories of compassion and cruelty could supply. Those who read Peter Singer's *Animal Liberation* (1975) found his descriptions of intensive farming and animal research both riveting and horrifying, and they found in his philosophy a moral ground for their feelings of outrage. The unfolding of that rage into a remarkable social movement is the subject of this book.

Chapter Two

Historical Roots

Everything about animal rights is controversial: its history is no exception. When the movement for animal rights began is difficult to say; many place its beginning with the publication in the mid-1970s of Peter Singer's book, *Animal Liberation*, while others date it in the early 1960s with the founding of the Hunt Saboteurs in Britain. There is truth in both of these claims, but there is a much longer history of struggle for animal rights that can teach us a great deal about today's movement. So we will set our sights much earlier, beginning with the humane[1] and antivivisection movements of the nineteenth century. That immediately raises a second controversy concerning the relationships between the animal rights movement and the humane movement. How separate have they been? How have they influenced each other? Is it possible to tell the story of the animal rights movement without also telling the story of the humane movement?

As we point out in other places in this book, the animal rights movement and the humane movement are distinct in a number of important ways. Generally, the two differ over the question of the extent to which society is justified in using animals as resources, as well as on such tactical issues as the use of confrontation, civil disobedience, and break-ins. Nevertheless, the connections between the animal rights and humane movements, both historical and contemporary, should not be neglected. Individuals move back and forth between the two movements, so that it is not possible to tell the story of one without reference to the other. Further, the humane movement flourished and accomplished a great deal during the British antivivisection movement. When that movement lost its vitality, the humane movement eventually lost momentum as well, and few reforms were achieved. With the resurgence of the animal rights movement in this century, the humane movement has experienced a revitalization as well. As we will show, the radical antivivisection movement and the animal rights movements have been highly beneficial to the humane movement. It is fair to say that the humane movement needs the animal rights movement, and that this is a very important thing if it is true, for those opposed both to animal rights and even to the reform and improvement of treatment for animals are currently investing their time, energy, and money in attempting to divide animal welfarists from the animal rightists. One tactic of those who stand to gain from animal exploitation—for example, product testing companies, the meat and dairy industry, the fur industry—is to divide the movement by portraying animal rightists as violent terrorists.

The Rise of Concern for Animals

Concern for animals has been voiced for centuries: the idea that it is morally wrong to eat animals has a thousand-year history in Greece: Pythagoras and his followers counseled vegetarianism, and Plutarch, Empedocles, Theophrastus, Plotinus, and Porphyry were all philosophical vegetarians. Saint Francis called for kindness, and Leonardo da Vinci refused to eat animals out of concern for their suffering.[2] But there was no political movement for animal rights during any of these times; da Vinci was teased by his friends for his concern for animals. In the latter portion of the eighteenth century the voices raised for animals were no longer so lonely. Works such as the Reverend Humphrey Primatt's "Dissertation on the Duty of Mercy and Sin of Cruelty to Brute Animals" (1776) and John Lawrence's "A Philosophical and Practical Treatise on Horses" (1796) are among the better known examples of a growing chorus of sentiment against cruel treatment of animals.[3] In 1780 the British philosopher Jeremy Bentham raised his now-famous challenge: "The question is not, can they reason? nor can they talk? but can they suffer?" Comparing the position of animals with that of black slaves, Bentham looked forward to the day when "the rest of animal creation may acquire those rights which never could have been withholden from them but by the hand of tyranny."[4] Bentham and other eighteenth-century reformers ushered in a new age that elevated concern for animals to a respectable sentiment.

In nineteenth-century Britain (and after the Civil War in North America) organized efforts began to translate this newfound sentiment into action to produce social change for animals. By the beginning of this century a large number of societies to prevent cruelty to animals were formed in the United States and Canada on the model of Britain's Royal Society for the Prevention of Cruelty to Animals (RSPCA), itself dating to 1824. These new societies provided an outlet for compassion by introducing and enforcing legislation to protect animals and educating the public about cruelty and kindness in our relation to working animals and pets. They built veterinary hospitals and provided ambulance services and shelters for abandoned and lost animals. They agitated for humane treatment for work animals and in the transportation and slaughter of cattle. And though animals had been used before for scientific purposes, the nineteenth century saw rapid changes in medicine that had tremendous implications for the growth of experimental uses of animals. In the latter half of the century, antivivisectionists organized into societies to oppose the emerging uses of animals in medicine and secured passage of the first law to regulate experimental uses of animals.

Though diet was never a major issue in the mainstream humane movement—vegetarianism being considered too impractical and extreme[5]—inevitably its connection to the new ideas about animals was noticed and acted on by some. As early as 1802 Joseph Ritson published *An Essay on Abstinence from Animal Food as a Moral Duty*, and in 1809 William Cowherd had made vegetarianism obligatory in his church based near Manchester. One of his followers, William Metcalfe, emigrated to Philadelphia and became a founder of vegetarianism in America. In 1842 the word *vegetarianism* was coined, and the Vegetarian Society was founded in Britain in 1847. By the end of the century vegetarianism became established among a minority of the middle class, receiving support and inspiration from the likes of Percy Shelley, Henry David Thoreau, George Bernard Shaw, Anna Kingsford, Howard Williams, and Henry Salt.[6] The influence of this nineteenth-century vegetarian circle on subsequent vegetarian thought must not be overlooked. Few have inspired vegetarianism in this century as much as Mohandas Gandhi. Yet Gandhi attributes his truly ethical commitment to vegetarianism to reading Henry Salt's *Plea for Vegetarianism* (1897); prior to that he had merely abstained from meat to comply with his vow to his mother, all the while secretly wishing that meat-eating was an acceptable practice to Indians.[7]

Why did compassion for animals become respectable, emerging as a mass movement in early nineteenth-century Britain and later in North America? Whatever the answer to this question—which is obviously quite complex—one important element is surely the fact that human rights were already in the air. Those who argue for animal rights—from Henry Salt in 1892 to Peter Singer in 1975—have frequently claimed that bias in favor of the interests of one's own species (or *speciesism*, a term dubbed by Richard Ryder) is cut from the same cloth as racism and sexism. We should not be surprised to find those who fight to end racism and sexism also opposing speciesism.

The nineteenth century saw both the advent of the woman suffrage movement and the movement to abolish slavery. The slave trade in Britain itself was abolished in 1807 and in its colonies by 1840. Influential figures in the suffrage and abolitionist movements in many cases went on to work to better the treatment of animals. Some of the charter members of the ASPCA were known for their anti-slavery positions: William Cullen Bryant, for example, is reputed to have been the one to suggest to Lincoln that he author the Emancipation Proclamation.[8] Similarly, the modern animal rights movement emerged along with the modern women's movement and the civil rights movement. Some people who had worked with these movements, as well as the movement to end the Vietnam War, went on to work in the animal rights movement. That movements for the rights of animals appear to wax and wane with movements for the rights of oppressed humans seems much more than historical coincidence.

Another important factor to consider is that the general view of the nature of animals was also changing during the nineteenth century. Charles Darwin's *Origin of Species* (1859) suggested much more continuity between humans and nonhumans than previous generations of thinkers had accepted. The Cartesian view of animals as unfeeling machines was giving way to the idea that animals are conscious, thinking beings.

James Turner has considered this question of the emergence of sentiment for animals in some detail. He argues that a number of converging causes help us make sense of the rapid rise of the humane movement. First, population had shifted in the century before: people were living more and more in cities and factory districts and were thus losing touch with their rural past. Animals represented a link to that more natural past. This makes further sense when we recognize the changing concept of nature in the preceding period. Earlier conceptions relate reason and nature (the nature of the mathematician-physicist Sir Isaac Newton), while by the end of the eighteenth century nature is more closely related to emotion, rationalization being a feature of human society over and against the natural world. Animals fit this picture nicely, for they were conceived as sharing our emotional nature more than our rational side, and thus "the defense of animals was, indirectly, a defense of nature and of man's emotional bonds with it" (Turner 1980, 33). Thus, changing conceptions of nature helped forge an association between animals and a past that was remembered as being more "natural" than the increasingly urban existence in Britain and later in America.

Second, industrialization and urbanization should have an even greater role in our understanding of the humane movement for yet another reason independent of these associations between animals and a lost rural tradition. Industrial society must have been shocking to those who initially made the transition from a more rural life: unemployment, slums, highly exploitive child labor, a more "rationalized" work (more tedious and specialized, the rhythms of which were dictated by needs of employers rather than the natural rhythms of seasons, planting, reaping, etc.). This dislocation must have heightened awareness of the suffering it caused. Thus, paradoxically, the suffering that was born of industrialization increased the sense of compassion. Some of this new humanitarian sentiment was directed to alleviate the human suffering that spawned it: child and female labor laws, the temperance movement (in part a response to the recognition that drink aggravated the suffering that led to it), the drive for universal public education, penal reform, education of the blind and deaf, treatment of the mentally ill, public health measures, endowment of libraries, founding of hospitals, and housing for the poor are all examples (Turner 1980, 34–35).

The motives in many of these "humanitarian" reforms were mixed. Prison reform was provoked as much by a concern for defending the social order as by compassion for prisoners, and slavery was opposed not solely on ethical grounds: for some the motivation was itself racial prejudice and distrust of the South as anything of a nobler origin. Turner suggests that we must understand growing concern for the suffering of animals in light of this mixture of motives for humanitarian reform in the period: "A deepened humane sensibility by no means suffices to explain the nineteenth century's great crusades. But it was a necessary ingredient. . . . Far from an aberration, animal protection embodied the temper of the age" (1980, 35). In making these connections to the growth of humanitarian sentiment and some of its sources, Turner appears to be on solid ground. If we distinguish the reasons a person has for acting and the causes that make him or her liable to regard these as good reasons for acting, then it is not at all paradoxical to suggest that much human action derives from mixtures of causes without suggesting that people are engaged in self-deception or hypocrisy.

But Turner also advocates a further thesis specifically about the application of this newly enlarged sentiment to animals. The problem he poses is this: Given the tremendous amount of *human* suffering, how could it have made sense to humanitarian reformers to devote so much effort to the animal cause? Briefly put, his hypothesis is that the growing sentiment of compassion for animals was primarily a safe response of the middle and upper class to changing conditions of human life. Industrialization and urbanization brought brutal factory working conditions, slums, unemployment, and child labor. The transformation from agrarian to industrial society removed people from their traditional connections to nature—and thus was accompanied by tremendous human suffering. But response to this suffering was difficult for middle- and upper-class people, as their own economic status was tied up with these changes. As a result, they needed ways to express the growing sentiment of compassion that would not undermine their own position: animals provided just such a safe object of concern. Thus, Turner's thesis is that concern for animals arose as a kind of displaced compassion for human suffering. We refer to this as the "Displacement Thesis."

The Displacement Thesis is not only of historical interest. For the charge is often leveled against those who work for the welfare of animals, that such work detracts from efforts to alleviate human suffering. The image of the misanthropic "animal lover"—who cares more about stray cats than starving children—is a favorite of those critical of the animal rights movement. But does this criticism have any basis in fact?

As we will show, quite the opposite is true. In fact, the evidence suggests that those who devote themselves to the welfare of one exploited group (whether human or animal) in many cases extend concern to other groups as well. For ease of reference let us call this "The Extension Thesis."

If the Displacement Thesis were correct, then we should expect that animal protection came in place of expressions of compassion for human beings. But this does not appear to be so. In addition to the charitable efforts on behalf of humans around the same time as the rise of the humane movement in Britain and America, which Turner himself mentions, Dix Harwood has pointed out that in Britain, philanthropic reform of various kinds had already emerged as a theme in the latter part of the eighteenth century. Readers of David Hume's *Inquiry Concerning Morals* (1751) might not find this surprising, given his emphasis (early in the eighteenth century) on the virtue of benevolence, but it is also evidenced by publications such as Jonas Hanway's *An Appeal for Mercy to the Children of the Poor* (1766). At the same time a variety of reform societies—such as the Royal Humane Society (founded by William Hawes in 1774 "to resuscitate people dragged out of the Thames and confidently given up for dead"), the Society for the Relief of Persons Imprisoned for Small Sums (which succeeded in obtaining legislation limiting certain types of imprisonment), the Society for Bettering the Condition of the Poor (established 1796), and the Philanthropic Society (founded in 1788 to assist foundlings)—were being created. A variety of institutions were endowed in the period: charity schools, schools for midwifery, and hospitals for foundlings, prostitutes, and very poor prospective mothers (Harwood 1928, 262n).

Even more damaging to the Displacement Thesis is the fact that not only charitable societies, but movements for liberation of colonial slaves and for women's rights emerged along with agitation on behalf of animals. And further, the individuals involved in these human-rights movements were in many cases simultaneously involved in the animal movement. To take but a few examples, William Wilberforce and Fowell Buxton, two founders of the SPCA in Britain, also fought against slavery. Frances Power Cobbe was the founder of the powerful antivivisectionist Victoria Street Society, and, as will become evident later in this chapter, many other British suffragists were also active antivivisectionists. In the United States Horace Greeley, the reforming anti-slavery editor of *The Tribune*, toasted women's rights and vegetarianism with Elizabeth Stanton, Susan B. Anthony, Amelia Bloomer, and Lucy Stone.

Thus, those who act on their compassionate feelings seem, on the whole, to be more, rather than less, sensitized to the plight of other beings not originally within the scope of their efforts. This is clearly borne out in the case of the anti-cruelty movement in America. In

1874, just eight years after the founding of the ASPCA, a case of child abuse was called to Henry Bergh's attention. Mrs. Etta Angell Wheeler, a social worker in New York, had been trying to have a child named Mary Ellen removed from physically abusive foster parents. The authorities were unable or unwilling to intervene to protect the child. Bergh agreed to take the case, and succeeded in prosecuting the foster parents and removing the child from their home. From this experience the American Society for the Prevention of Cruelty to Children was formed, the first of its kind in the world.[9] Hundreds of the anti-cruelty societies that were subsequently formed in the United States on Bergh's model incorporated both child and animal protection functions.[10]

More recently, the trend of cross-fertilization of human and animal liberation movements has continued. Those active in the peace and civil rights movements during the 1960s—Tom Regan and Henry Spira, for example—now enrich the animal rights movement. Alice Walker, Dick Gregory, Cesar Chávez, and Alex Pacheco all extended their original concern for oppressed humans to the oppression of animals. And not only individuals but whole organizations, such as Feminists for Animal Rights, and Gays and Lesbians for Animal Rights, provide strong evidence for the Extension Thesis and against the Displacement Thesis.

In rejecting the Displacement Thesis and arguing for the Extension Thesis, however, we must recognize that a heightened concern for human oppression is, undoubtedly, only one of many complex forces that led to the rise of the British antivivisection movement. As we shall see, other forces, including a deep suspicion of the new science of medicine, were also important.

Nineteenth-Century Britain

Early Progress for Animals.   At a much more concrete level, it is clear that the most immediate impetus for many who founded the humane movement in nineteenth-century Britain was the extensive cruelty to animals that was a part of daily life at the time. Baiting of bulls and other animals was common entertainment. Children tormenting animals for amusement set cats on fire and set animals on each other in all sorts of fights. The cruel treatment of large domestic animals was routine. Horses were publicly beaten and worked to death, and cattle were cruelly driven.[11] These displays inspired attempts to legislate an end to cruelty: one of the earliest in 1809 would have prohibited bull baiting but was defeated in the House of Commons after having passed the House of Lords. Lord Thomas Erskine came in for quite a bit of ridicule for introducing the bill but nevertheless reintroduced it in the next session, only to encounter even stronger opposition.

In 1822 Richard ("Humanity Dick") Martin, M.P. from Galway, introduced "An Act to Prevent the Cruel and Improper Treatment of Cattle," which "sought to punish people who wantonly and cruelly beat or ill-treated the horse, mare, gelding, mule, ass, ox, cow, heifer, steer, sheep or other cattle by a fine of not more than five pounds or less than ten shillings, or imprisonment not exceeding three months." "Dick Martin's Act," as it came to be known, was limited in scope—it had to be extended by amendments in 1833 and 1835 to protect domestic animals; to prohibit stoning or beating cattle in driving them; to prohibit baiting and fighting of dogs, bulls, bears, badgers, and cocks; and to forbid keeping of animals longer than three days in "knacker's yards" (slaughterhouse yards). A few years after this act was passed similar acts appeared in the United States—in New York State in 1829 and in Massachusetts in 1836 (Schultz 1924, 12–13).

Nevertheless, a significant difference existed between the American and the English situations until the 1860s. Martin's Act became law on 10 June 1822. Though it made a historic breakthrough in the field of legislation to protect animals, what made it distinct from its American cousins was not the precedent it set but that Martin soon followed its passage with an announcement of a meeting of people interested in "preventing, as far as possible, the cruel treatment of animals," leading within two years to the formation of the Society for the Prevention of Cruelty to Animals (SPCA), which included among its aims the prosecution of the more flagrant incidents of cruelty that its constables uncovered (Coleman 1924, 27, 31). This crucial move helped turn Martin's legislation into a powerful tool for change. And so did the nature of the organization he formed. From the start, the SPCA had influential backing: at the first meeting three ministers and five members of Parliament—and no women—were present. This elite and powerful support continued, and by 1840 the SPCA had become the Royal Society for the Prevention of Cruelty to Animals (RSPCA), as it had achieved the further clout of Queen Victoria's patronage (Turner 1980, 44). The aforementioned New York and Massachusetts statutes were as advanced as the English act at the time, but prosecution of cruelty cases has never been among the priorities of law-enforcement agencies in the United States or Britain. In both Massachusetts and New York the real beginnings of any effective animal movement did not emerge until a quarter century later, with the formation of organizations that, like Martin's, obtained the legal powers to arrest and prosecute violators of the anti-cruelty statutes.

The Antivivisection Movement's Rise and Fall.   It was not only mistreatment of horses and cattle that attracted the attention of the SPCA, however. Experimentation on animals was becoming more frequent, especially on the Continent, and when the French physiologist François Magendie visited London in 1824 for public lectures and demonstrations, his use of live animals created considerable controversy. There can be no doubt that Magendie's experiments—performed before the advent of anesthetics—caused protracted and intense suffering. Tales of the suffering of horses used repeatedly for practice surgery at the veterinary schools in France caused further concern, and in 1857 the RSPCA sent a delegation to France to complain to Louis-Napoleon. By the 1860s the RSPCA had developed a policy focused on the prohibition of painful experiments, while accepting those performed under anesthesia. During this period the British medical societies remained sympathetic to the RSPCA's mission and themselves condemned use of animals in practice and demonstration.[12]

It was not until the 1870s that a mass awareness of the issue of vivisection arose. The practice was becoming more common in Britain, and the press and public began to see little distinction between experimentation on the Continent—which had long been abhorred as cruel—and in Britain. In 1873 the physiologist John Burdon Sanderson published the *Handbook for the Physiological Laboratory* detailing experimental techniques of various gruesome sorts on animals and making no mention of anesthesia. Subsequent testimony of vivisectors revealed that many gave little thought to the pain they caused their subjects and often failed to administer any form of painkiller. This book, together with a few other notorious cases, led the RSPCA closer to a completely antivivisectionist position (French 1975, 47, 55).

A pivotal event occurred in Norwich in August 1874. At the British Medical Association meeting a French experimentalist, Eugène

Magnan, was invited to lecture on the physiological effects of alcohol. After his lecture he commenced a demonstration of the induction of epilepsy in a dog by intravenous injection of absinthe. As the dog was injected, objections were raised both by doctors and laymen present, and someone cut the dog loose. General confusion followed. The RSPCA formally charged Magnan and the three Norwich doctors who had invited him under Martin's Act but lost the case. Magnan was back in France and unavailable for prosecution, and the three doctors were acquitted on the grounds that they had not been directly involved in the demonstration (French 1975, 56).

In some historian's views, this affair was crucial in galvanizing the antivivisection movement. The RSPCA was, by the 1870s, a large, multifaceted organization unprepared to move too far ahead of public opinion. The strength they derived from the influential support they had always enjoyed also proved an incentive to conservatism and an obstacle to those who wanted to push the organization to take positions that were too radical. But there was a growing segment of the population who were radically opposed to vivisection. Journalist and suffragist Frances Power Cobbe recognized, in the wake of the Norwich affair, that Martin's Act was too weak to deal with the issue of vivisection, and in 1875 she drew up a memorial with many influential signatories, urging the RSPCA to take action to restrict vivisection (French 1975, 64). The RSPCA responded conservatively, proposing fact-finding, and Cobbe decided to take her business elsewhere.

It was largely as a result of the conservative nature of the RSPCA that Cobbe decided in 1878 to form her own antivivisection society, which came to be known as the Victoria Street Society (French 1975, 86). In these early events, we see the prototype of a pattern that has been repeated many times: when humane organizations move too slowly and conservatively to satisfy their more radical reformers these segments split off and form their own societies. Indeed, in 1898, when Stephen Coleridge took over the Victoria Street Society and focused on restrictionist, rather than abolitionist, legislative reform, Cobbe founded yet another abolitionist organization, the British Union for the Abolition of Vivisection (French 1975, 163), which exists to this day.

Legislation to restrict vivisection—the Cruelty to Animals Act—was finally passed in 1876, but with heavy lobbying from the medical community it was weakened considerably from the original form proposed by Cobbe and her supporters. Nevertheless, the bill had the backing of the RSPCA, whose members feared that this might be the last opportunity to get any legislation at all. The legislation required all those performing experiments on live animals to obtain a yearly license through the Home Office, and it restricted painful experiments in various ways. The original form of the legislation had prohibited the use of cats and dogs, but this was modified under pressure (French 1975, 126).

The Cruelty to Animals Act is a historic milestone and did indeed restrict the use of animals in research. It was an inconvenience to researchers, causing delays and sometimes denial of licenses. But the few prosecutions tried under the act were unsuccessful. It was much weaker than the antivivisectionists would have liked; the Victoria Street Society was founded to lobby for complete abolition of vivisection. Bills for the complete abolition of vivisection were introduced in Parliament every year from 1876 to 1884—but all of them failed.

During this time the biomedical community became organized, with the Association for the Advancement of Medicine by Research forming in 1881. This organization was able to convince the home secretary to allow it to inspect applications under the Cruelty to Animals Act, and under its auspices the number of licenses granted steadily grew—from 42 in 1882 to 638 in 1913 (French 1975, 164).

In the years that followed formation of the Victoria Street Society, the antivivisection movement attracted a remarkable range of support. This is well illustrated by the "Brown Dog Riots" of 1907. A few years earlier, two women, Lizzy Lind-af-Hageby and Liese Schartau, enrolled in University College medical school in London to learn of vivisection firsthand so they could expose it. They witnessed a throat operation on a dog that they observed to also have a recent abdominal wound, and recounted their experiences in *The Shambles of Science* (1903), which Stephen Coleridge, now president of the National Antivivisection Society, helped them to publish. Recognizing that what the women reported was a clear violation of the 1876 Cruelty to Animals Act—which forbade multiple experiments on the same animal— Coleridge charged the physician involved, Professor William Bayliss, with violation of the act, and Bayliss in turn sued Coleridge for libel. In the end Bayliss won his libel suit, and Coleridge was fined 2,000 pounds, which was paid in short time by readers of one of the many newspapers that sided with the antivivisectionists.[13]

Three years after the trial, Louisa Woodward, secretary of the Church Antivivisection League, met Lizzy Lind-af-Hageby, and the two decided to present the Battersea Council with a drinking fountain to commemorate the dog. Battersea, a working-class borough of London famous for its Home for Dogs, also contained one of the many antivivisection hospitals of the time, referred to affectionately as "the Old Anti" by its many patrons. The doctors in this hospital had all pledged to perform no vivisections. The fountain was accepted by the mayor and council and was unveiled on 15 September 1906. The story would have probably ended there, had the statue not included a rather provocative inscription: "In Memory of the Brown Terrier Dog Done to Death in the Laboratories of University College in February, 1903, after having endured Vivisection extending over more than Two Months and having been handed over from one Vivisector to Another Till Death came to his Release. Also in memory of the 232 dogs Vivisected at the same place during the year 1902. Men and Women of England, how long shall these Things be?" (Lansbury 1985, 14).

The ranks of the antivivisectionists by this time included not only such notables as George Bernard Shaw and Queen Victoria but many women, especially suffragists, as well as members of the working class. When the statue was attacked by medical students in what came to be known as the Brown Dog Riots of 1907, it was the police and working-class men of Battersea who defended it and "the Old Anti" as well. The students wanted the inscription removed—pressure was brought to bear at all levels of government to do so—but the Battersea Council stood firm, maintaining that the inscription was founded on ascertained facts. Failing that, the students tried on a number of occasions to destroy the statue, again without success. They turned in their frustration to disrupting antivivisection meetings with jeering and sometimes violence. At one meeting Lind-af-Hageby held, over 100 of the students succeeded in getting past the guard of Battersea workers, resulting in a violent confrontation with fist fights, smoke bombs, and many arrested student rioters. By now the cost of defending the statue was becoming unappealing to the council, which had seen a shift in control from Socialists and Progressives to Moderates in the election of 1908, and at 2 A.M. on 10 March 1910 the statue was removed by four councilmen guarded by 120 police. A few days later, over 3,000 antivivisectionists demonstrated in Trafalgar Square for the return of the brown dog, but it was too late: the statue had been destroyed (Lansbury 1985, 16–21).

As the story of the Brown Dog Riots illustrates, the nineteenth-century antivivisection movement appears to have had two sources. On the one hand, antivivisectionists were reacting to new ideas (such as vaccination) that seemed obviously wrong and dangerous. At the same time, members of the working class and women in general responded to the oppression of animals in vivisection that so clearly reminded many of their own situation.

As Turner has pointed out, prior to 1880 animal experimentation played little role in the training of physicians or in the development of therapies. It is not surprising, then, that one could find physicians who spoke out against vivisection, not only on moral but also on medical grounds. Vivisection in the last third of the century seemed especially objectionable for a number of reasons. That vivisection was performed in the name of advancing civilization, by cultivated and educated men, threatened the Victorians' deep faith in moral progress, as it seemed to carry society in the opposite direction: it "engenders cruelty or indifference to suffering. Therefore, it reverses the order of the refining forces of civilization," and "if we destroy pity, which it took thousands of years to develop, we have much to fear from the cruelty of a man who has brain but no heart" (Cobbe, quoted in Turner 1980, 97).

Indeed, vivisectors' relation to pain was suspect, and it thus undermined the medical profession. Physicians represented healing: they were supposedly dedicated by profession to the alleviation of illness and suffering. Vivisectors represented the antithesis of this image: "How could one dedicated to comforting the miserable and alleviating pain deliberately torture a sentient fellow creature?" (Turner 1980, 97).

In addition to these sources of anxiety about what vivisection would do to society and the medical profession, we must also recognize the importance of the medical revolution that was occurring at the time both vivisection and its opposition arose in the last century. Today the idea of microscopic organisms transmitting diseases is familiar, but this was unbelievable to most people 150 years ago. When the new germ theory was championed by the likes of Louis Pasteur, Joseph Lister, and Robert Koch, it was met with stiff opposition, not merely from antagonists of science but from within established science itself. The new theory represented a significant shift in outlook, a new paradigm, and such paradigm shifts represent revolutions that are usually resisted by those working within the conventional framework of a science.[14] Thus arose resistance to inoculation,[15] for to the already strange idea that invisible organisms were the cause of diseases this added the paradoxical claim that injection with some of these germs would actually help one avoid becoming infected. In fact, despite the discovery of numerous bacterial pathogens in the 1880s, the germ theory had little in the way of practical advances to contribute to the physician's tools until much after the vivisection debate had begun in earnest: the first widespread application of bacteriology for public health in the United States was the introduction of diphtheria antitoxin in 1894.[16] As the germ theory of disease was "notoriously the child of animal experimentation" (Turner 1980, 113), this suspect theory was linked with the moral dangers mentioned above, making resistance to it all the more reasonable at the time.

Combined with these facts about the shift in medical paradigm and its effects is the symbolic power of vivisection. The working class was not generally sympathetic to woman suffrage, fearing the loss of their own jobs. But antivivisection brought together the working class, suffragists, and antivivisectionists, as we have seen in the example of the Brown Dog Riots. These people appear to have been united by fear and disgust over the emerging medical establishment and the identification of the suffering of vivisected animals with their own plight. The new experimentally oriented doctors performed dissections on the cadavers of criminals—they were officially entitled to a certain percentage of corpses from those hanged—and families struggled to protect their recently deceased from this fate. William Hogarth's popular engraving *Four Stages of Cruelty* (which warned against cruelty by showing the progress from childhood cruelty to animals to adult criminality, culminating in the criminal's own dissection at the hand's of medical students) was influential in associating dissection and vivisection in the popular mind with horror, as was some popular literature, such as Mary Shelley's *Frankenstein* (Lansbury 1985, 57–58).

Quite simply, the working poor feared winding up dead or alive as the victims of vivisectors. And these fears were not without some justification. For example, in 1883 William Murrell and Sidney Ringer administered large doses of sodium nitrate to hospital outpatients at Westminster Hospital before this had ever been tried on animals (Lansbury 1985, 58). Similarly, women viewed the vivisection of animals as an extension of the treatment they themselves received at the hands of physicians. Under the Contagious Diseases Act of 1864, suspected "common prostitutes" were detained and forced to undergo gynecological exams to see whether they had venereal diseases. If found to be infected, they would be confined in a special venereal ward of a hospital for up to three months, and by the revisions of 1869, up to nine months.[17] Working-class women came to see their treatment in gynecological exams in the same light, as "being treated like a prostitute, with no more consideration for her sense of modesty than if she had been taken from a whorehouse" (Lansbury 1985, 86). During this time women were strapped down and subjected to humiliating examinations and mutilating surgeries: ovarectomies, clitoridectomies, and hysterectomies, among others. These surgeries were often performed on poor women without anesthetic—just as they were with vivisected animals—long after anesthetic was available and commonly employed for other surgeries (Lansbury 1985, 87). The emerging science, coupled with Freudian psychology, pathologized women's sexuality and prescribed such medical interventions as surgery on the bones of the nose to treat so-called female sexual aberrations such as the tendency toward masturbation.

In short, both women and the working poor saw their own oppression in the torture of animals under the vivisector's knife. It was a special form of cruelty to which these groups reacted, and this defined a fundamental difference between the antivivisectionists and the humane movement as represented by the RSPCA—a difference that exists to this day. The antivivisection movement challenged an entire institution, and the institutionalized cruelty and oppression it sanctioned. The humane movement, as represented by the RSPCA, focused more often on private, individual cases of cruelty—especially cruelty as practiced by the working class—and was content to reform and regulate the institutional cruelties.

Given the increase in the number of experiments performed on animals in the years following the skirmishes surrounding erection of the statue in Battersea—reaching into the millions today—the medical students won the war against the antivivisectionists. The fact that the advocates of experimental medicine organized and successfully resisted efforts to limit their activities is one crucial factor in this story. In both Britain and the United States medical defense societies, such as Britain's Association for the Advancement of Medical Research (AAMR), were formed shortly after the first attacks of antivivisectionists, and they succeeded in attaining powerful allies in Parliament and state and federal legislatures. The AAMR's undermining of the Cruelty to Animals Act by gaining control of the licensing process is a clear example of this success.

Perhaps equally important to the rising political power of the medical profession were the successes that experimental medicine began to enjoy in the 1890s in connection with bacteriology. While rejected at first, such innovations as the antitoxin for diphtheria, Pasteur's treatment of rabies, and Lister's development of antiseptic surgery could not ultimately be ignored. Antivivisectionists turned to sanitation and public health: cleaning up slums, improving sewerage, maintaining pure water supplies, promoting healthier diets, and eliminating vice and intemperance were all offered as answers to disease.

In fact, these alternatives were certainly not just wishful thinking. Sanitation was a much more significant source of improved health in the previous half century than experimental and clinical medicine together had been. It has been forcefully argued that medical intervention has played a much smaller role in reducing mortality from infectious diseases than traditional medical histories have suggested. Thomas McKeown has shown that introduction of vaccines and drug therapies can only explain a small percentage of the reduced mortality from the major infectious diseases, since the mortality rates were already showing a steady decline prior to such interventions. McKeown argues that improved sanitation, nutrition, and public health measures in the nineteenth century must be given the lion's share of the credit for reducing deaths from infectious diseases.[18]

The relevance to the debate about vivisection is clear: if bacteriological advances played a crucial role in the reduction of mortality from infectious diseases, then animal experimentation was also crucial, for the bacteriological revolution was built on numerous forms of animal experimentation. In fact, it is difficult to see how the germ theory of disease could have been established without infecting some living organisms, as Pasteur did in his classic demonstrations relating to anthrax. The presence of microorganisms in diseased individuals was acknowledged even by those skeptical about the claim that germs were causally involved in acquiring diseases. Clearly, McKeown's arguments are important, and the issue raised is sufficiently complex that we cannot do it justice here, but it is worth noting that one complexity frequently left out of the discussion is the degree to which public health measures and sanitary advances were tied up with the developments in bacteriology. One brief example of the complex relation will have to suffice here.

Water filtration had been used as early as 1842 in the United States (in Richmond, Virginia) and earlier in Europe, initially motivated by the desire to reduce the odor and turbidity of water, which make it not only unpleasant to drink but, according to the popular "miasmatic" theory, a potential cause of disease. Filtration was believed able to eliminate the disease-producing factors. This assumption turned out to be largely correct: when properly performed, filtration can eliminate most water-borne causes of infectious disease. Thus it might seem that water purification is one area in which sanitary reform succeeded in contributing to the reduction in mortality independently of the developments of bacteriology.

In fact, the usefulness of filters turned out to depend on factors that could not be predicted prior to the introduction of bacteriological methods. This was brought home rather strikingly in the case of the cholera outbreak in 1892 in the German cities of Hamburg and Altona. The two cities are situated side by side on the Elbe River, and both depended on the river water. Hamburg extracted its water from above the city; Altona extracted its water downstream from where Hamburg had introduced the sewage of its 800,000 inhabitants. To compensate, Altona had installed a filtration system, whereas Hamburg used the clear river water unfiltered. When cholera broke out in 1892, Hamburg's death rate was nearly six times higher than Altona's. The following winter, after the outbreak had subsided, a number of cases of cholera appeared in Altona, leading to an investigation of the operation of the filters. The number of bacteria in the filtered water had increased twentyfold, indicating that something was wrong with the filtering process. One of the filters had been cleaned during a frost, after which bacteria had not been trapped by the filter. Understanding that this was the source of the problem depended both on being able to identify cholera bacilli (Koch discovered the bacillus in 1883), and on understanding how filters create a barrier to bacteria when they are operating properly.

A reasonable prediction would have been that filtration is largely ineffective in eliminating microorganisms, since the interstices between the grains of sand are considerably larger than typical microorganisms. Surprisingly enough, when bacteriological studies of the filtering process were conducted, it was discovered that upwards of 90 percent of the microorganisms in unfiltered water were removed in the filtration process. Studies in Europe and the United States in the 1880s and early 1890s showed which features of filtration were particularly relevant to the number of microorganisms in the filtered water. One particularly important result was the discovery that the buildup of a slimy deposit (itself composed of bacteria) on the sand in the filters forms a barrier through which bacteria do not pass. Consequently, a freshly cleaned filter permits most of the bacteria to pass through for the first day or so. The frost present during the cleaning of the Altona filter delayed the buildup of slime, and thus reduced the efficiency of the filter. This is something that could be understood in 1892, after the cholera bacillus had been identified, and methods for identifying it in water had also been developed.[19] There are numerous such examples of the interplay between the results of the bacteriological revolution and the quest for sanitary reform. While it is undoubtedly true that sanitary reformers in the nineteenth century helped eliminate many sources of cantagion without benefit of the germ theory, once bacteriology came into its heyday in the 1880s the public health movement was transformed by it (Duffy 1990, 193ff). Consequently, the competition typically posed between public health and the results of medical experimentation may be something of a false dilemma. In the end the new experimental medicine did not compete with, so much as complement, the alternatives.

While Britain had established the foundations for the humane movement during the nineteenth century and exported this movement throughout the colonial world, the antivivisection movement ceased to be a vital and mass movement after the turn of the century. The medical establishment had effectively organized a lobby in the form of the Association for the Advancement of Medical Research. The antivivisectionists had based their case not only on the immorality of vivisection but also on its scientific worthlessness. At first, resistance to the new experimental medicine was highly reasonable, but eventually the medical community was able to muster extensive argument for its value. In a not very distant past, as Charles Adams wrote in 1882, "The entire field of Human Knowledge was conceivably within the grasp of any one first-class human intellect" (quoted in Turner 1980, 107). But antivivisectionists were discovering the hard way that science, as it grew more abstruse, was becoming more and more the province of a small group of experts. It was increasingly easy to misunderstand what scientists did, and antivivisectionists occasionally made things worse, much to the delight of advocates of vivisection, by appealing to outdated evidence or showing lack of familiarity with basic medical facts (Turner 1980, 106).

To cite one example, W. W. Keen, a Philadelphia surgeon and outspoken advocate of animal research, cites numerous such cases in *Animal Experimentation and Medical Progress* (1914). Referring to the British scene, he points out alleged confusions in Frances Power Cobbe's *The Nine Circles*, even after the book had been revised by a Dr. Berdoe: in a discussion of an experimental stimulation of the sciatic nerve, the antivivisectionists lose credibility by mistaking these to be experiments on the spinal cord.[20] The British Medical Association declared a national commitment to promoting vivisection, dozens of pamphlets promoting vivisection were written, and anatomist Richard Owen wrote a book entitled *Experimental Physiology: Its Benefits to Mankind* (1882). These tactics succeeded, and subsequent attempts to restrict or eliminate vivisection failed. By World War I, the first wave of the animal rights movement was at an end.

Despite the failure of the nineteenth-century antivivisectionists to achieve their goals, the Brown Dog statue serves as a symbol of the ongoing fight to end vivisection. A modern statue stands today in Battersea Park—just up the street from the still operating Battersea Home for Dogs (which now, as then, refuses to supply dogs for use in research). The statue was re-erected in 1985 as a result of the efforts of Londoner Jose Parry, with help from the extant British Union for the Abolition of Vivisection. The new statue bears the original controversial inscription that led to riots, as well as an updated inscription on the other side reminding visitors of the exponential increase in animal experiments in the intervening time.

The Movement in the United States

Early History.   It is commonly thought that much of the U.S. tradition of concern for animals derives from precedents in Britain, and there is much truth in this view. The earliest legislative effort to protect animals from cruelty is actually American, however. In 1641 the Puritans of Massachusetts Bay Colony voted to enact the "Body of Liberties," a document containing 100 "liberties," including two provisions that legally protect animals. Sec. 92 provides "That no man shall exercise any tyranny or cruelty toward any bruit creatures which are usually kept for the use of man." Another section added, "If any man shall have occasion to lead or drive cattle[21] from place to place that is far off, so that they be weary, or hungry, or fall sick, or lame, it shall be lawful to rest and refresh them for a competent time in any open place that is not corn, meadow, or inclosed for some particular use" (Barnes 1975, 16, 18). The "Body of Liberties" was compiled by a Puritan minister, Nathanial Ward, who was enlisted for the task owing to his familiarity with the Common Law of England. Ward was born in England, where he studied law before being driven out for heresy. Sec. 92 was used in at least one case to prosecute against cruelty to an ox, but Ward's ideas did not spark organized

Eighty years after the original statue of the brown dog was destroyed, Jose Parry shows the new one she had erected in Battersea Park, London. *Photo by Susan Finsen*

concern for animals. In addition, cruelties were occasionally prosecuted as "nuisances" under the common law.[22]

Following passage of Martin's Act in Britain, further legislation began to appear in the United States. A measure was passed in New York State in 1829 providing that "every person who shall maliciously kill, maim or wound any horse, ox or other cattle, or any sheep, belonging to another, or shall maliciously and cruelly beat or torture any such animal, whether belonging to himself or another, shall upon conviction, be adjudged guilty of a misdemeanor," and a similar act was passed in Massachusetts in 1836 (Schultz 1924, 12–13). While these statutes were similar to Martin's Act, they did not signal a serious anti-cruelty movement at the time, for no organizations sprang up to encourage their enforcement until nearly 30 years later.

Anti-Cruelty Societies.   George Angell and Henry Bergh are the best known of many figures in the early days of the humane movement in the United States. They both became concerned in the mid-1860s about the cruelty they witnessed in the daily lives of work animals and sought to do something about it. Bergh, heir to his

Henry Bergh, founder of the American anti-cruelty society, the ASPCA. *Courtesy ASPCA*

father's ship-building estate, had been appointed by President Lincoln to St. Petersburg as secretary of legation and acting consul, but he left the position in 1864. While in Russia, the story goes, he observed peasants beating their horses, and had found that he could use his position to intervene on behalf of the animals. On his way back to New York, Bergh visited London, where he spent time visiting the RSPCA. The British model apparently made an impression on him, for in February 1866 he followed in Richard Martin's footsteps by announcing a public meeting, followed in April by a trip to the legislature seeking a charter to incorporate the American Society for the Prevention of Cruelty to Animals.

Like its British model, the ASPCA was permitted by its charter to employ agents to arrest violators of the anti-cruelty statute and was able to supply its own prosecutors for such cases as well. Immediately upon receiving the authority to do so, Bergh went forth to personally enforce the law. He rapidly became notorious for defending abused and overworked carriage horses in the streets of New York City, fearlessly stopping the cruel whippings and overloading that were a common practice. Transport of cattle was also an early concern, and Bergh pursued the arrest and prosecution of a butcher for tying the legs of calves and piling them in a cart. The butcher was convicted and fined $10 and forced to serve a day in jail. This conviction was the first for animal cruelty in the United States (as opposed to the colonies), but before the anniversary of the first year of the ASPCA Bergh was to follow this conviction with many more, including successful prosecutions for overloading carriages, cruel treatment of livestock, cock fighting, and dog fighting. By the end of the first year he had successfully appealed to the New York State legislature to limit the time cattle could be left on rail cars to 28 hours; subsequently it was reduced to 24 hours (Coleman 1924).

A few years later George Angell founded the Massachusetts SPCA, with much the same aims and police and prosecutorial powers, though from the start Angell gave greater voice to the importance of humane education.[23]

While Bergh and Angell are appropriately identified as founders of the American humane movement, there were others with similar ideas trying to get something going about the same time. For instance, Caroline Earle White appears to have had the idea of creating an organization in Philadelphia on the model of the RSPCA before 1866 but was prevented from doing so by the Civil War. After learning of the formation of the New York society, she visited Bergh, who encouraged her to get together with Colonel M. Richards Muckle, who had placed notices to form such an organization in the *Bulletin* in 1866.[24] In Massachusetts, when George Angell (moved to action on learning of a horse race from Brighton to Worcester in which two horses were literally run to death)[25] called in 1868 for support in forming a society, he discovered that Emily Appleton had already set out to accomplish the same end: she had visited Bergh, collected 90 signatures of influential people willing to become patrons, and had drafted a charter and submitted it to the state legislature (Angell 1892, 9–10).

In January 1866 the *New York Times* published an editorial calling on the wealthy and idle to turn their efforts toward formation of societies for the prevention of cruelty; indeed, after Bergh began organizing his society, many of this class answered the call. The charter members of the ASPCA included such illustrious individuals as J. J. Astor, Jr., George Bancroft, John Dix, Peter Cooper, Francis Cutting,

Caroline Earle White founded the American Antivivisection Society in 1883. As a woman, she could not serve as an officer. *Courtesy American Antivivisection Society*

John Van Buren, and Hamilton Fish. The list is packed with prominent financiers, bankers, merchants, industrialists, clergy, former senators, governors, and journalists (McCrea 1910, 200).

The founding of the ASPCA represented the beginnings of an organized movement to protect animals in the United States. But public sentiment against brutality to animals surely existed before that time. Beginnings of legislative efforts to protect animals in various locales around the country were seen well before 1866. As we have mentioned, New York State and Massachusetts had established prohibitions of cruelty in the 1820s and 1830s. In 1855 a Pennsylvania law, introduced by Senator William A. Crabbe, made "wanton cruelty to animals in the city of Philadelphia" a misdemeanor.[26] And on 24 June 1865 this editorial was published in the *New York Times*:

CRUELTY TO ANIMALS—A correspondent very properly reminds us, when we quote illustrations of the cruelty practiced toward dumb animals in England, that it would not be amiss to look at home. It is only too true that poultry dealers and wholesale butchers (many of them, at least,) permit the practice of a system of needless torture, by their assistants, in bringing their livestock to market, or in preparing it for the stalls. The preliminary process of dressing fowls, as described by our correspondent, is scarcely less horrible than the atrocious practice of vivisection; and the manner in which the smaller class of live cattle are dragged or driven to the shambles, is an outrage upon the natural feelings of anyone not utterly hardened by familiarity with cruelty in its most barbarous forms.[27]

Had there not been such sentiment at the time, it would be difficult to explain the rapid rise of such a movement nationwide: within a few short years of the founding of the ASPCA in 1866, societies modeled on Bergh's cropped up all over the country: Pennsylvania (1867), Massachusetts and San Francisco (1868), and Illinois and Minnesota (1869) were among the many early followers. By 1877 the American Humane Association was founded to provide national communication and coordination of the local and state groups, which numbered in the hundreds by the turn of the century (McCrea 1910, 10–15).

The Rise and Fall of Early Antivivisectionism. It is clear that the American humane movement was heavily influenced by its British model. It should come as no surprise that the English antivivisection movement also inspired an American counterpart. Indeed, the humane movement took up this issue early on, with Bergh, Angell, and White opposing all forms of vivisection. In the early years of the ASPCA Henry Bergh tried in vain to achieve legislation against vivisection. When Philadelphia surgeons attempted in 1871 to secure dogs for experimental use from the newly established Pennsylvania SPCA, they were refused. Appalled at the idea and encouraged in her efforts by Frances Power Cobbe, Caroline Earle White in 1883 founded the American Antivivisection Society (AAVS), whose first effort was to regulate vivisection. The medical establishment rallied in opposition, however, and no such legislation was allowed to pass. Within a few years the AAVS altered its purpose and fought for nothing less than total abolition (Coleman 1924, 204–205; Turner 1980, 93).

Unlike its British counterpart, the first wave of the American antivivisection movement did not generate a large following. Vivisection was not the vital issue in the United States that it had become by the 1870s in Britain, at least partly because American science lagged sufficiently behind the European scene at the time, so that little vivisection was occurring in the United States (Turner 1980, 92). Nonetheless, activists considered it important to try to prohibit it before it gained too great a foothold. In the early years of the movement, Henry Bergh introduced antivivisectionist bills before the New York State legislature almost annually. And just as regularly these bills went down in defeat.

For a time it seemed that restrictive or abolitionist legislation had a reasonable chance of being enacted. For example, in 1894 George Angell and the MSPCA, in a cooperative effort with antivivisectionist groups, succeeded in securing legislation to prohibit the exhibition of vivisection or dissection in public schools in Massachusetts.[28] In 1896 Representative James McMillan of Michigan introduced a bill to Congress to regulate vivisection in the District of Columbia. Passage of this legislation seemed promising, as it was endorsed by six Supreme Court justices, leading Washington clergymen, eminent academics, and practicing physicians (Rowan 1984, 50). In addition, the Senate hearings were being conducted by New Hampshire Senator Jacob Gallinger, a homeopathic physician who sided with antivivisectionists. Nevertheless, the bill was strenuously opposed by the National Academy of Sciences, the American Medical Association (AMA), and many scientists and doctors, and the bill died in the House (Benison, Barger, and Wolfe 1987, 173).

Indeed, it appears that proponents of animal research had learned well from the British lesson. They formed the Council on Defense of Medical Research in 1908 (Roberts 1979, 26), an effective lobbying force for vivisection. They distributed numerous pamphlets on the value of animal research, disseminating these to family physicians and the public as well. The council had watchdogs in every state where antivivisection activity was organized, and it made sure to give persuasive testimony before state congressional committees. This testimony included detailed descriptions of the value of animal research as well as claiming that animal research was already adequately self-regulated. The history of arguments for and against animal research during this time appears, in fact, to be very similar to that current in modern debates.

In contrast, proponents of antivivisection appear to have been less organized and less effective. As William Gary Roberts has argued, some sought abolition, while others sought to regulate research. When bills to regulate research were being debated before congressional committees, this conflict gave rise to inconsistent and confusing testimony on the part of antivivisectionists.[29]

In addition to the political ineptitude and disagreement among the antivivisectionists, the progress of medicine during this period militated against abolitionist legislation. As Turner has argued, public perception of the benefits of medical research was rapidly altering during this time. Diphtheria antitoxin, developed in 1894, had apparently lowered mortality rates considerably. The medical establishment's success in promoting this and similar developments manifested itself in repeated victories against the antivivisection movement (Turner 1980, 115; Roberts 1979, 61).

In the process of defending itself, the medical establishment made considerable gains, including learning to lobby congress effectively and to influence public opinion in its favor (Benison, Barger, and Wolfe 1987, 168–201). Indeed, it is arguable that one of the chief effects of the early efforts of the antivivisection movement in the United States was to help organize and politicize the medical establishment. It is quite instructive, especially in light of the current extensive efforts of the AMA to discredit the animal rights movement, to note the successful strategies employed by the medical establishment in combating the first wave of antivivisectionism. Prominent surgeons such as W. W. Keen and W. B. Cannon served as eloquent advocates of the greater humanity of the scientists. Humanists and antivivisectionists were anxious to point out the detriment to moral character that cruelty brings—a view that goes back at least as far as Immanuel Kant and William Hogarth a century and a half before. Then president of the American Antivivisection Society, the Reverend Dr. Floyd W. Tomkins, urged that "vivisection tends to weaken character . . . [and as] [n]othing which hurts the character can be right" this cinches the

case against vivisection (quoted in Keen 1914, 234). But now provivi-
sectionists turned the argument on its head. Keen, for example, wrote
an article entitled "The Influence of Antivivisection on Character," in
which he argued that antivivisection arouses violent passions, fosters a
spirit of cruelty to human beings, and lessens reverence for truthfulness. In the last case, Keen cited many purported cases of antivivisectionist distortions in descriptions of experiments, and the failure to
correct these in subsequent editions after the errors had been pointed
out (Keen 1914, 234–85).

The major weapon in the vivisectionists' arsenal, however, was and
remains the appeal to the benefits of medical research. In 1914 Keen
was able to cite a litany of cases in which animal experimentation had
played some role in the genesis of major medical advances. Keen
argued that the very sanitation and public-health measures championed as alternatives to animal research by the antivivisectionists
required an understanding of bacteriology in order to know which
kinds of measures might be useful. But bacteriological knowledge
(such as that involved in identification of the tubercle bacillus by
Koch) had been obtained through animal research (Keen 1914, 282).

Not only did the antivivisection movement face legislative defeats in
the wake of attacks by the biomedical community, but, like its British
counterpart, the U.S. antivivisection movement was disowned by the
more conservative humane movement. An international conference of
humane organizations (under the auspices of the American Humane
Association) met in 1900 and formally expelled all antivivisectionist
organizations. For a number of reasons this was not really a surprising
move, despite the antivivisectionism of the humane movement's
founders. After Bergh's death in 1888 the ASPCA gradually ossified,
taking over the care of stray dogs and cats, as did other anti-cruelty
societies in the 1890s. Preoccupied with these day-to-day problems,
they became less and less capable of dealing effectively with the com-
mercialized cruelties that were emerging. The accounts written early
in this century by leaders and historians of the humane movement
make it absolutely clear that antivivisection was held at arm's length
by the mainstream humane movement. For example, both Francis
Rowley and William Schultz, in describing the vivisection controversy,
paraphrase arguments concerning the reality of the benefits proclaimed by research advocates. While they reject the argument that
research does not truly benefit human health, no comment is made on

why we should not refrain from experimentation for moral reasons (Rowley 1912, 60–63; Schultz 1924).

In Britain and the United States the humane movement withdrew from the institutional cruelties in farming, vivisection, and exploited wildlife. Both the SPCAs and the American Humane Association—which had originally been formed in order to deal with the cruelty involved in livestock transport—had attracted support from rich and powerful patrons, as had the RSPCA. And, as in the British context, this tended to thwart criticism of institutionalized cruelty (Ryder 1989, 174–75).

The emerging peace with researchers was well expressed by none other than Bergh's own nephew, himself treasurer of the ASPCA, when he said in 1908, "I have found every disposition on the part of representative men of the [medical] profession to more than meet us halfway in any intelligent and honest effort to properly restrict the practice [of vivisection]." The young Bergh suggested that humanitarians and researchers should "unite in an earnest and well-meant effort to bring about such changes as may not interfere with the legitimate and necessary workings of science" (quoted in Schultz 1924, 237). This cooperative approach was mirrored elsewhere in the movement: delegates to the American Humane Association in 1914 assured observers from medical research that they wished to "leave vivisection alone" (Turner 1980, 118). This strategy was clearly flawed, however, as the "cooperation" was clearly one-sided. Vivisection forces actively fought against all attempts at regulation or reform of animal experimentation, arguing that the status quo was quite adequate. They were quite explicit in arguing that no concessions, oversights, or compromise with animal advocates should occur, since such compromise would merely undermine research and provide a "foot in the door" for antivivisectionists (Roberts 1979, 61).

It is possible that the split between the humane and antivivisection movements would not have been so decisive had the antivivisection movement been more successful in its earlier attempts. But the overall conservatism of those in the humane movement makes it likely that the two movements would have gone their separate ways in any event. As we have seen, the humane movement avoided challenging the assumptions that underlie institutionalized exploitation. For example, tremendous energy and concern was directed to issues of transportation and slaughter reform from the beginning of the humane movement, but the idea that vegetarianism might be a response to this exploitation seems rarely, if ever, even to have been entertained. *The Humane Idea* (1912), by Francis Rowley (who became president of the MSPCA after Angell's death), is unusual in the humane movement literature in even acknowledging vegetarianism as an ethical idea. Rowley cites Williams, Salt, Porphyry, and Plutarch, all of whom made significant ethical cases for vegetarianism, and, in discussing the slaughter reform issue, even acknowledges that "after the last word is said about the ranchman and the railroad, about the callous drover, the butcher whose hands must drip with blood, the packer who grows rich out of his traffic, —we come face to face with ourselves. But for us there would be no demand and no supply" (1912, 59).

One supposes that in saying this Rowley would be laying the groundwork for a discussion of the possibility of withholding economic support from this exploitation; instead, he simply states, "Upon us, then, rests the moral obligation to do the utmost that is within our power to see that these victims of our appetite and desire are slain in what shall be to them as painless and merciful a death as the noblest humanity can devise" (1912, 59). To cease eating animals was not an option to be seriously entertained. Even the most enlightened among the humane movement seem not to have given serious consideration to the idea that animals might not exist simply to serve as resources—however humanely used—for human consumption, even though there were eloquent voices at the time (such as Henry Salt's) saying just that.[30]

It should be acknowledged, however, that the conservative approach of the humane movement was not without its successes. By 1907 every state in the union had an anti-cruelty statute on the books, and by 1923 they covered a wide gamut of issues, including docking horses' tails; failure to feed, water, or shelter; abandonment of decrepit or disabled animals; maliciously killing or injuring another's animal; cock fighting; prohibition of certain traps; failure to visit traps; bristle burs; cutting off more than half an ear of domestic animals; cruelty in filmmaking; and careless exposure to barbed wire (Schultz 1924, 100).

By World War I the first wave of animal rights sentiment in the United States—if antivivisectionism can be so classified—had been contained. It appears that the chief reasons for the containment pertain to the effectiveness of the biomedical community itself, though undoubtedly there are other factors as well. The "great leaders" had grown old and died, and to some extent movements are inspired by their leadership. Richard Ryder argues that wars interfere with the advance of such movements, and no doubt there is a disruptive effect of such events.

Whatever the complex social factors, the antivivisection movement was not able to make significant advances during the two wars and the postwar eras. Whenever efforts were mounted, the antivivisectionists found able foes poised to attack them. When, for example, an antivivisection initiative was placed on the 1920 California ballot, the research community mobilized with a strong response, and the measure was defeated by a two-to-one vote (Rowan 1984, 51). A similar bill introduced about the same time in Congress, designed to prohibit the use of dogs in research in Washington, D.C., was not given serious attention, never making it to the Senate floor for debate (Roberts 1979, 68).

After World War II the institutional abuse of animals increased, both because of the vast increase in animal research on both sides of the Atlantic and because of the advent of factory farming. In the area of research, more and more animals were being used, and government funding of scientific research was increasing. Passage of the Public Health Service Act in 1944 paved the way for funding to grow from less than $1 million in 1945 to almost $1 billion in 1963 (Rowan 1984, 52). Factory farming got its initial boost from the discovery of vitamins A and D, which enabled farmers to confine "broiler" chickens indoors without previously needed sunlight or exercise. These "advances" encouraged farmers to maintain larger flocks, but the intensification also resulted in greater losses to contagious disease and the problems resulting from the stress of overcrowding. Given the strong demand for chicken at the time, large feed and pharmaceutical companies were motivated to seek solutions, which were fast in coming: a machine to debeak chickens (so they could not cannibalize each other under stressfully overcrowded conditions), hybrid feeds that put weight on faster, mechanized feather pluckers, and antibiotic additives are examples of the technological solutions to the new confinement-caused problems (Mason and Singer 1980, 1–2).

These abuses remained largely hidden from the public, and the humane societies took little notice of them. Indeed, the ASPCA cooperated in the sale of pound animals to research laboratories during the 1950s. Passage of the Humane Slaughter Act in 1958 marks one of the few advances for animals of this decade, and on slaughter issues it was one of the few advances the humane movement was able to achieve in nearly a century. A variety of slaughter-related practices had been criticized for some 90 years.

In 1910 Roswell C. McCrea wrote of agitation for "humane slaughter" reform (258). That same year a law passed in Massachusetts allowing the MSPCA to inspect slaughterhouses. The next year a vigorous campaign to repeal the law had to be fought off (Schultz 1924, 36). The Humane Slaughter Act succeeded largely owing to the efforts of the Society for Animal Protective Legislation (SAPL), founded by Christine Stevens in 1955, and also to the persistence of Senator Hubert Humphrey, who authored the bill, saw it through Congress, and demanded that it be enforced.[31] The law requires packers selling meat to the government to provide either anesthetization or an electrical or mechanical stun to all animals prior to slaughter, except those used for kosher meat.[32] SAPL was also instrumental in passage of the 1959 Wild Horses Act, prohibiting poisoning of horses and burros, as well as use of aircraft to round them up for slaughter. While these are important advances, the post–World War II period appears overall to be a time of little advance for animals.

It should also be pointed out, however, that part of the difficulty was beyond the control of the humane organizations. The political climate at this time was very conservative, and those who fought for human rights—much less animal rights—did not receive a sympathetic hearing. On factory farming issues, the postwar, postdepression climate was not one ripe for challenging the application of technology to produce larger quantities of food at cheaper prices, and certainly agribusiness did a good job persuading the American people that animal foods were essential to human health.[33]

Nevertheless, the failures of both the British and American humane movements to make significant progress in improving conditions for animals in the eras following the decline of the more radical antivivisection movements cannot be attributed merely to such external social factors. The failure to challenge the legitimacy of exploitive institutions inevitably focused the humane movements on issues of individual cruelty and away from the social structures that continued to promote them. While prosecution of individual cruelty and rescue of individual animals are worthy goals, they are inherently conservative and cannot lead to progress in the overall welfare of animals unless they are coupled with the stronger challenges provided by those willing to take on the institutions and ideologies of oppression themselves.

The Modern Animal Rights Movement

Human rights issues were once again in the air in the 1960s; both the civil rights and women's movements emerged during this time. In the United States the movement protesting the Vietnam War brought an intellectual climate conducive to the challenge of "morality as usual," and the seeds of animal liberationist sentiment once again found fertile ground in both the United States and Great Britain. While many in the movement date their own awakening to animal rights issues in the mid-1970s, with the publication of Peter Singer's *Animal Liberation*, the resurgence of the movement began in the 1960s on both sides of the Atlantic.

In the early 1960s agitation against blood sports was increasing in Britain, with the Hunt Saboteurs forming in 1963. The group's formation was highly significant for a number of reasons. For one thing, it appears to be the first organization to speak openly and uncompromisingly of members as proponents of rights of animals in the modern sense.[34] For another, it employed highly visible, confrontational tactics of direct action. And, finally, it represented a significant broadening of the animal movement to the working class—something that had not occurred since the Brown Dog Riots (Ryder 1989, 183–88). Concern for the environment also increased throughout the 1960s, with a number of major environmental organizations forming in 1969. Cleveland Amory founded the Fund for Animals in 1967, launched campaigns against hunting and trapping, and encouraged a revitalization of the ASPCA in New York.

By the early 1970s animal rights activity was becoming more widespread than just the Hunt Saboteurs in Britain. Richard Ryder coined the term *speciesism* in 1971, and the leadership of the RSPCA fell into the hands of Ryder and other progressives in 1970. By 1972, the Animal Liberation Front (formerly the Band of Mercy) was in operation in Britain. But it was not until the end of the Vietnam War that the animal rights movement really moved to the United States.

While a complex of changes in social climate in the United States undoubtedly provided the conditions in which animal liberation could grow, specific events drew public attention to these issues. In particular, a severe irritant had been injected into the complacent humane movement. The biomedical research establishment had moved aggressively during the late 1940s and early 1950s to obtain access to research animals through pounds and shelters. For example, the

Metcalf-Hatch Act in New York State *required* municipal pounds to sell animals to research. As Andrew Rowan has argued, this broke a long-standing truce between the humane movement and the research establishment. Those who were frustrated with the conservatism of humane organizations began to break off and form their own organizations. For example, Helen Jones began by working with the American Humane Association (AHA), but in less than a year she left to join Fred Myers and Larry Andrews in forming the Humane Society of the United States (HSUS). In a pattern reminiscent of Frances Power Cobbe, she eventually left HSUS as it became too compromising; she founded the Society for Animal Rights, known today as the International Society for Animal Rights.[35]

It was not until the mid-1960s, however, that these issues came into national focus. Bills to regulate research had been introduced at the federal level for a number of years, but two events outside the usual legislative debate helped mobilize public pressure more than anything. The first set of events related to the Lakavage family, who had been unable to locate their lost dalmatian, Pepper, until they noticed a newspaper story about the arrest of an animal dealer in Northampton County, Pennsylvania, for improperly loading his truck with dogs (including two dalmatians) and goats to be sold to laboratories. The animals were temporarily held by the Northampton SPCA and photographed while the animal dealer, William Miller, procured a more suitable vehicle. When shown the photographs, Mrs. Lakavage identified one as Pepper, but by then Miller had retrieved his load of animals and left for New York City. Tracing the dog led the family to a large animal dealer in New York, a Mr. Neresian, but Neresian would not cooperate with the family's attempt to find Pepper, even after being approached by New York Representative Joseph Resnick. Angered at Neresian's arrogance, Resnick, along with Senators Magnuson and Clark, introduced legislation to Congress to regulate trade in dogs in 1965. In the meantime, Pepper's trail led to Montefiore Hospital in New York, where she had been used and cremated before the Lakavages could retrieve her.[36]

Resnick's bill (which required licensing of animal dealers and laboratories) might have passed into obscurity, as so much animal legislation does, had it not been for a number of magazine stories exposing the egregious abuse of animals by animal dealers selling to research labs, as well as the charges of theft. Cole Phinizy wrote articles detailing the stories of the Lakavages' and other stolen dogs that appeared in *Sports Illustrated* (where he was a senior writer) and *Reader's Digest.* Soon thereafter *Life Magazine* published a photo essay ("Concentration Camps for Dogs") showing a Humane Society raid on a dealer in Maryland. As a result of this publicity and lobbying from humane organizations, the Laboratory Animal Welfare Act was passed in 1966. At the hearing for the bill, Congressman Resnick stated, "I am not an antivivisectionist, and the issue of vivisection is nowhere involved in this legislation. Neither is the issue of animal care in the laboratory. This bill is concerned entirely with the theft of dogs and cats, and to a somewhat lesser degree, the indescribably filthy conditions in which they are kept by the dealer" (Phinizy 1965, 41). While the law was intended to leave animal research alone, focusing solely on licensing of animal dealers, housing, and transport, it represented some slight improvement. Amendments to the act in 1970 and 1976 added a variety of provisions, such as a requirement that pain-relieving drugs be used except where this would interfere with experiments (Rowan 1984, 56–57).[37]

The issue of animal research thus became the central focus for early animal rights protests in the United States, and some (e.g., Sperling 1988) see this issue as *the* central issue of the modern movement, as it was with the nineteenth-century British and American antivivisectionists. This perception is misleading, however, for the current movement is much more multifaceted, and the arguments for animal rights are central in a way unprecedented in the earlier movement. Undoubtedly, this is due in large measure to the forceful arguments and fact-finding provided by Singer and Regan during the 1970s.

In 1975 Peter Singer published his highly influential book, *Animal Liberation.* Singer made many of the same arguments regarding the relation between speciesism, sexism, and racism that had been made by Jeremy Bentham and Henry Salt in previous centuries, and he coupled them with graphic, well-documented descriptions of the conditions of animals in factory farms and research laboratories. The combination of straightforward argument with hard-hitting fact was highly effective. Furthermore, Singer initiated an intellectual controversy that led animal rights issues into the universities, especially into serious academic philosophical discussion. But Singer was not working alone: at about the same time Tom Regan was writing his first article about animals, "The Moral Basis of Vegetarianism." Shortly thereafter, Regan became an important influence within academic philosophy's dialogue over the moral status of animals. His influence outside of academic circles spread much more rapidly when his *The Case for Animal Rights* was published in 1983.

Henry Spira: Inspiration for the Movement.   The conceptual integrity provided by these philosophical works paved the way for a new perception of the movement. A veteran of union and civil rights activism, New York teacher Henry Spira had begun thinking about animals around 1974, and at the same time fortuitously read Peter Singer's first article on animal issues, the *New York Review of Books* review of Stanley Godlovitch, Rosalind Godlovitch, and John Harris's *Animals, Men, and Morals.* Finding Singer's argument direct and powerful, Spira pursued the opportunity to sit in on Singer's class at New York University when Singer came shortly thereafter as a guest professor.

Spira's first effort at animal activism was directed at animal experimentation. He and a small group of activists had been looking for an appropriate goal: "a single significant injustice" to fight, and "moreover, that goal must be achievable." In fact, they "wanted an issue which we merely had to describe in order to put our opponents on the defensive." In 1975 he received a leaflet distributed by an antivivisectionist organization, United Action for Animals (an important source of Singer's information concerning experimental uses of animals when he wrote *Animal Liberation*), which described an experiment being conducted by the Museum of Natural History with government funding. The experiments involved blinding, deafening, and destroying the sense of smell and removing parts of the brains of cats to discover the effect on their sexual behavior. The current experiments were part of a series that had been going on for some 20 years, and they seemed to fit the criteria well. Spira's group used the Freedom of Information Act to research the experiments, and then had scientists evaluate the experiments. Museum officials refused to talk with the group, so the group went public, publishing reports in local newspapers, setting up pickets in front of the museum that lasted 18 months. Ultimately they generated enough controversy to convince Ed Koch, then a New York congressman, to tour the laboratories and submit his observations to the *Congressional Record.* Koch apparently had some difficulty understanding why the government would wish to fund this particular experiment:

Then I said to this professor, "Now tell me, after you have taken a deranged male cat with brain lesions and you place it in a room and you find that it is going to mount a rabbit instead of a female cat, what have you got?"

Henry Spira began organizing protests and coalitions in the 1970s, helping to vitalize the movement. *Photo by Jim Mason*

There was no response.
. . . I said, "How much has this cost the government?"
She said, "$435,000."[38]

One hundred twenty members of Congress joined Koch in questioning the funding of these experiments, and some other scientists also distanced themselves from the research. The museum was taking a

Protesters at the Museum of Natural History in New York City (pictured here in 1976) persevered for 18 months until the cat experiments at that institution were halted. *Photo by Dan Brinzac*

public relations beating, and finally the National Institutes of Health (NIH) halted funding for the project.

Spira led a group that accomplished what no one had to that point: they did not just protest objectionable research but actually succeeded in getting it stopped. Within two years of first learning of the experiments, the laboratory had been dismantled. The unprecedented had been accomplished through a carefully orchestrated campaign targeting an obviously vulnerable bit of animal exploitation. Helen Jones reports that, for the first time, the American press used the term *animal rights activists* rather than *animal lovers* in describing these events (1988, 74).

From there Spira went to work on the Metcalf-Hatch Act, which permitted researchers to seize unclaimed animals from shelters in New York State to use in research. Following the expansion of federally funded research in the post–World War II era, the research community became aggressive in promoting pound seizure legislation. The first law requiring municipal pounds to sell to research was passed in Minnesota in 1949, followed by Baltimore and Los Angeles (1950), the state of New York (1952), and several other states. The public support for the practice appears to have been fairly strong during the early 1950s, since pro-pound seizure laws were passed by public referendum in Los Angeles, Baltimore, and Illinois by comfortable margins. The practice of "pound seizure" has been objectionable to both animal rights advocates and humane groups for a long time, at minimum because it frustrates the purposes of shelters in providing safe haven for lost animals, and a humane death if that is necessary.

Others had worked for repeal of these hated laws before. Initially, the American Humane Association attempted to negotiate with the National Society for Medical Research (NSMR), but the pledge to keep the negotiations secret was immediately betrayed by the NSMR, bringing this tactic to an end and causing formation of two new organizations: the Animal Welfare Institute (1951) and HSUS (1954). In Rhode Island the first prohibition of pound seizure was passed in 1972, followed by New Jersey in 1974. The major turning point, however, was the repeal of the Metcalf-Hatch Act, spearheaded by the Society for Animal Rights and Citizens for Animals, and succeeding in 1979 with a larger coalition led by Henry Spira.

Spira succeeded in bringing about repeal of the Metcalf-Hatch Act by trying an angle no one had tried: he lobbied the legislator who was well known to be the chief obstacle to repeal of the law. Senator

Lombardi had on many occasions not allowed the issue to pass through his committee. Spira convinced Lombardi that the issue should be openly debated on its merits, regardless of the senator's personal view on animal experimentation. The appeal to Lombardi's sense of fairness succeeded—the law was debated and ultimately repealed in 1979. The biomedical research establishment felt sufficiently threatened that the Association for Biomedical Research (later called the National Association for Biomedical Research) was formed to combat the animal rights movement and promote animal research.

In the 1980s Spira was also to lead a coalition of groups fighting product testing, and he continues today with a group called Animal Rights International. Henry Spira is clearly one of the modern animal rights movement's early heroes. His successes inspired—perhaps even helped create—the young movement, showing that victories are possible if campaigns are carefully conducted.

The vigor and conceptual integrity of the animal movement soon revitalized the humane movement. Both the HSUS and the RSPCA took on strong roles in exposing and condemning institutional cruelties during the 1970s. The RSPCA condemned the fox hunt for the first time in 1976 and joined the International Fund for Animal Welfare (IFAW) and Greenpeace in their campaigns against the Canadian seal kill in 1977.[39] In the United States John Hoyt, president of HSUS, announced a new era in 1976, hiring animal rights defender Dr. Michael Fox (a British native trained in veterinary science and ethology) as HSUS's science advisor. The organization took on institutionalized animal cruelty with new vigor.

Edward Taub and the Silver Spring Monkeys.   One of the dramatic cases that helped create a mass animal rights movement—and also helped catapult the young organization People for the Ethical Treatment of Animals (PETA) into prominence in the movement—is the case of the "Silver Spring monkeys." Realizing that firsthand experience in a laboratory would be helpful to the young organization PETA, co-founder Alex Pacheco perused a USDA directory of registered animal research facilities and selected the Institute for Behavioral Research (IBR) in Silver Spring, Maryland, purely out of convenience: it was close to his home. The George Washington University student was taken on as a volunteer by head researcher, Dr. Edward Taub, almost immediately. Knowing nothing of the research or conditions of the laboratory, Pacheco was in for something of a surprise. The conditions he found at the laboratory were shocking, even to someone who had gone "underground" to learn how to expose animal research:

On 11 May, 1981 I began work and was given a tour by Taub himself. . . . As we went through the doors . . . , I had my first indication something was wrong. The smell was incredible, intensifying as we entered the colony room where the monkeys were kept. . . . I saw filth caked on the wires of the cages, faeces piled in the bottom of the cages, urine and rust encrusting every surface. There, amid this rotting stench, sat 16 crab-eating macaques and one rhesus monkey, their lives limited to metal boxes just 17 and 3/4 inches wide. In their desperation to assuage their hunger, they were picking forlornly at scraps and fragments of broken biscuits that had fallen through the wire into the sodden accumulations in the waste collection trays below. The cages had clearly not been cleaned properly for months. There were no dishes to keep the food away from the faeces, nothing for the animals to sit on but the jagged wires of old cages, nothing for them to see but the filthy, faeces-splattered walls of that windowless room, only 15 ft. square.

In the following days the true nature of the monkeys' sad existence became apparent. Twelve of the sixteen monkeys had disabled limbs as a result of surgical interference (deafferentation) when they were juveniles. Sarah, then eight years old, had been alone in her cage since she was one day old. . . . According to a later count, thirty-nine of the fingers on the monkeys' deafferented hands were severely deformed or missing, having either been torn or bitten off.

Many of the monkeys were neurotic. . . . Like a maniac, Sarah would attack her foot and spin around incessantly, calling out like an infant. Domitian attacked his arm mercilessly and masturbated constantly. . . . The surgery room had to be seen to be believed. Records, human and monkey, were strewn everywhere, even under the operating table. Soiled, discarded clothes, old shoes, and other personal items were scattered about the room. Because of a massive and long-standing rodent problem, rat droppings and urine covered everything, and live and dead cockroaches were in the drawers, on the floor and around the scrub sink.

No one bothered to bandage the monkeys' injuries properly (on the few occasions where bandages were used at all), and antibiotics were administered only once; no lacerations or self-amputation injuries were ever cleaned. Whenever a bandage was applied it was never cleaned, no matter how filthy or soiled it became. . . . The monkeys also suffered from a variety of wounds that were self-inflicted or inflicted by monkeys grabbing at them from adjoining cages. I saw discoloured, exposed muscle tissue on their arms. Two monkeys had bones protruding through their flesh. . . .

. . . Even though I had made it plain to Taub that I had no laboratory experience, within a week of starting work I was put in charge of a pilot study. . . .

Taub called the study a "displacement experiment." The monkeys . . . were deprived of food for two or three days, and I was . . . to record events and feed them about fifty raisins each. After some weeks I was to withhold food for three days and then, instead of giving them the raisins I was just to show them the raisins but not allow them to eat, and then record their frustrated reactions.

. . . I asked Taub and [his assistant] Yakalis three times what the purpose of the experiment was and what I should keep my eyes open for. On each occasion they responded that they hoped to find something "interesting," in which case they "could get [grant] funding."

. . . After about a month I was put in charge of yet another experiment: "the acute noxious stimuli test." I was to take a monkey from the colony and strap him in a homemade immobilizing chair, where he would be held at the waist, ankles, wrists and neck. The acute noxious stimuli were to be applied with a pair of haemostats (surgical pliers) clamped and fastened onto the animal, and locked to the tightest notch. I was to observe which parts of the monkey's body felt pain.[40]

Taub had received federal grants to study the rehabilitation of impaired limbs, but Pacheco's observations, if accurate, threw grave doubts on the possibility that any results Taub's lab might produce would be reliable or reproducible. Though the state anti-cruelty laws usually exempt animal experimentation from their scope, a revision of the Maryland statute had eliminated the exemption. On learning of this, Pacheco began collecting evidence. He had been sneaking fruit to the monkeys to supplement their inadequate diet, but now stopped the secret feeding so the monkeys would appear as they had without his intervention. He approached five individuals with expertise that might help bolster the case: Dr. Geza Teleki, an ethologist and primatologist; Dr. Michael Fox, veterinarian, ethologist, and scientific advisor to HSUS; Dr. Ronnie Hawkins, a physician who had experience in laboratories with primates; Dr. John McArdle, former primate researcher who now worked with HSUS; and Donald Barnes, a psychologist who had done military research with primates and ultimately became director of the National Antivivisection Society (NAVS). Armed with photographs and affidavits, Pacheco brought the evidence to the Silver Spring police. On 11 September 1981 a scientific laboratory in the United States was raided by the police for the first time. The monkeys and the files were confiscated, charges were pressed against Taub on 17 counts of cruelty to animals—one for each monkey. The NIH suspended Taub's funding, pending an investigation, and called on Taub to account for his expenditures and research results.

In the initial week-long trial, Taub was convicted of six counts of cruelty for failing to provide proper veterinary care for six of the monkeys, with the court finding the remaining charges based on psychological suffering, lack of cage space, and sanitation problems unconvincing evidence of cruelty. Nonetheless, the conviction was unprecedented: not only had the local police been willing to investigate, the prosecutors took the case forward, and a researcher had been convicted of cruelty. A major battle had been won—researchers were on notice that their activities were not immune from legal recourse for cruelty to their animal subjects.

The conviction, however, was not to stand for long. Taub appealed, and the second trial—which excluded all evidence unrelated to the six counts Taub had been convicted on—resulted in the conviction (after a two and a half day jury deliberation) being reduced to just one count. Taub appealed again, and the Maryland Court of Appeals reversed the conviction, ruling that the state anti-cruelty laws do not apply to researchers who receive federal funding.

The story does not end there, for the question of what would happen to the Silver Spring monkeys was unresolved. Initially, the police confiscated them and turned them over to PETA, which had prepared a refuge for them in the basement of an activist's home when the National Zoo had been unwilling to help and local animal shelters were unable to help. Within a few days of his arrest Taub's attorneys motioned for the return of his "property." Relying on recent inspections of the laboratory by the USDA in which only "minor deficiencies" or "no deficiencies" were reported, and without hearing the testimony of PETA's experts, Judge David Cahoon granted the motion. The Silver Spring monkeys were to be turned over the next day. But the monkeys disappeared that night, leading to warrants for the arrest of Ingrid Newkirk, Lori Lehner (in whose house the monkeys had been housed), and Jean Goldenberg, of the Washington Humane Society/SPCA. Lehner spent a night in jail, but in the morning it was determined that insufficient evidence existed against the three, and the arrests were dropped.

The dilemma facing PETA was that the monkeys were the key evidence in Taub's upcoming trial. After some negotiation, an agreement was reached with the police: they would be turned over to the police, who would not turn them over to the IBR; but Judge Cahoon ordered them returned to IBR without the further hearing that had been negotiated. A few days after their return, one of the monkeys (Charlie) died, allegedly of a heart attack. The police confiscated the body and sent it to Cornell University for a necropsy. The cause of death could not be determined because vital organs were missing, including the heart, lungs, kidney, a testicle and several glands. At this point Judge Cahoon ordered the monkeys taken from IBR and placed at the NIH's primate quarantine center in Poolesville, Maryland. While there, another monkey (Hard Times) had to be euthanized because he was paralyzed from the waist down and in great pain, and another (Nero) had to have an arm amputated.

The saga of the Silver Spring monkeys did not end there. The surviving 15 monkeys became something of a cause célèbre in the animal rights movement. For the next eight years a battle was waged between PETA and the NIH in the courts and the press over the disposition of the monkeys. PETA offered to place the monkeys in a primate sanctuary in Texas, Primarily Primates, at its own expense for the rest of their lives, but the NIH rejected this plan. Courts ruled that PETA and other animal protection groups lacked the necessary legal standing to sue on behalf of laboratory animals, rulings that PETA unsuccessfully appealed. By the beginning of 1991, nine of the 17 original monkeys had died. Of the 15 living after Charlie and Hard Times died, five were sent to the San Diego Zoo, of which four are still living; 10 went to the Delta Regional Primate Center (Tulane University), where Paul, Brooks, and Billie were all euthanized in 1989 or 1990. Three (Augustus, Domitian, and Big Boy) were all killed following further experiments at Delta in the summer of 1990. Sarah, Allen, Nero, and Titus remained under NIH control at Delta 10 years after the case originally broke.

The fact that Taub's conviction was overturned and the monkeys never freed from the NIH dampened but did not overturn the conclusion that a victory of sorts had been won by PETA. The case was remarkable for a number of reasons. It was the first time the police had cooperated with an animal rights organization, raided a laboratory, and presented evidence to prosecute a scientific researcher. The conviction was unprecedented, and even though it was overturned, animal rights advocates took solace in the fact that it was overturned on a "technicality"; in their eyes the jury that had seen the evidence had spoken clearly about the cruelty in Taub's laboratories.

The exposé of the lab sent a broader message as well: the IBR had received funding from the NIH (the government agency which provides the vast majority of funding for animal research in this country) and had even received recent stamps of approval from USDA inspectors. Nevertheless, if Pacheco's evidence was to be believed—as PETA's independent experts, the police, prosecutors, and the juries did—the public could not rest assured that the law and the government agencies responsible for enforcing it would meet even the most minimal moral requirement that animals used for medical research be treated humanely, with any suffering being imposed only reluctantly, as a matter of necessity.

And further, the willingness of activists to do undercover investigation, and the ease with which extreme conditions at laboratories could be brought to public attention, made activists realize that they did not have to remain helpless in their opposition to the giant institution they were questioning. Important lessons could be learned from this campaign, exemplifying qualities that ultimately led to PETA's prominent position in the movement: careful investigation, a narrowly defined target and correspondingly well-defined demands or expectations, and unyielding persistence.

"Unnecessary Fuss": The University of Pennsylvania Head Injury Lab. "Unnecessary Fuss" was to become the rallying cry of another major event in PETA's history. PETA has served on a number of occasions as liaison between the Animal Liberation Front (ALF) and the media, as the ALF could not present their own results and case to the press very readily, given the illegal, underground nature of many of their actions. On 28 May 1984 such a raid was made on the laboratory of Thomas Gennarelli at the University of Pennsylvania. Gennarelli had been receiving approximately $1 million per year in federal grants for 13 years to study head injuries of the type received in sports and automobile accidents. For many years the grants had gone into the development of a device that could deliver precisely measured blows to the heads of baboons, so that subsequent investigations could differentiate between severity of blows in an objective, reliable manner. After the device was ready, the research involved cementing the device onto the heads of baboons, and then delivering blows of different force to the baboons. Learning of the experiments, a local group, the Pennsylvania Animal Rights

Coalition (PARC), and the national group, Fund for Animals, denounced them. Gennarelli met with the groups but refused to let them inspect the laboratory.

The ALF raiders were greeted with a surprise when they entered the lab: the researchers had maintained a record of their research on videotape. Rather than disturbing the laboratory or liberating any animals, the raiders simply removed some 60 hours of videotapes, recognizing their value to the movement. And in fact, that value was immense. The ALF's press release called the tapes the "Watergate tapes of the animal rights movement." PETA (to which the ALF had delivered the tapes) offered the Department of Health and Human Services (HHS), the branch of government that has oversight of the NIH, the opportunity to view the entire 60 hours of tapes, but HHS officials declined. Despite NIH Director Dr. James Wyngaarden's public assurances that Gennarelli's lab was "one of the best in the world," an inspection at this time revealed 74 violations of the Laboratory Animal Welfare Act.

By September, PETA had produced and made public a documentary based on 30 minutes excerpted from the tapes. Gennarelli had been quoted in a newspaper interview in 1983 as saying he did not want his work publicized because it could "stir up all sorts of unnecessary fuss among those who are sensitive to these sorts of things," so the documentary was ironically titled *Unnecessary Fuss*. And indeed it did stir up quite a bit of fuss. The tape showed a brutal experiment, and the impact on most viewers on seeing the baboons receiving numerous intense blows, as well as their subsequent stupors and inability to stand or even hold their heads up certainly accounts for the tremendous power of the tape to move audiences. The tapes not only packed this tremendous emotive force but also revealed numerous violations of the Federal Animal Welfare Act (e.g., surgeries that were not aseptic, animals left unattended on the operating table, researchers smoked while performing surgery), and a cavalier attitude of the researchers toward the intense suffering that the baboons must surely have undergone. One of the most damning aspects of the excruciating 30 minutes was a scene in which researchers were shown removing the device from a number of the baboons' heads. After spending millions of taxpayers' dollars to develop a device that would deliver precisely measured blows to the head, and after imposing severe suffering on dozens of baboons, the researchers confounded their own results by using hammer and chisel to remove the cemented devices from the heads of the baboons. Any precise measure was now meaningless in light of the additional, unmeasured blows from screwdriver and hammer. The words of "Sonya," a spokesperson for the ALF, expressed the widespread feeling: the videotapes revealed "the callousness, wastefulness, inhumanity, and arrogance of the animal experimentation industry."[41] Throughout the year following the break-in, efforts were made by animal rights activists and organizations to shut down Gennarelli's lab from a variety of directions. In November 1984 law professors from the University of Pennsylvania (led by Professor Gary Francione, a longtime animal rights activist) attempted to initiate a dialogue with the research committee of the university but were not allowed to show the committee *Unnecessary Fuss* or to bring an independent scientific advisor to the meeting. In January 1985 it was revealed that the head of the research committee, Dr. Jacob Abel, had previously worked with Gennarelli on a head injury project. In April 1985 a mass demonstration drew 1,500 people to the university campus. In June the university appointed a "blue-ribbon" committee to investigate allegations against the lab. The report, issued in August, maintained that there were no problems, no wrongdoing at the lab. It was later discovered that one of Gennarelli's grant applications mentioned the chair of the blue-ribbon committee, Truman Schnabel, as having been instrumental in the "planning and implementation of the Head Injury Clinical Research Center."

Having tried unsuccessfully to get HHS officials to view the tapes in their entirety, PETA took their case to Congress, which was soon to be considering an appropriations bill for the NIH. They succeeded in securing two showings of *Unnecessary Fuss* on Capitol Hill, and in May 1985 some 60 members of Congress petitioned HHS Director Margaret Heckler to stop funding for Gennarelli's lab, still without success. A number of animal rights organizations joined the cause, with the International Society for Animal Rights (ISAR), the National Antivivisection Society (NAVS), and the American Antivivisection Society (AAVS) all helping to fund a series of newspaper advertisements in the home districts of the 13 members of Congress on the Health and Human Services subcommittee of the House Appropriations Committee, which had the power to amend the appropriations bill and thereby deny funding to Gennarelli's lab. All these efforts failed, and, despite the heat, Gennarelli's lab was continuing with its research.

In fact, throughout this period local law-enforcement agencies in Pennsylvania were turning up the heat on the animal rights activists, rather than the laboratory. Pacheco and members of the Pennsylvania Animal Rights Coalition who had held a joint PARC/PETA press conference in October 1985 were served with subpoenas to appear before a grand jury investigating the break-in and theft of the tapes. Activists maintained that the investigation involved numerous violations of their civil rights.[42]

It was clear that "normal, legal channels" were not succeeding in bringing about any relief for the baboons. By July 1985 the laboratory had been exposed, protests had occurred, and members of Congress had even petitioned HHS Director Heckler to interrupt funding of the lab—but all to no avail. PETA turned to civil disobedience. The 100 protesters had been through a day-long training session, involving coaching by veterans of civil disobedience protests, attorneys from the Animal Legal Defense Fund (ALDF), and PETA leaders.[43]

Initially, the activists' plan was to occupy NIH offices and present their demands of the NIH: to halt funding of Gennarelli's lab, to stop using baboons in the lab, and to include an animal advocate on the NIH grant committee. On 15 July 101 activists went into the eighth-floor offices of Murray Goldstein, director of the NIH division that funded the lab, and sat down, intending to remain until arrested and removed by police for trespassing. They expected to be there a few hours at most. After a few hours NIH personnel had abandoned the surrounding suite of offices, and the protesters now occupied these as well. All contact with the activists was cut off (*Agenda*, September 1985, 1, 8–11).

Apparently, the NIH had decided to wait out the protesters, who they figured would certainly give up after a day or so without food or contacts. The activists were not to be defeated so easily: they hauled food up the eight stories in a basket tied to a rope. Then a congressman's wife ended the food and telephone embargo with a well-placed phone call of her own. Banners hung from the windows of the NIH building, and outside a candlelight vigil was maintained by supporters each night. Alex Hershaft of the Farm Animal Reform Movement (FARM) initiated a hunger strike on the third day to increase the pressure on the NIH. On the fourth day, HHS Director Heckler announced she was suspending delivery of funds to Gennarelli's lab until an NIH investigation was complete. Her action, she claimed, was based on a preliminary report of the investigating team, which stated that there were indications that the laboratory had failed "to comply with the Public Health Service Policy for the care and use of laboratory animals." (Later, activists who were part of the protest were to cite a different account of Heckler's acquiescence, stating that Heckler finally viewed *Unnecessary Fuss* as a result of the sit-in, and before the 30-minute film was over she had called to cancel Gennarelli's funding.) At any rate, the activists emerged victorious from the building on July 18 (*Agenda*, September 1985, 1, 8–11).

A few days after the sit-in James Kilpatrick viewed *Unnecessary Fuss* and was moved to write a passionate piece in his nationally syndicated column entitled "Brutal Research Techniques Unacceptable." The conservative columnist wrote: "though I am no antivivisectionist, I found [the film] appalling. . . . [I]t was high time for someone to rescue these baboons from the hands of their tormentors." Kilpatrick's column was followed by editorials expressing support for the activists and concern about controls on research in major media sources such as the *Washington Post* and the *New York Times*, the latter advocating passage of the Dole-Brown bill to impose tighter controls on laboratories, currently under consideration by Congress. NBC's "Nightly News" and "Today Show," Cable Network News, and other broadcasters showed portions of *Unnecessary Fuss*, giving many viewers a glimpse of the horrible suffering wrought by Gennarelli's research.

The campaign had lasted over a year, but the persistence and careful planning had paid off. The campaign had a specific, limited focus, although media coverage appropriately related the issues in question to larger questions about control of animal research. Numerous channels were pursued to close the lab, civil disobedience being employed only when it was clear that other avenues were blocked. Despite the Philadelphia district attorney's (unsuccessful) attempt to discover who had conducted the raid, little criticism of the ALF's break-in has been raised. In fact, the break-in became a classic example in the argument for the underground activities of the ALF—after all, had they not entered illegally and stolen the tapes, the movement would never have had the crucially damning information that ultimately closed the lab down.

Thus the modern animal rights movement was launched by a number of successes that dramatized what the new philosophies were pointing out: that the plight of animals was not the aberrant behavior of occasional acts of cruelty but exploitation at the hands of respected, government-sanctioned institutions as business as usual. Additionally, these early actions dramatized just how far we have come from the early days of the ASPCA, when prosecution of individual wrongdoers (once anti-cruelty statutes were on the books) and public education seemed the promising routes.

Chapter Three

Many Hands on Many Oars: Organizations, Tactics, and Politics

On 10 June 1990 thousands of animal rights activists and sympathizers from hundreds of animal rights organizations from all over the United States gathered in Washington, D.C. The event was originally the brainchild of Bill Dyer of Last Chance for Animals, who had envisioned it as a massive protest against pound seizure. The dimensions of the project grew, and the organization and coordination of the event were eventually handled by Peter Link and Tom Regan, who widened the focus to include all animal rights issues. The March for Animal Rights began with a rally at a park area near the White House called the Ellipse. Numerous information booths of a variety of organizations and the banners of dozens of states and animal groups could be seen all over the Ellipse. Activists had come to Washington—many from quite a distance and at considerable personal expense—to listen to movement leaders, to join in a rally with thousands of like-minded people, to march from the White House to the Capitol with the hope that the sheer force of their numbers would make their message reach millions of Americans.

Hundreds had come for the entire weekend of activities, including an activist workshop (PETA's "Animal Rights 101") and performance of a multimedia show, "Bless the Beasts," and many stayed through Monday to participate in lobbying efforts with Congress. So many people participated that the marchers who began from the White House covered the three miles to the Capitol before the last participants had even started walking. Official estimates of the turnout from the press, the Park Service, and march organizers ranged from 24,000 to 75,000. The sheer number of activists who gathered on that day is testimony to the strength of the movement. The virtual explosion of new animal rights organizations in the 1980s is remarkable. In addition to a number of large organizations with a national focus, there are hundreds of smaller organizations throughout the country, some with a national focus, some local or regional. These organizations represent a vast diversity of perspectives and approaches. There are organizations that focus on a single type of animal exploitation, such as vivisection (NAVS, New England Antivivisection Society), factory farming (Farm Animal Reform Movement, Humane Farming Asociation, Farm Sanctuary, Farm Animal Care Trust), or Fur(Lynx). There are organizations of professionals (Psychologists for the Ethical Treatment of Animals, Veterinarians for Animal Rights, Physicians' Committee for Responsible Medicine, Actors and Others for Animal Rights, Society for the Study of Ethics and Animals). There are organizations connecting animal rights with other liberation causes (Feminists for Animal Rights, Gays and Lesbians for Animal Rights, Incurably Ill United against Vivisection), and organizations with religious affiliations (International Society for Religion and Animal Rights, Buddhists Concerned for Animals, Jews for Animal Rights, Unitarian Universalists for the Ethical Treatment of Animals).

Some organizations focus on particular tactics, such as passing pro-animal legislation and fighting in court for animals (National Alliance for Animal Legislation, Society for Animal Protective Legislation, Humane Legislative Network, Animal Legal Defense Fund, United Action for Animals, Animal Rights Law Clinic), distributing educational materials as widely as possible (Argus Archives, NAVS, Animal Rights Network) or funding works of art that focus serious attention on animal issues (Culture and Animals Foundation). Some organizations focus on abuses of specific animals (Humans against Rabbit Exploitation, Friends of the Wolf, Wolves and Related Canids); others provide sanctuary for specific types of abused animals (Primarily Primates, Horse Sanctuary, Farm Sanctuary, Wolf Sanctuary). Some organizations are focused on particular campaigns, such as ending product testing (Coalition to Abolish the Draize), ending pound seizure (Pro Pets), ending dissection in the classroom (Student Action Corps for Animals), or ending hunting (Committee to Abolish Sport Hunting, Hunt Saboteurs).

Some groups focus on providing alternatives to the exploitation of animals, and showing connections between animal exploitation, environment and health (EarthSave). And many local groups around the country are working at the grass-roots level, such as the chapters of the North Carolina Network for Animals, Houston Animal Rights Team, and Citizens to End Animal Suffering and Exploitation. In southern California alone there are a number of local groups working toward similar goals, sometimes in a coordinated effort: Last Chance for Animals, Orange County People for Animals, Animal Emancipation, San Diego Animal Advocates, and Californians for the Ethical Treatment of Animals. These are just some examples of types of organizations; within each of the preceding categories are many worthy and active organizations we have not mentioned.

Thus, the task of describing the organizations that make up the movement is utterly daunting. No attempt can be made here to be comprehensive, and inevitably the work of hundreds of dedicated activists and organizations will be passed over or mentioned only briefly. Our goal can only be to provide descriptions of a representative sample of organizations and tactics, so that the true diversity of the movement is reflected. This is especially important because stereotypes and one-sided descriptions of the movement abound (e.g., Susan Sperling's *Animal Liberators*). We will begin by describing a brief history of the first few of the most widely known and influential organizations; even here it is impossible to be comprehensive. We will then turn to examining some special focus and regional organizations.

The 1980s: A Mass Movement for Animals Is Created

In the first few years of the 1980s a number of organizations that have now achieved national prominence evolved. Within a few short years People for the Ethical Treatment of Animals (PETA), Trans-Species Unlimited (TSU), Farm Animal Reform Movement (FARM), Mobilization for Animals (MFA), In Defense of Animals (IDA) and many other organizations with national, regional, or local focus were formed. In part this is not surprising, since a wave of interest in animal rights issues was sweeping the nation at the time, stimulated most clearly by publication of Peter Singer's *Animal Liberation* in 1975 and a spate of related works dealing either with philosophical concerns or the concrete problems of factory farming, hunting, animal experimentation, and the like.

But this concurrence was also not entirely coincidental. A growing number of people in the late 1970s shared the new philosophical concerns but had no effective way to act toward their goals short of pursuing personal life-style changes such as vegetarianism. The upsurge in interest in animal rights and the institutional critique implicit in that notion needed to be transformed into more organized efforts to give an outlet for activism. There were certainly activists and campaigns worth noting, such as the campaign to end the cat experiments at the Museum of Natural History in New York, but there seemed insufficient focus, little in the way of an analysis of how the struggle for social change should occur, and few outlets for individuals to become involved. In short, the newfound respect for animals was not yet a mass movement.

In the summer of 1980 this was all to change. Alex Hershaft, a former environmental chemist, had become a leader in the vegetarian movement in the mid-1970s. At the time, the leadership of the vegetarian movement, though ethically motivated, were not thinking about animal rights. As Hershaft puts it, "We had no concept of animal rights. I only knew you shouldn't slit an animal's throat and eat it." Beginning in 1975 a small but growing number of people would come to vegetarian conferences and agitate for inclusion of an animal rights agenda: "These people had read Peter Singer's book and opposed all forms of animal exploitation. Feminists saw connections between oppression of animals and oppression of women. . . . They had a whole agenda, which was very foreign to us at the time. They were the crazies sitting at the back of the room and disrupting proceedings. Yet we tolerated them because they seemed to make sense. Little by little, I talked to them one on one and read some of the literature, and eventually joined their ranks."[1]

Hershaft began to see the need to bring the two forces together: the vegetarian movement had more resources and organizing experience, while the animal rights agitators had a certain spark of enthusiasm then lacking in the vegetarian movement. So, in the summer of 1980, Hershaft brought together a number of people at the New York apartment of one of the vegetarian movement leaders, with little more agenda than Hershaft's notion that these people should put their heads together and see what they could create. The most immediate outcome of the meeting was a plan for a conference the following summer at Cedarcrest College in Pennsylvania, to be called "Action for Life." The title of the conference expressed the common concerns of these forces: activism and respect for life (Hershaft interview, June 1990).

Out of the first conference a number of organizations emerged, with the specific intent that different organizations would have different foci. Alex Hershaft created FARM, a natural progression for the former director of the Vegetarian Information Service. Alex Pacheco and Ingrid Newkirk transformed PETA from a local student group to a national organization, while George Cave created Trans-Species Unlimited and Richard Morgan Mobilization for Animals. Additionally, Doug Moss and Jim Mason's information service for animal rights activists, the Animal Rights Network (which published the *The Animals' Agenda*), and Henry Spira's coalition that waged a highly visible and partly successful campaign against the Draize and LD50 tests each got a boost from the conference (Hershaft interview, June 1990).

The Action for Life conferences continued for seven years, with many current activists in the movement finding their inspiration or direction at one of the early conferences. The conferences typically involved training sessions for activists, networking of different groups, ceremonial activities (awards, keynote speakers), showing of videos, and rap sessions—periods of open discussion of sensitive issues (e.g., maldistribution of wealth among organizations, killing as a solution to problems of overpopulation of companion animals, relation between animal rights and controversial issues such as abortion).

Along with the growing readership for writers such as Singer and Regan and the emergence of activist organizations, a number of specific events and campaigns helped create the support and publicity necessary to a mass movement. The uproar over the Museum of Natural History's experiments on cats in the 1970s, the plight of the Silver Spring monkeys, and the revelations of the University of Pennsylvania's Head Injury Lab all helped mobilize national support for the fledgling movement.

People for the Ethical Treatment of Animals.   Two groups are most widely associated with work for animal rights: the Animal Liberation Front (ALF) and People for the Ethical Treatment of Animals (PETA). These names are widely recognized and identified with the movement by people who know little else about them. PETA was founded by Ingrid Newkirk and Alex Pacheco in 1980. Through a

Alex Pacheco, co-founder of People for the Ethical Treatment of Animals. *Courtesy People for the Ethical Treatment of Animals*

series of carefully focused campaigns, PETA grew to an organization with an annual budget in excess of $7 million and over 300,000 members in less than a decade. Pacheco writes of its founding, "We decided the time was right for a grassroots movement for animal rights. . . . Although we would fight for all the animals, our primary focus would be on those animals largely ignored by traditional humane societies—animals used for experimentation, food and fur" (Pacheco 1990, 37).

PETA's offices reflect the dedication and no-nonsense orientation of the organization. The converted warehouse provides cramped quarters for the approximately 90 employees. In sharp contrast to the plush offices of some of the older animal welfare organizations, Pacheco's tiny office is bare-bones and utilitarian. The walls are decorated with PETA posters and photographs of Pacheco and various famous people. We spoke with Pacheco about PETA's history, strategies, and Pacheco's own involvement with animal rights.

Pacheco had thought at one point that his future lay in the priesthood, primarily as an avenue to work on social issues. A chance visit

Ingrid Newkirk, co-founder of People for the Ethical Treatment of Animals. *Courtesy People for the Ethical Treatment of Animals*

to a slaughterhouse led him to animal rights. Appalled by what he saw as he entered the slaughterhouse, Pacheco educated himself about animal issues. Ultimately this led to his departure from his studies for the priesthood—disillusioned, as he was, at the lack of sympathy among fellow students and instructors for his growing concerns about animal exploitation. Dedicating himself to a life of activism for animals, he spent the next few years "apprenticing" with those already active in a variety of settings: with the Hunt Saboteurs in Britain, aboard the *Sea Shepherd* in the Atlantic, and learning from activists, especially Nellie Shriver and Constantine Salomone (who, interestingly, is the person Alex Hershaft mentioned to us as the one who ultimately convinced him that what the animal rights "crazies" at the back of the room were saying made sense).

PETA has been in the forefront of a number of events that have helped create headlines for the animal rights movement and in turn has itself benefited from the attention. It has exposed many specific cases of institutionalized cruelty and has been an important force in helping to influence corporations to eliminate or reduce animal testing on cosmetics and in promoting the availability and marketing of cruelty-free alternatives. But what has probably been most significant in helping PETA to attain its position within the movement are a series of campaigns involving narrowly defined goals, specific targets, and a great deal of persistence.

The lesson of the value of persistence is one that co-founder Ingrid Newkirk brought with her to PETA. As a child in India, she had witnessed a great deal of animal suffering and had promised herself someday to do something about it. Years later as an employee in a filthy, mismanaged dog pound, she was to begin to make good on that promise. After a year of attempting to implement changes at the shelter, she told a television reporter about the shelter's conditions, and when the story hit the local news, she was fired. Banding together with other local concerned citizens who had heard of the story, she worked day and night until the shelter was put under new and caring management. This experience, according to Newkirk, taught her that persistence pays off: "There had been so many days when it had seemed hopeless to me, when I had felt out-manned, out-gunned, out-financed. But I had used every waking moment to work for what I believed in, and that had been a bigger card than the opposition could offer. I have never felt intimidated by the enormity of the opposition since."[2]

During the next few years Newkirk initiated anti-cruelty law-enforcement programs, wrote legislation, testified on animal protection bills, and learned all aspects of animal welfare work. Like Pacheco's, Newkirk's transition to animal rights came in response to concrete exposure to animal suffering:

One day, driving back late at night from investigating an appalling cruelty case in which a horse had been locked in a stable without food or water until he had died, it suddenly dawned on me that I spent about 14–16 hours a day rescuing dogs, cats, raccoons, and horses only to come home to eat lambs, chickens, and cows. I stopped eating animals then. Later, I visited a chicken slaughterhouse on the Delmarva Peninsula and saw first-hand how the animals died. During those first years, when the smell of Kentucky Fried Chicken might have weakened my new vegetarian resolve, I would remember the screams and the panic of those conscious birds and the look in their eyes as they headed for the knife. (Newkirk 1985, 46)

In 1976 Newkirk became director of cruelty investigations for the Washington Humane Society/SPCA. Two years later, while working to improve conditions at the District of Columbia's dog pound, she met Alex Pacheco. He gave her a copy of *Animal Liberation* and made fun of her for eating dairy products and eggs. At this time, Newkirk says, "My feelings for animals fell into place" (Newkirk 1985, 47). Shortly thereafter she and Pacheco founded PETA.

Initially, PETA sponsored chapters around the country, and many of these were highly visible in their regions. But in the mid-1980s PETA decided to close its chapters and maintain only a central office in the Washington, D.C., area. The decision reflected PETA's growth in size and influence and the difficulty of maintaining a single, focused position. Of particular concern to PETA's leadership was the problem of control of what the organization does when offices are scattered throughout the country, staffed mainly by volunteers who are not answerable in the end to an employer. Pacheco explained the importance of this move in our interview with him:

If I could get one thing through the heads of the people who want to be effective, [it's that] it's a political world, it's a business world. The world is run on politics, decisions are financial. That's the world that needs to be addressed. We're in the business, figuratively speaking, of selling compassion, of getting people to change life-styles and become more civilized. And the only way to get through to America is to do it the same way the politicians and business people do it . . . by being politically savvy and business savvy, using all the modern techniques of selling a concept and selling a philosophy. . . . It doesn't matter if you're grassroots or not—you should still be professional, savvy and smart.

Pacheco believes that this "professionalization" of the movement has been crucial in its growth and successes. We were interested to learn that PETA requires new employees and college students participating in its internship program to read Singer's *Animal Liberation*. When asked how PETA views the relation between the philosophical debates over animal rights and PETA's own work, Pacheco stated that the philosophical contribution of people like Singer and Regan is important in giving the movement a sense of legitimacy, and in introducing some people to its ideas. He is less interested, however, in getting lost in the details of the philosophical debate:

What got me and most everybody I know involved was just the pain and suffering of the animals. It wasn't anything academic or philosophical. It was in the gut and in the heart, something very fundamental. Something a five-year-old has. . . . It's not elaborate. And that's what keeps us in this. The anger that we have over the injustice, the cruelty to helpless creatures that don't deserve it. . . . People don't have to adopt the whole philosophy . . . they just have to care. Whatever they call us, that's what guides us.

The whole problem is a business problem. The reason animals are in the predicament they are in today is that it's a good business proposition. . . . I used to think if we could just switch the minds of the politicians, that's where we should go. . . . Then I found out the hard way that the politicians are just like the businessmen—they're out selling to their customers. Whatever their customers want, they provide. They don't lead their customers around—they would go out of business. The politicians, the companies . . . they're going to follow the masses, and whatever the masses want they will provide. [Consequently,] every American has to go through the same process as we did before we will succeed.

Over the past decade PETA's work for animals has been prodigious. To name but a few accomplishments, PETA has exposed cruelty in numerous product testing companies, at Carolina Biological Supply, at a Montana fur farm, and at General Motors, which until recently performed crash tests using animals. PETA's undercover investigations have repeatedly brought to light gross violations of basic law and decency, and in each case the organization has effectively brought pressure and publicity to bear. PETA's effective and thorough research and investigation have become a model for the movement. Their educational and direct action tactics make it highly visible—a library of hard-hitting documentary videos, educational and training materials, a course on activism ("Animal Rights 101"), street theater, and demonstrations—and effective enlistment of celebrities (such as Paul McCartney, the late River Phoenix, Berke Breathed and Kevin Nealan) and direct action keep a steady media spotlight on the organization.

PETA has frequently found evidence from ALF raids on its doorstep and has acted as a media connection for the underground group. In addition, Ingrid Newkirk has recently published a book about the ALF. The perception that PETA is itself involved in illegal ALF activities has led the FBI to investigate PETA's leadership and various staff members. As this book goes to publication, Alex Pacheco and Ingrid Newkirk have both been asked to submit fingerprints and handwriting samples, and the threat of indictments against PETA appears real (Burd, 1993).

Trans-Species Unlimited.   One of the organizations that emerged from the meeting in New York in the summer of 1980 was Trans-

Species Unlimited (TSU). Founded by Dr. George Cave and Dana Stuchell, TSU established offices in New York City, Chicago, Philadelphia, and Harrisburg and Williamsport, Pennsylvania, where the main headquarters were located until 1991. They have been quite active in the New York-Pennsylvania area, as well as being highly supportive of and influential in helping to create a national grass-roots movement. TSU is well known in the animal rights community for its use of direct action, its endorsement of confrontational tactics, its various campaigns (including its leadership of the Campaign for a Fur-Free America, ongoing demonstrations against an annual pigeon shoot in Hegins, Pennsylvania, and its success in getting Cornell University to abandon plans to use cats to study barbiturate addiction, despite already having federal funding lined up for the project), and also for its outspoken criticisms of other groups and trends in the movement.

In 1990 TSU changed its name to Animal Rights Mobilization! (ARM!) and announced that it was launching a new focus for the organization—to build a coalition of local grass-roots groups and provide support services (such as literature that could be distributed and information sharing among the groups). The aim was to both maintain the autonomy and identity of local organizations around the country while providing some of the support and services that only a larger, more centralized organization can afford. This seemed a rather natural outgrowth of TSU, as it had itself always concentrated on grass-roots campaigns, building large local groups of supporters in each of the cities in which it had set up offices. Co-founder Cave had earlier urged greater coalition building on the part of the movement. The direction Cave sees for the movement seems somewhat contrary to the vision of PETA, which has become more centralized, more "businesslike" over the years.

George Cave has been a vocal critic of the use of money among animal organizations, especially the high salaries paid animal welfare organization officers. Inevitably, as organizations proliferated and the animal rights movement grew in influence, questions about use of funds by some organizations have been raised. These questions arise partly because new supporters of animal rights wanted to know where their money could do the most good, but they were also surfacing because some within the movement were questioning the propriety of some expenditures. Primarily, the latter questions have concerned the larger, more conservative animal welfare organizations, as well as some organizations that seemed to be primarily in the business of fundraising. According to *Animal Rights Reporter*—a publication that provides information (and much disinformation) about activities and organizations within the movement to its opponents (see Chapter 5 for more about this publication)—in 1988 George Cave helped form the Coalition against Animal Welfare Fraud, denouncing the high salaries paid to officers of animal welfare organizations such as HSUS, as well as their tremendous assets, demanding that the money "be given to grassroots animal rights groups, which have a record of dedication and commitment to the animals, in contrast to HSUS's record of fraud, theft and deception."[3] *Animal Rights Reporter* also reported that about a dozen protesters highlighted the issue by protesting outside of HSUS's annual conference in October 1988. Helen Jones, president of the International Society for Animal Rights (ISAR) and one of HSUS's founders, joined the picketers, who were referring to HSUS President John Hoyt as the "Jimmy Bakker of the Animal Welfare Movement."[4]

A report published in *The Animals' Agenda* in 1991 listed major organizations' income, overhead, assets, and compensation of their top officers for 1989 based on 1990 IRS filings. Leaders of many organizations received little or no compensation, but for others the charge made by Cave and others that some organizations were paying exorbitant salaries was substantiated. For example, in 1989 HSUS President John Hoyt was reported to have received compensation of $146,927, the fourth highest salary paid by an organization within the animal/environmental movement. Also drawing top compensation among leaders of such organizations were John Kullberg of the ASPCA ($130,000), John Sawhill of the Nature Conservancy ($180,000) and David Ganz of the North Shore Animal League ($163,700). Among the organizations with budgets over $10 million, the World Wildlife Fund (WWF) clearly ranks top in the report in terms of numbers of highly paid officers—the top 12 salaries paid to WWF officers average $89,000, coming to over $1 million just in compensation of their officers.

By comparison with the high salaries paid to officers of the wealthier organizations, PETA Chairman Alex Pacheco drew a salary in 1989 of $21,000, and George Cave and Dana Marie Stuchell of TSU were paid salaries of $15,000 each in the same year. A number of leaders of important animal rights organizations drew no salary at all, including Ingrid Newkirk (national director and co-founder of PETA), Shirley McGreal (chairwoman of the International Primate Protection League), Cleveland Amory (founder and president of the Fund for Animals), Alex Hershaft (founder and president of FARM), and

Christine Stevens (founder and president of the Animal Welfare Institute).

Agenda's report also examined the percentage of budget allocated to administrative overhead—an important category in determining whether money is going for the projects that attracted contributions in the first place. The report revealed that the North Shore Animal League (NSAL) spends only 60 percent of its nearly $20 million budget on programs, using some 40 percent on overhead, as contrasted with 18 percent for overhead for HSUS and 24 percent for PETA. This surprised few familiar with NSAL, as it has come in for much criticism within the movement for its fundraising appeals, which are often reminiscent of the Publisher's Clearinghouse Sweepstakes. HSUS and ASPCA are well-established, national animal welfare organizations, known for their moderate stances, educational literature and nonconfrontational approaches. Both have been at the forefront of the humane movement historically (ASPCA since the 1860s and HSUS since the 1950s) and have achieved considerable influence and respect on a variety of animal welfare issues. NSAL, on the other hand, is known for its "no-kill" animal shelter on the north shore of Long Island, and this is well-known nationally only because of the aggressive, direct-mail fundraising NSAL has done over the years.

Farm Animal Reform Movement. FARM has two aims—one long-range and the other of a shorter range. In the long run FARM seeks to bring about the end of exploitation of all animals, especially those raised for food. That, of course, means the end of consuming animals as food and food-producers. In the shorter run—until people stop eating animals—FARM hopes to bring about better conditions for animals while they are raised, transported, and slaughtered.

Formed in 1981, Farm Animal Reform Movement (FARM) is among the smallest of the national animal rights organizations in terms of membership and fundraising. Somewhat surprisingly, FARM founder and director, Alex Hershaft, claims this as FARM's strength. Keeping FARM small, Hershaft contends, enables him to do what he thinks he does best: conceive new ideas and respond to immediate needs.

A good example of the advantage of maintaining a small-size organization can be seen in what Hershaft called the Compassion Campaigns he waged during the 1984, 1988, and 1992 presidential elections. As the presidential campaigning began, Hershaft realized that no animal rights organizations were working to influence the party platforms or the campaign positions of the major candidates. So he took on the task, advocating not just for farm animals but across the spectrum of animal rights issues. The campaign took FARM to the early primary states, to party platform hearings, and to the national conventions.

Among the other things Hershaft does is to offer advanced training seminars for activists. In one such seminar, which he calls "Anatomy of a Successful Campaign," Hershaft maintains that, on most issues, campaigns for social change must go through four developmental stages before actual reforms take place. If reforms are to succeed, activists need to understand these phases and to see which phase they are in.

According to Hershaft, the first phase functions to alert the public to the issues. As the public is woefully ignorant of the ways in which animals are raised for food, this is obviously a crucial step in creating any public support for change. Alerting comes in many different forms—from the straightforward pamphlets, fliers, and brochures to pickets, demonstrations, and civil disobedience. The latter is properly viewed as falling within the informational stage, according to Hershaft, because the underlying message of demonstrations and civil disobedience is that the participants undergo some degree of discomfort for the purpose of publicly displaying the seriousness with which they regard this issue. As if to say, "I feel so seriously about this that I'm making a personal sacrifice—so pay attention." During this phase the main goal is to inform a large segment of the population of the issues while maintaining a positive image. The activities of the Compassion Campaigns fit into this phase and are crucial in informing lawmakers, politicians, and those who are politically active generally. Since opponents do not yet feel pressure, they will tend to ignore the campaign, which is one indication that a campaign is in the first stage.

The second stage is one of discussion. It is not (or at least not always) enough to inform the public of the problem. After all, the attitudes about animals that activists confront are deeply ingrained ones. So rational discussion and debate, consciousness raising, and a continuing effort to inform the public through media and literature characterize this stage. As with stage 1, it is important to maintain a high moral ground. Activists continue their presence in the chambers of decision makers and hold press conferences. Since the issue's existence and importance are taken more seriously at this stage, the opposition takes it more seriously and attempts to discredit it. The active involvement of the opposition is a key indication that a campaign is in this second phase.

The third stage, according to Hershaft, is that of public acceptance. This acceptance means that public attitudes have been changed while actual behaviors and laws have not. For example, the public may find the conditions of battery hens deplorable but still buy eggs produced on battery farms. At this stage the focus on lawmakers, lobbying, and boycotts is especially important. The degree of public acceptance causes the opponents to become more aggressive—for example, characterizing activists as terrorists and attempting to appeal to public fears. At the same time, activists become more complacent, since they see they have won public acceptance. One important reason that activists should learn about these phases is so that they understand that the work is not finished at this stage.

The fourth stage is that of reform, in which the gains made in stage 3 are actually implemented. Through lobbying of lawmakers to pass effective legislation, and following legislation through to the phase of appropriation and enforcement, activists finally achieve genuine changes in behavior and in conditions for animals. During this phase the opposition will do almost anything to oppose activists, including pressuring governors to veto bills that have passed and pressuring legislators to block appropriations. Activists at this phase need to maintain cohesion and avoid infighting in order to see the process of reform through to completion.

Hershaft believes that many activists flounder because they fail to pay attention to what sorts of activities are appropriate to the stage of development their campaign is in. Yet, he points out, it is often difficult to tell what stage one is actually in. Activists are too close to the issues they address, and they do not always have a very good sense of the public's response to what they do.

Having such an analysis of the process of social change enables Hershaft to understand what to do and what to make of the results. For example, he maintains that on most farm-animal issues, we are of necessity still in stage 1: the public simply lacks sufficient knowledge of how food is produced in this country to proceed very far with programs to change factory farming. As a result, much of what Hershaft does is educational, and it is in such terms that he understands whether he succeeds. Thus, even though no significant pro-animal items appeared in the final party platforms as a result of the

Compassion Campaign, Hershaft considered the extended opportunity to inform a large number of influential people of the problems animals face a tremendous step forward.

American Antivivisection Society.   While the 1980 Action for Life conference helped spark the movement by giving rise to several important national groups, it is important to recognize that there were already well-established organizations with a committed animal rights philosophy. A notable example is the American Antivivisection Society (AAVS), established in 1883. For over a century the AAVS has worked to end vivisection, primarily through public educational efforts. Currently headed by James Clark, this organization employs the talents of academically well-qualified scientists and scholars, such as John McArdle and Bernard Unti, whose research provides the animal rights movement with high-quality materials to make the case against animal experiments. AAVS publishes carefully researched monographs and pamphlets dealing with vivisection, pound seizure, patenting of genetically engineered animals, alternatives to dissection, and more general animal rights issues, such as speciesism and vegetarianism. The literature is distributed for free or at cost to grass-roots organizations, and it is a clear part of AAVS's philosophy to support grass-roots efforts.

While AAVS emphasizes education rather than such direct-action tactics as protests, this organization has actively supported and worked together with the newer animal rights organizations. For example, AAVS was an active supporter and participant in the March for Animal Rights in 1990. While committed to the goals of animal rights, the tactics for achieving these goals remain those of the more traditional welfare organizations—namely, research and education.

Fund for Animals.   Like AAVS, the Fund for Animals was an animal rights organization doing important work for animals before there was an animal rights movement. How there could be such organizations before their time is often to be attributed to the leadership of dynamic individuals, and such is certainly the case with the Fund for Animals. Cleveland Amory has been its leader and inspiration since its founding in 1967. Both he and his organization provide an interesting problem for those who seek a sharp boundary between animal rights and animal welfare work, for they are a blending of both. Amory was influenced by Anna Sewell's *Black Beauty* and by his

Cleveland Amory, founder of the Fund for Animals, with his companion cat, Polar Bear. *Courtesy Fund for Animals*

aunt who rescued homeless dogs.[5] His own thinking seems to reside squarely between the two traditions of animal rights and animal welfare. The fund was one of the first organizations to popularize the notion of animal rights with its "Animals have rights, too" T-shirts and bumper stickers, but Amory says that it was not really his idea and he was not sure what it meant.[6]

Amory finds the phrase difficult in some cases, conjuring up images of "bears marching down the street toward the Capitol and then marching in to take seats and raising their paws to vote." Regardless of his misgivings about the terminology, Amory's views often express animal rights ideas with a refreshing wit. For example, in a "Today Show" interview in 1963, Amory announced the formation of a new club—one to be called the "Hunt the Hunters Hunt Club." As Amory put it,

All the club ever tried to do was to define the word "conservation" for the hunters the way they have always defined it for the animals. We were shooting them, in other words, for their own good. But from the beginning the hunters made no effort to understand this, even though we made clear we never used words like "shooting" or "killing." Instead we used the hunters' own words—words with which they would feel comfortable—"culling," "trimming," "harvesting," or just "taking." We wanted them to understand that if we didn't take them, in no time at all there would be too many of them. They would be crowding the woods, and the fields and the roads, and they would be breeding like flies. . . .

The hardest criticism we had to take was that the "Hunt the Hunters Hunt Club" had no season on hunters. Nothing could have been further from the truth. The club's very second rule forbade members to take hunters "within city limits, in parked cars or in their dating season." (1990, 212–13)

Early on, the fund took on tough and successful campaigns, such as the fight to end the Canadian seal hunt, using both political lobbying and direct action tactics. (A memorable early example of Amory's "direct action" is the quite direct threats that the rather large Amory made personally to carriage horse drivers in New York City who whipped and mistreated their horses, which he recounts in a film produced by Tom Regan, *Voices I Have Heard* [1987]). In 1979 the fund's activities took on a new dimension when it won an injunction against the U.S. Park Service's plan to kill hundreds of burros in the Grand Canyon. The fund was suddenly faced with the prospect of rescuing 577 feral burros, and needing a place to keep them while good homes were found. In response, it purchased 200 acres of farmland in northeast Texas, which subsequently became Black Beauty Ranch. Over the years Black Beauty Ranch has become a sanctuary for thousands of animals rescued by the fund. For example, when the navy threatened to shoot burros at China Lake Naval Weapons station in California, the fund sued and won the right to remove the animals. And when the army sought to shoot 4,700 goats and 300 feral pigs on San Clemente

Island, Amory's friendship with Secretary of Defense Caspar Weinberger prevailed, and the animals were taken to Black Beauty Ranch, where many lived out the rest of their lives.

The fund's ability to intervene at a legal level (bringing lawsuits and injunctions to prevent killing and abuse of animals) as well as in a rescue capacity through its sanctuary makes it highly effective. In addition, the fund has regional offices and wildlife rehabilitation sanctuaries, and it continues to work on many legislative fronts. Examples of recent successful campaigns the fund was involved in include playing a major role in settling a lawsuit that will gain federal Endangered Species Act protection for 401 imperiled species; leading an international tourism boycott that prompted the state of Alaska to abandon its aerial wolf gunning plan; halting, by threatening litigation, a coyote-killing contest on national forest lands in North Dakota; and compelling the Texas Parks and Wildlife Commission to disallow hunting in eight state parks in Texas. One of the fund's great strengths is its willingness to form coalitions with other organizations, be they animal rights organizations or animal welfare organizations. Over the years the fund has worked with environmental organizations such as IFAW and Greenpeace, animal welfare organizations such as HSUS, and animal rights organizations such as Mobilization for Animals.

Rutgers Animal Rights Law Clinic.   A number of organizations have focused on animals and the law. There are political action committees (such as PAW PAC and the Humane Legislative Network in California) that promote animal legislation and keep members informed of the voting records of elected officials. With tremendous effort some changes have occurred—a number of which we discuss in the next chapter. But to this date little substantive change has come for animals by way of the legislative process. Our legal system does not currently recognize animals as being capable of possessing or asserting legal rights.

Nonetheless, existing laws do occasionally provide an avenue to broaden protections of animals, or at least to advance the activities of the movement. Recognizing this, longtime animal rights advocate Gary Francione (a professor at the Rutgers University Law School) founded the Rutgers Animal Rights Law Clinic in 1990. The clinic, connected to the law school but funded by private donations, provides both an educational and an advocacy function. Students in the law school can enroll in a seminar that promotes discussion of developments in the law relating to animals and ways that existing law can help promote their interests; the clinic also takes on cases—sometimes by providing backup research for local attorneys, and sometimes with Professor Francione acting as attorney.

In the first two years of its operation, the clinic took on a number of cases, often, but not always, relating to issues in universities. For example, the clinic staff advises thousands of students who inquire about their right to refuse vivisection or dissection in classes and reports that most cases are resolved without litigation. In a number of cases the clinic has negotiated on behalf of students and achieved settlements securing the right to alternative assignments. There have also been a number of cases relating to gaining access to information about what is going on in laboratories—information that many in the movement feel is essential to making their case to the public.

In cases in New York, Minnesota, and North Carolina the clinic prepared or helped prepare litigation aimed at creating open access to Institutional Animal Care and Use Committees (IACUCs) and their files. In each of these states "sunshine" laws grant citizens rights to attend meetings of governmental bodies and access to their documents. As of 1985, amendments to the Federal Animal Welfare Act require most research institutions to determine compliance with the act through the local IACUC system. Though many animal rights advocates regard this system as providing little in the way of substantive advance for animals, they nonetheless see it as an opportunity to gain access to information about local research activities. In many places, however, such committees have not allowed citizens to attend meetings or have any access to files. The New York courts ultimately ruled that access under state law was not guaranteed, since the IACUCs (created by federal law) did not perform a function for the State of New York. In North Carolina, on the other hand, access to research protocols reviewed by the committee was successfully achieved through the courts.

Animal Legal Defense Fund. The Animal Legal Defense Fund (ALDF), directed by attorney Joyce Tischler, combines advocacy of legislation to protect animals' interests with court cases. One noteworthy case the ALDF was involved in succeeded in expanding the coverage of the Laboratory Animal Welfare Act to include rats, mice, and birds. Prior to 1992, one common criticism of the federal law relating to laboratory uses of animals was that its minimal protections did not even extend to mice, rats, and birds, while rodents make up some 80 percent of the animals used in U.S. laboratories. The act itself explicitly mentions dogs, cats, monkeys, guinea pigs, hamsters, rabbits, and "such other warm-blooded animals" as the secretary of agriculture (who is charged with enforcement of the act) finds is being used for research, but the USDA had always interpreted the act as not regulating research with mice, rats, and birds. The ALDF sued and won: in January 1992 U.S. District Judge Charles Richey determined that the USDA had acted capriciously in excluding rats, mice, and birds.[7]

The ALDF is regarded by some within the movement as moderate, and perhaps the suit to extend this law case exemplifies the point, for the Federal Animal Welfare Act, while providing some protection of animals (e.g., requiring certain cage sizes and exercise for certain species), does not in any way challenge and provides very little limitation on the use of animals in laboratories. Thus, including rats, mice, and birds within its scope does little to advance the rights of such animals. It is not surprising, therefore, that Barbara Rich, vice-president of the National Association for Biomedical Research (an organization set up to defend and promote research with animals), was little troubled by the ALDF's victory. Rich noted that extending the rules currently applied to animals covered by the law to rats, mice, and birds "would mean different record-keeping and reporting [procedures], but I don't see it as a big problem" (Anderson 1992, 191).

Culture and Animals Foundation.   Since the beginnings of the movement in the 1970s, Tom Regan has been at the forefront in bringing academic, artistic, and cultural depth to animal rights issues. His books, articles, and anthologies have been an important force in making animal rights a topic of serious and central concern in colleges and universities throughout the country. While others, such as Singer, had viewed traditional Western religion as an obvious anathema to animal rights, Regan maintained (as had the British scholars S. R. L. Clark and Andrew Linzey) that a thorough reexamination of the question of religion and animals was in order. In 1977 Clark published an important work along these lines, *The Moral Status of Animals* (which examines the relation between Christianity and animal rights), and in 1984 Regan organized an international conference in London on Religion and Animals, the proceedings of which are published as an anthology, *Animal Sacrifices*.

It was this same commitment to a serious cultural reexamination of the dominant view of animals that led Regan to found the Culture and Animals Foundation (CAF) in 1985. If the arts express the fundamental ideas of an age, and are even crucial in shaping and developing them, then artists courageous enough to challenge the dominant view of our relation to animals ought to be supported. Audiences ought to confront the issue of their complicity in animal exploitation not only from the demonstrators who challenge them for wearing their furs *outside* theaters but from the stage as well. Since its formation, the CAF has funded many talented visual and performance artists, such as Sue Coe, whose powerful images of the suffering of farm animals have been described as a combination of illustration, documentary, propaganda, and fine art. Coe provides a strong social critique of oppression generally—for example, in her graphic series *How to Commit Suicide in South Africa* and *Police State*. The CAF has also supported scholarly works of fiction, poetry, and cultural critique and has produced two award-winning documentaries: *We Are All Noah* and *Voices I Have Heard*, both directed by Tom Regan. Carol Adams's *The Sexual Politics of Meat* (1990) was also supported by the CAF. Each year the CAF sponsors the Triangle Animal Awareness Spolito Festival for the Animals in Raleigh, North Carolina, bringing together artists, literary figures, historians, cinematographers, musicians, and scholars for four days of discussion, exhibition, and performance.

Animal Emancipation.   Local and regional organizations, while much less well known and visible, carry much of the burden of work for animal rights. Such groups are often eclectic, taking on a variety of local as well as global issues. Animal Emancipation (AE) is such a group, having a tiny bank account, no paid staff, and a remarkable record of achievements. Founded as a student group in 1988 by Denise Ford and Simon Oswitch, the Ventura, California, organization is involved in virtually all aspects of animal rights work. For example, it has rescued and found homes for hundreds of abandoned dogs and cats, rehabilitated wounded wild animals, relocated animals slated for extermination, conducted campaigns against area rodeos, protested against furs, filed litigation against animal abusers, conducted educational campaigns regarding factory farming, investigated and protested against animal research activities in the University of California system, conducted training seminars on numerous issues, and hosted vegetarian feasts for the homeless.

AE's successes are numerous: it has obtained a ban of the steel-jawed leghold trap on 90 percent of Santa Barbara County's public lands, closed two local fur showrooms, closed down an annual rodeo, succeeded in getting veal off the menu of an area market, and collaborated in documentary efforts resulting in a prohibition against Circus Vargas's use of chimpanzees.

But among all the situations AE has taken on, none has been as extensive nor as difficult as the campaign against the use of animals in research and classroom instruction at the University of California at Santa Barbara (UCSB). AE has uncovered a number of invasive federally funded experiments whose scientific value AE has questioned. In addition, AE claims the Institutional Animal Care and Use Committee is out of compliance with federal law on several counts (and at least one member of the committee, who resigned in protest, agreed). AE has also exposed extensive and unnecessary use of animals in biology, psychology, and pharmacology courses. In response, AE claims that UCSB researchers and administrators have made personal attacks against members of AE, focusing much of the brunt of their public denunciation against AE president Denise Ford. The attacks are reported to draw attention to Ford's health problems in an attempt to argue that she has made use of the benefits of animal research while at the same time criticizing it. In addition, AE members report that anonymous harassment (leaving of dead animals in cars, threatening phone calls, etc.) has become part of their daily life. Threats of legal sanctions, media attacks, and arrests have not dissuaded the group from continuing its campaign against vivisection at UCSB.

North Carolina Network for Animals.   Founded in 1983 by English Professor Nancy Rich, North Carolina Network for Animals (NCNFA) is a multifaceted, grass-roots organization that takes on issues such as vivisection, furs, factory farming, and individual cases of animal abuse. Tactics of the organization are also diverse, including investigative work, protests, letter writing, and public education. NCNFA is unusual organizationally, with a statewide board of directors coordinating 10 chapters throughout the state. This structure allows each group autonomy to address local issues, while assuring coordination and unity over more global issues and projects, such as statewide legislation. The NCNFA also coordinates efforts with other organizations, such as the Culture and Animals Foundation and PETA. For example, NCNFA was actively investigating Carolina Biological Supply for several years before PETA sent in an undercover investigator, leading to federal indictments.

Like other grass-roots organizations, NCNFA takes on local causes, such as the sale of animals from shelters to research and the uses of animals in research at area universities. One target NCNFA has shown much interest in is University of North Carolina at Greensboro's Walter Salinger, whose 20-year research program blinding cats and kittens has subsequently drawn widespread publicity.

Last Chance for Animals. An organization as different from PETA as it is from FARM, Last Chance for Animals (LCA) is an example of an organization that focuses most of its energy on a single issue (antivivisection) and primarily employs a single kind of tactic (direct action). Originally named "Second Chance for Animals," LCA was founded by Chris DeRose, Margo Tannenbaum, Regina Eshelman, and Maxine Lake. Though not all of the founders are still with this highly visible Los Angeles group, DeRose has continued as president. The group has a wide following in southern California and, like PETA, a nationwide membership as well. The group sponsors a variety of events—from cruelty-free fairs to undercover investigations, demonstrations, and various forms of direct action. Perhaps two things stand out about LCA: its direct-action tactics and its understanding of the mass media (perhaps somewhat natural for a number of the major figures in LCA, including DeRose, Jack Carone, and Tannenbaum, who have experience in acting or working with the mass media).

One of the tactics of the animal rights movement that has understandably attracted quite a bit of attention is civil disobedience, both for its drama and for the difficult moral questions it poses.

Civil disobedience has enjoyed a long tradition in this country, going back into the early nineteenth century (with Henry David Thoreau's refusal to pay taxes that went to support slavery and war), and more recently in the civil rights movement, the anti-war movement, the anti-nuclear movement, the women's movement, the anti-abortion movement, and AIDS activism. Last Chance for Animals has embraced civil disobedience as one of a number of important direct-action techniques available to the movement. While LCA is not the

Last Chance for Animals protesting the mistreatment of elephants at the Los Angeles Zoo in 1992. *Courtesy Last Chance for Animals*

only group that employs civil disobedience, its use of the tactic has been a prominent feature of LCA's strategy: LCA was formed with the express intention of using direct action to confront animal exploitation.

Last Chance for Animals distinguishes civil disobedience from other forms of direct action by the fact that the former involves some form of disobedience of the law. LCA requires its members to participate in training sessions before they can participate in civil disobedience. The training sessions cover a variety of concerns—from the nature of the act of civil disobedience as understood by LCA (e.g., its commitment to nonviolence) to the more practical preparations required by a group planning to submit to carefully orchestrated arrest.

As part of the training, activists view a videotape on civil disobedience produced by the leaders of the group: DeRose, Aaron Leider, Mary MacDonald Lewis, and Carone. The video is itself a statement of LCA's philosophical position on civil disobedience and is revealing of the group's general approach. The video makes clear that LCA's leadership is committed to a hierarchical view of activism. Decision making is top-down, with individual activists separated from the decision-making process by at least one layer (captains) during civil disobedience.

Participants in a particularly sensitive action would not know the nature of the target or any specifics of their plan until they were safely on a bus heading to the destination. LCA's leaders maintain that this approach is needed to retain the element of surprise and frustrate efforts at infiltration, either of which could make civil disobedience ineffective. Activists are advised in advance that their participation must be based on complete trust of the leader's judgment, and that they must accept orders during an action when they are delivered.

Under its first name, Second Chance for Animals, the group staged a series of protests in 1985 at Cedars-Sinai Medical Center in Los Angeles to call attention to the center's use of animals from the San Bernardino City Shelter. The first protest took place in San Bernardino on 17 August, with activists chaining themselves on the shelter's roof. After refusing to leave, three protesters were arrested. A month later a well-publicized protest at Cedars-Sinai attracted widespread national publicity and involved 11 arrests, with protesters chaining themselves to the truck used to transport dogs from the shelter to the medical center. By October (having now changed its name to Last Chance for Animals at the request of another organization bearing the "Second Chance" name), the group moved the focus of its protests to San Bernardino again, where it worked to pressure the city council to discontinue its sales of shelter animals to research. After numerous requests to speak before the city council had been denied, the group disrupted a city council meeting to demand that a hearing be set on the issue of the sale of animals from the shelter. The council agreed to a hearing, and the group agreed to leave the chambers. On 8 November LCA returned to Cedars-Sinai to protest the treatment of animals at the facility, and DeRose and nine other activists were arrested after chaining themselves to the roof of the center's entrance.[8] Finally, LCA members showed up in force at the city council hearing on the pound seizure issue on 9 January 1986.

This series of hard hitting and ongoing protests did, in the long run, achieve results. Feeling intense pressure both from the animal rights community and the researchers wishing to buy dogs from the shelter, the council put the issue to a public referendum. While the measure to ban the sale of animals was narrowly defeated, the ensuing modifications in shelter policy put virtually all animals out of the reach of researchers, and continuing pressure from LCA and other San Bernardino activists finally ended pound seizure in that city in July of 1991.

In addition to civil disobedience, LCA's direct-action efforts include intensive undercover investigations similar to those of PETA. Such an investigation of a dog theft ring selling animals to Cedars-Sinai and Loma Linda University led to the conviction of Barbara Ruggiero, Frederick Spero, and Ralf Jacobsen.[9] Ruggiero received the longest sentence for dog theft to date: six years in prison. In a subsequent investigation, LCA has uncovered a second dog ring in Oregon. DeRose's training in police work is clearly a useful asset to the group.

The Animal Liberation Front

The ALF has the unfortunate job of trying to pry open the door to let ordinary people see what it is that researchers are so afraid of us finding out. We are the underground, the French Resistance, in many ways.

—"Valarie," ALF activist

It is sometimes said that the Animal Liberation Front (ALF) is not an organization but a state of mind, and if one wishes to "join" the ALF, there is no way to do this other than to raid a laboratory or factory farm and to take credit for this action in the name of the ALF. The ALF is certainly not an *organization* in the usual sense of the word. Yet based on the few published sources (interviews with ALF "members," media accounts of raids, and two recent books—Ingrid Newkirk's *Free the Animals* and Rik Scarce's *Eco-warriors*) the loosely knit cells of the ALF in the United States do seem to share a number of strategies and philosophies beyond the "state of mind" that leads them to liberate animals. Furthermore, the ALF may not be so open-ended as the state of mind criterion suggests. The ALF raids that have attracted so much attention in recent years do not appear to have been either spontaneous or amateurish. Those involved have managed to escape apprehension for years, and it was only in the fall of 1992 that the FBI arrested and charged some alleged ALF members. The professionalism surrounding the ALF is reputed to include training, experience, and a complete veil of secrecy, such that even ALF spokespersons do not know the identity of ALF activists or about any of their plans in advance of a raid. Nevertheless, even if shared philosophy and strategy were not enough to qualify the ALF as an organization, its profound influence on events in the movement qualifies it for serious examination.

Animal Liberation Front raider with a liberated dog. *Courtesy Animal Liberation Front Support Group of America*

Given the secrecy surrounding the ALF, our account is necessarily incomplete in some ways. We cannot, for example, say anything about the personalities of those in the ALF. Ingrid Newkirk has painted a vivid picture of "Valerie," the alleged founder of the ALF in the United States, along with a compelling story of the history of the organization and its many successful raids. But the account is necessarily fictionalized in many ways, in order to avoid revealing the actual identities of ALF members. Readers of her book are left to surmise which features have been altered and which are fact.

Unquestionably, the direct-action, illegal tactics of the ALF are the most controversial of any in the animal rights movement. There are many who see the ALF as a dangerous terrorist organization with the potential of destroying the movement by discrediting it as violent. There are also many who see the ALF as the most dedicated and important arm of the movement, providing information available through no other means and liberating animals where all other efforts have failed. Others feel deeply ambivalent about the ALF, lauding its successes and at the same time fearing the possible repercussions of the ALF image. Examining the history of liberation groups is highly useful in understanding the sources of these complex and conflicting perspectives.

There have been a number of organizations with broadly liberationist tactics operating in Great Britain, France, Germany, Holland, Canada, and Australia. The first of these was formed from within the Hunt Saboteurs Association in Britain. In 1972 Ronnie Lee and Cliff Goodman, both "Hunt Sabs," decided to embark on a campaign of direct action against vehicles and other property used by the hunt. To do this they formed the Band of Mercy, which began by carrying out raids on fox hunt kennels in the south of England, and in autumn of 1973 the group expanded its campaign to attacking other forms of animal abuse. In November of that year it carried out arson attacks (causing over 45,000 pounds worth of damage) on a laboratory being built for the Hoechst drug company at Milton Keynes.[10] They followed with the successful sinking of a seal hunter's vessel and numerous attacks on lab-animal suppliers. After the arrest of some key members of the Band of Mercy in connection with a raid on Oxford Laboratory Animal Colonies, the activities of the Band of Mercy came to a halt. Nevertheless, the publicity surrounding the imprisonment of members of the Band of Mercy brought out the support of a new group of activists. Together with the remnants of the Band of Mercy, this new group formed the Animal Liberation Front in Britain in June 1976.

The newly formed ALF carried out 10 raids against animal research targets in 1976 and rescued beagles from the Pfizer laboratory in Sandwich. This group restrained itself from damaging property unless it was directly connected with animal abuse; nor did they attack homes of vivisectors. In one raid when a considerable amount of money was discovered, they are reported to have refrained from taking it for fear of being considered common thieves (*Against All Odds*, 11). In 1977, 14 laboratory raids were carried out, and more than 200 animals were taken from laboratory suppliers.

The first U.S. ALF raid occurred in 1977, when the "Undersea Railroad" released two porpoises from a Hawaii research lab. This deed had more of the character of traditional civil disobedience than an ALF action, as it lacked the clandestine nature of other raids to come. Two years later the ALF rescued five animals from the New York University Medical Center. According to the *New York Post* (15

March 1979), three women and a man disguised themselves in white smocks and posed as faculty members. They entered the unlocked laboratory and took a cat, two guinea pigs, and two dogs. In their press statement the spokesperson for the group stated that during months of observation of the laboratory she had seen many animals left bleeding and in pain after experiments. She stated, "We're not against working to save human lives. We're just against the attitude that animals can just be used for any kind of experiment, without regard for the fact that they're alive." The unlocked laboratory, the surprised and confused response of NYU (whose spokesperson stated, "We're sorry that anyone would resort to criminal trespass to draw attention to something that is a matter of public record"), and the moderate statement from the ALF all stand in marked contrast to subsequent ALF raids.

In 1979 liberation actions occurred in France and Holland, and distinct groups began operating in Britain. These actions were carried out by independent groups, operating with a variety of tactics and with differing philosophies and politics. Some groups, such as the Northern Animal Liberation League (NALL), believed in exposing vivisection to the public rather than causing damage. Their approach was to involve large numbers of activists in daylight raids, in contrast to the British ALF, which used the minimum number necessary. The French "Commando Lynx" were different from other groups in not being vegetarians and operating with ad-hoc "commandos" rather than using a small group of experienced people. During the 1980s not only the NALL but the EALL (Eastern Animal Liberation League), WALL (Western Animal Liberation League), the SEALL (South East Animal Liberation League) and Animal Rights Militia (ARM) sprang up in Britain. Because these groups differed in both their tactics and philosophies, there are no general answers to questions such as, "Do animal liberators believe in causing property damage, attacking the homes of animal abusers, using sabotage such as bombs or poisoning of products? Or are they merely intent on exposing animal abuse and rescuing animals?" These questions have been answered differently by the various liberation groups, although for the most part these groups were committed to nonviolence.

Nonetheless, in the late 1980s a number of acts of violence by the British underground groups led to something of a backlash within the animal rights movement. In addition to an incident in which a public scare was created by a false report that Mars candies were poisoned, a number of department stores with fur salons were bombed, causing extensive damage and threatening lives. Opposed to violence, and afraid that it would undermine the progress the movement was making, other groups disavowed the violent tactics.

In the United States the ALF appears to have consistently held to a philosophy of nonviolence, while distinguishing between property damage and violence toward living beings. An anonymous interview with a member of the ALF involved in the 4 July 1989 raid of John Orem's Texas Tech laboratory is representative of many statements made by ALF members. In answer to the question, "Would you ever harm a person?" the ALF member states, "No. The ALF will break things, but we will never harm a living being. The vivisectors are terrorists. Every day they cut, shock, burn, poison and drive insane thousands of frightened, helpless, innocent animals. They kill without a thought. Our aim is to slow down and eventually stop their violence."[11]

In destroying laboratory equipment used in animal experimentation, the ALF regards itself as destroying the tools of violence and hoping to divert money that would otherwise be used to exploit animals. As the animal liberator Sarah H. puts it, "Economic sabotage entails the destruction of devices used to torture animals, it raises the cost of animal abuse, and provides irrefutable proof that a raid did, in fact, occur. This proof, in turn, serves to corroborate our documentation in the eyes of the public. And, in the final analysis, is it not a moral act of mercy to destroy an instrument of torture?"[12]

Thus, ALF raids are focused on one or more of three goals: liberating animals, obtaining information (such as videotapes and records of experiments that reveal the exploitation of animals), and destroying equipment used in exploitation of animals and diverting research funds. While some people consider destruction of property a form of violence, a clear distinction should be made between violence to living beings and destruction of property. Thus far, no credible reports have linked any ALF action to violence against people in the United States. As a result, the ALF enjoys broader support from within the animal rights movement in the United States than have similar groups in Great Britain in recent years.

In fact, the U.S. ALF's philosophy and tactics reflect a number of lessons learned from the British experience. Many people who participated in the British raids found themselves doing long prison terms. For example, Ronnie Lee received a 10-year prison sentence, Sean Crabtree and Roger Yates each received four years. Most of the British Leagues became so enmeshed in legal battles that they folded.

The need to avoid a repetition of the British experience has led to the highly professional and closed nature of the ALF, though it appears that the U.S. government is employing tactics similar to those used by the British to separate the radical end of the movement from the moderate. Even those involved as media spokespersons (in particular, the British ALF Support Group) found themselves serving prison sentences: Robin Lane was sentenced to 18 months in prison for publishing reports of ALF activities that were interpreted as "inciting" and conspiratorial. In the United States PETA leaders Alex Pacheco and Ingrid Newkirk are currently under investigation by the FBI for possible criminal connections to the ALF.

The success of the ALF operations in the United States is no doubt attributable not only to training, advance reconnaissance, and research but also to assistance from insiders (known as "hands"), who are disturbed by the conditions they have witnessed. As Sarah describes it,

Frequently regular access is provided by employees who find animal abuse morally indefensible. With multiple access assured, our routine is always the same—first, all documentation is copied and replaced while the confinement conditions are videotaped and photographed. Once the evidence is secured and new homes for the animals pre-arranged, then the raid, the liberation itself, occurs. We conduct many more raids than are reported to the police or media. Most institutions will report a raid only if they cannot conceal it or they believe they can exploit it to their benefit. (McFarland 1990, 41)

The raids themselves give a clearer sense of the nature of the ALF. The following descriptions provide a sample of the types of activities the ALF has undertaken, along with the outcomes of the raids, where this is particularly significant. The sampling is quite small—to date there have been well over 100 known raids in the United States.

• In December 1984 the ALF raided the City of Hope National Medical Center in Duarte, California (famous for its cancer treatment center for children), removing dozens of animals from filthy cages. The video taken by members of the ALF revealed animals lying on freezing cold, damp floors, with open and infected wounds. Cats were caged on the roof of the building with no shelter from rain or wind. A large dog who had given birth to puppies had stood helplessly by while her puppies died of exposure and starvation. The dog was unable to nurse her puppies since she had been exposed to high doses of radiation, and had been forced to give birth to her puppies on a nearly freezing floor (Newkirk, 1990). Subsequent USDA inspection revealed the facility to be in violation of numerous Federal Animal Welfare Act regulations, including failure to establish adequate veterinary care, maintain adequate surgery areas, consult a veterinarian regarding use of anesthetics, and monitor and shelter dogs properly after surgery. The facility was fined $11,000 by the USDA and required to build a new $380,000 research facility and hire a full-time veterinarian.[13]

- On 21 April 1985 the ALF took more than 1,000 animals from the laboratories at the University of California at Riverside, destroyed computer equipment, and painted graffiti on the walls. During this raid, the tiny stump-tailed macaque, named Britches by her liberators, was rescued, and the crude sutures with which her eyes had been sewn shut were removed by a veterinarian. Videotapes of Britches's original condition and recovery were made into a film (*Britches*) by PETA.

- On 26 October 1986 the ALF raided the University of Oregon's research facility in Eugene, liberating 264 animals and inflicting more than $50,000 in damage. As in the University of Pennsylvania raid, documentation, including pictures taken by the researchers themselves, revealed numerous violations of the Laboratory Animal Welfare Act, as well as a callous disregard for the suffering of research animals. In one now infamous photograph, a researcher (subsequently fired) is shown smoking and drinking beer while holding a newborn macaque. The picture reveals the infant monkey was a terrified participant in a mock cesarean section delivery, staged for the apparent amusement of all present.[14]

- On 23 June 1988 the ALF raided a Santa Rosa, California, veal farm, liberating two baby calves who were stressed and sick, having lived their short lives in tiny restraining wooden crates in total darkness. The ALF reported finding over 60 calves lying in their own excrement, suffering from chronic diarrhea and respiratory disorders. The calves were spirited away to safe homes.

- On 16 April 1987 the ALF entered the University of California's new diagnostic laboratory at Davis, still under construction. They set it on fire and fled. The building, designed for agricultural research, burned to the ground causing $3.5 million in damages.[15]

- On 14 January 1990 the ALF raided the office of University of Pennsylvania cat researcher Adrian Morrison, an outspoken defender of animal research and head of the anatomy laboratory at the University of Pennsylvania School of Veterinary Medicine. The ALF took files, videotapes, slides, and computer disks in the raid.[16] The files revealed the extent of Morrison's efforts in attacking the animal rights movement in his correspondence with researchers who had come under scrutiny, as well as his own 25 years of exposing cats to extreme temperatures and electrically burning out sections of their brains (Newkirk 1992, 368–69). The raid generated negative publicity, both for Morrison and the animal rights movement. Zoe Weil of the American Antivivisection Society expressed disappointment that the raid had occurred, since AAVS had been conducting its own above-board investigation of Morrison's research and had planned to reveal that Morrison's research had not been beneficial in any way to human health problems such as sleep disorders and sudden infant-death syndrome, contrary to his own statements. In fact, researchers simply did not cite Morrison's work. Weil feared that this information would become lost in the publicity regarding the raid.[17] Morrison has subsequently been given a newly created position at the NIH as director of laboratory animal care and a spokesperson for laboratory animal research (Newkirk 1992, 370).

While no U.S. ALF raids to date are known to have physically harmed any individual, there have been ALF actions (such as the arson at the University of California at Davis) in which the methods used placed people in danger. Furthermore, researchers who have been the targets of raids claim both psychological and professional harm. That they have been professionally harmed is obvious: their laboratories have been destroyed, their animals removed and research interrupted, and their reputations damaged. In many raids such information as photographs, videotapes, and documents relevant to establishing those research projects as fraudulent, illegal, and callous were obtained. In the wake of adverse publicity, researchers have received threatening telephone calls and had their homes picketed by outraged activists. Some have abandoned their research. For example, an examination of government-funded research grants reveals animal research at the University of California at Riverside has decreased quite dramatically in the years since the massive ALF raid. This sort of result is, of course, the forseeable and sought-after end of such raids.

Whether one agrees with the tactics of the ALF, there can be no question that the information brought to light in numerous raids has played an important role in educating all of us about what happens in some laboratories. It has also had a galvanizing effect on the movement. The images of animals removed from laboratories in such raids—of their miserable living conditions and the pain they have endured—serve as powerful symbols for activists, and the ALF's success in removing even a few animals is empowering to those who feel helpless in the face of powerful institutions. Implicated vivisectors provide a personal face for the evils of institutional animal suffering and a concrete target as well.

Conclusion

While we have inevitably left out many important organizations, we hope this chapter has illustrated the vast diversity of individuals, tactics and beliefs that characterize the movement. Activists cannot be neatly categorized or labeled, and discussion within the movement generates an evolving set of ideas. Others who have written about the animal rights movement[18] have suggested that it contains a division between "fundamentalists" and "pragmatists." The fundamentalists insist "that people should never use animals for their own pleasures or interests, regardless of the benefits" and pursue their goals with a self-righteous, missionary zeal. Pragmatists, on the other hand, "feel that certain species deserve greater consideration than others, and would allow humans to use animals when the benefits deriving from their use outweigh their suffering" (Jasper and Nelkin 1992, 9).

While there are, to be sure, individuals in the movement who fit the "fundamentalist" description, the comparison to a religious crusade does not accurately reflect the diversity of approaches or the climate of intellectual discussion within the movement. (Indeed, the demographics of the movement, which is highly educated in comparison with the overall population, belie this sort of comparison.) Those with the most strident or self-righteous positions often attract the most media attention, given the desire of the media for sensational stories. But it is important to distinguish philosophical positions (a strict rights perspective as opposed to a more utilitarian view, for example) from the strategies employed to achieve these ends. There are groups with an abolitionist philosophy, such as AAVS, which employ very conservative and pragmatic tactics, and those with a more "pragmatic" agenda that have engaged in direct action (e.g., FARM, Coalition to Abolish the Draize). As James M. Jasper and Dorothy Nelkin mention in *The Animal Rights Crusade* (1992), many shift tactics depending on the issue or political arena. But, as Tom Regan long ago pointed out, the very diversity of the movement, with "many hands on many oars," is one of its strengths (*Agenda,* March–April 1984, 5).

Chapter Four

Issues and Campaigns of the 1980s

A number of important organizations and influential leaders emerged in the animal rights movement in the 1980s. Individuals like Henry Spira and organizations like PETA have succeeded in becoming influential leaders because of well-focused campaigns and a number of dramatic cases, such as the Silver Spring monkeys, which helped to focus energy, attention, and passion on individuals in a context that otherwise threatened to make animal victims abstractions through the sheer weight of their numbers and their invisibility behind the closed doors of laboratories and factory farms. After all, the Silver Spring monkeys had names, and the faces of the baboons in *Unnecessary Fuss* are unforgettable. But in addition to these very useful focal points for the young movement, a number of campaigns emerged in the 1980s that concentrated not so much on identifiable individual victims but on larger-scale institutional exploitation as such.

In this chapter we discuss three major areas of activism: fur, factory farming, and the scientific uses of animals. These do not represent all the important issues animal rights activists have taken up: for example, we do not discuss anti-hunting activism or efforts to end the exploitation of animals in sport and entertainment. Rather than trying to cover all possible topics, we discuss cases that exemplify the kinds of activism most typical of the animal rights movement and the sorts of challenge that it faces in achieving its goals.

The Anti-Fur Campaign

The fur trade, in so far as it is a supply of ornamental clothing for those who are under no necessity of wearing fur at all, is a barbarous and stupid business. It makes patch-work, one may say, not only of the hides of its victims, but also of the conscience and intellect of its supporters. A fur garment or trimming, we are told, appearing to the eye as if it were one uniform piece, is generally made up of many curiously shaped fragments. It is significant that a society which is enamored of so many shams and fictions, and which detests nothing so strongly as the need of looking facts in the face, should preeminently esteem those articles of apparel which are constructed on the most illusory and deceptive principle. The story of the Ass in the Lion's skin is capable, it seems, of a new and wider application.

—Henry Salt, *Animal Rights Considered*
in Relation to Social Progress (1892)

The anti-fur campaign is one campaign in which activists can claim to have made progress, having had a significant impact on the industry, and it has helped to further mobilize the animal rights movement. Given the extreme nature of the suffering of animals trapped or ranched for their fur and the lack of any necessity for this use of animals, the external conditions for success have been favorable. The campaign has its roots in activism throughout the 1960s against the hunting of seals which helped publicize the plight of fur-bearing animals to the world.

Probably the most well-known success in the fight against fur is the case of the Canadian seal hunt. Every year until 1983 large numbers of harp seal pups were clubbed to death off Canada's east coast. The baby seals ("whitecoats") were selected because their fur is pure white (it turns darker as they mature). Each year in July hundreds of thousands of whitecoats would be rounded up on land and driven to locations where they could not escape back into the water, then clubbed to death. In the peak years of the late 1970s some 200,000 seals were slaughtered annually.

The seal hunt had been opposed by the humane community since the first decade of this century. But it was not until someone with the vision and persistence of Brian Davies came along that real progress against it was made. Davies, who had been asked to inspect the hunt for the Canadian government in 1965, was so outraged by what he saw that by 1969 he had formed the International Fund for Animal Welfare (IFAW) to work to end the seal hunt. Under Davies's leadership the

IFAW, along with the Sea Shepherd Society, the Fund for Animals, Greenpeace, and other groups created an international effort against the hunt. Davies mobilized world opinion by shuttling reporters and photographers by helicopter to the remote location, despite physical attacks from seal hunters, threats to his life, arrest, fines and imprisonment (the government passed a law forbidding helicopter flight near the seals in order to cut off the negative publicity). Dramatic events— such as activists spraying the pups' coats with green paint to make them worthless as garments—were employed over many years. Many years of demonstrations, lobbying, testimony before governmental hearings and public outcry (including letters and cards to European Community officials from some 3.5 million people) led, in 1983, to the EC imposing a two-year ban on importation of seal fur. The ban was extended another four years in 1985. The seal hunt is all but dead— killed by the EC's ban and the international outrage produced when people saw "the scenes of infant seals being clubbed, skinned and left in a bloody, steaming mass as their mothers looked on helplessly" (Ryder 1989, 226–30; *Agenda,* May 1985, 14).

The fur industry was targeted early on by animal rights as well as animal welfare groups, because it, like the cosmetics industry, sells unnecessary products that depend very much on their appeal as fashion, and therefore the industry is vulnerable to campaigns that associate it with cruelty and suffering. As in other areas, the fact that both animal welfare groups such as HSUS and animal rights groups such as In Defense of Animals (IDA), Trans-Species Unlimited (TSU), and PETA have worked toward the goal of eliminating sale of furs does not mean that they have employed the same tactics or worked particularly closely together. Nonetheless, fur is an area in which animal rights groups are claiming that much progress has been made, and the campaign against fur has gained much momentum in the latter half of the 1980s.

Legislative attempts to prohibit trapping, especially with the steel-jaw leghold trap, have played a role in the campaign. In many other countries the leghold trap has been banned, but so far little success has been met in achieving similar results in the United States. A number of cities and states have considered bans on the leghold trap, and legislative efforts continue in a number of places. In 1930 Massachusetts voters banned devices that "cause continued suffering" to trapped animals. Since that time, no other state has banned traps by popular vote. Attempts to put the issue to a public vote in Oregon, Ohio, and (in November 1992) Arizona all failed. The Arizona ballot, spearheaded by Arizonans for Safety and Humanity on Public Lands, would have prohibited all kinds of trapping on public lands. It was defeated in a battle that saw the National Rifle Association and Wildlife Legislative Fund of America (a group headquartered in Ohio) outspending Arizonans for Safety and Humanity on Public Lands 10 to 1.[1] Attempts at a more local level have, on the other hand, sometimes succeeded. Thanks to the efforts of the Good Shepherd Society, Grass Valley, California, banned the steel-jaw trap a couple of years ago. Thus far, the real significance of legislative efforts in this country has been in helping to educate the public about the connection between animal suffering and fur. While activists would welcome a ban on the leghold trap—the most commonly used method in the United States—the entire industry is inherently objectionable to animal rights advocates, as imposing unjustifiable suffering and death of animals in the name of fashion and profits.

The anti-fur campaign has primarily focused on convincing consumers to avoid fur products. The most significant portion of the campaign, both in terms of energy and results, has been directed at eliminating consumer demand for furs. Unlike the more complex case of toxicity testing, the fur industry depends absolutely on marketing animal "products" directly to retail customers, and as a result the fur industry is highly sensitive to any negative associations consumers make with its product. Recognizing the importance of image and their weakness in this respect, fur industry defenders strive to avoid any association of furs with living animals. On the other side, animal advocates have focused much energy on making sure that just that connection is within public awareness.

Lynn Kentish and Mark Glover formed the British group Lynx in 1985 after Glover left Greenpeace in protest of its pulling back from the anti-fur campaign. Lynx's specific aim is to transform the public's understanding of fur from its traditional image as luxury to an awareness of its brutality. They embarked on a highly successful advertising campaign (credited with helping to bring the British fur market into tremendous decline) that has served as model for many here in the United States, and Lynx has itself opened offices in the United States. In one image Lynx has used for billboards, advertisements, and bumper stickers, a woman is seen dragging a fur coat behind her, blood trailing from the coat. The caption reads: "It takes up to 40 dumb animals to make a fur coat. But only one to wear it." An American group, Friends of Animals (FoA), produced an advertisement showing a paw in a leghold trap, with the caption: "Get a feel for fur. Slam your fingers in a car door." In this country the visible inhumanity of trapping—especially the steel-jaw leghold traps—has become reasonably well-known to the public. Animal defenders recognize that focusing exclusively on the inhumanity of trapping would not be a completely successful strategy, however, as the fur industry has responded with the claim that many fur garments are made from "ranch-raised furs." Recognizing the power of words, marketers are careful to identify coats as "ranch mink" and the like. This response served the industry well, as the public is largely ignorant of the suffering and lack of humane regulation of fur farming, and also because this response appeals to the commonly held bias that animals who were specifically bred for a purpose owe their lives as a kind of gratitude—after all, ranch mink or foxes would not have even lived a day if it were not for the human desire to turn them into coats - so they have no complaint (this kind of argument was dubbed "the logic of the larder" by nineteenth-century reformer Henry Salt). When asked about wearing her fur despite the opposition, one woman expressed it this way: "I approve of wearing furs, provided they are not from endangered species. Furs *[sic]* that are grown and ranched for the purpose of making coats are fine with me."[2]

From year to year the proportion of trapped to farmed furs shifts, but approximately one-fourth of the fur coats made in the United States in 1986 came from animals bred and raised on fur farms.[3] Nonetheless, animal advocates needed to educate the public about the nature of fur ranching as well as trapping in order to succeed. And, though that makes the issue a bit more complex, it is equally clear that ranch furs are objectionable.

While there has not been a coordinated national campaign—the animal rights movement rarely acts as the monolithic, centralized entity its opponents would like the public to believe it is, nor does it act sufficiently as a coalition when it would serve it well to do so—it is reasonable to date the beginning of the anti-fur campaign to Trans-Species Unlimited's Campaign for a Fur-Free America.

While there had certainly been much anti-fur activity prior to the Campaign for a Fur-Free America, including the very important and courageous effort to end the Canadian seal hunt, TSU's entrance marked perhaps the first attempt to promote massive use of direct-action tactics against fur in this country. TSU's campaign was kicked off in December 1985 with a 21-city "Sitdown for Wildlife," in which activists staged sit-ins in major department stores. Since that time other groups, such as Los Angeles's Last Chance for Animals, have also employed civil disobedience in stores that sell furs. Demonstrations that have not aimed to cross the legal barrier have been a more frequently used tactic of the anti-fur campaign. Though demonstrations occur throughout the fur season, one event has become a national tradition within the animal rights movement: "Fur-Free Friday" rallies activists to express their opposition to fur on the busiest shopping day of the year, the day following Thanksgiving. Since the mid-1980s demonstrations have been organized annually across the country, drawing ever larger numbers of protesters. In New York, for example, a handful of protesters were in evidence in 1986; by 1988, 2,000 were marching down Fifth Avenue in a parade led by Bob Barker, whose courageous opposition to furs had led him to refuse to host the Miss USA Pageant the year before until assured that furs would not be used to costume contestants. In 1989 some 3,500 activists came out for New York's Fur-Free Friday. Each year the number of demonstrations nationwide has grown as well—with activists in over 100 cities coming out for the 1990 Fur-Free Friday. The event was preceded that year by an 18-kilometer "Run against Fur," sponsored by FoA in Connecticut, and a concert in Orlando, Florida, sponsored by PETA and ANIMALiberation. Originally organized by TSU, Fur-Free Friday is now coordinated by In Defense of Animals, a California group led by veterinarian Eliott Katz.

The anti-fur campaign has been characterized by a division on the question of tactics. TSU's "Speakouts against Fur" exemplify a tactic that has been controversial both within and outside the movement. Dana Stuchell of TSU described the approach this way:

We meet and separate people into two's and three's. We don't say "Be obnoxious or aggressive"; we tell them "Do what's comfortable, but do something." People average 20 to 50 confrontations a day; thousands of New Yorkers have been confronted. We encourage people to be as loud as possible; they may not convert the fur-wearer, but other people may hear and start to think. The purpose is to embarrass the person; when people find it's unpleasant to wear fur, they'll stop. You're dealing with very selfish people; you have to give them a selfish interest for not wearing fur. Most people in fur coats just think it's attractive or prestigious. They need to know how many people feel it is a symbol of moral backwardness.[4]

And the tactic has turned media heads—a rash of articles in dailies such as the *New York Times* and *Washington Post* have responded by interviewing fur-wearing women and commenting on the manners of the protesters. In one memorable column Yona Zeldis McDonough wrote, "What is even more offensive than the opinions is the rudeness with which they are expressed. Didn't the mothers of these women tell them that shouting at strangers shows an appalling lack of manners? . . . It seems ironic that the champions of animal rights have so little regard for human rights."[5] Others have a different sense of the relative importance of etiquette and morality: Andy Rooney seemed to endorse confrontational tactics in a column that suggested that the humane community ought to make those who wear fur "the objects of public scorn" rather than continuing the 100-year old battle to ban leghold traps (*Agenda,* April 1987, 6).

But not all within the movement are convinced of the wisdom of confronting fur wearers with any kind of animosity or even apparent disrespect. For some the issue is primarily a question of what works— whether confrontational tactics will ultimately help or hurt a movement whose opponents are all too happy to characterize animal rights activists as fanatics who, lacking a sense of proportion, put the interests of animals before all else. Some activists therefore urge a more toned-down approach. Says poet and animal activist Ann Cottrell Free, "You don't want to come across as a hard-driven fanatic; the appearance of fanaticism could destroy us all. You want to get the middle group out there; many of them have come into this way of thinking; we need to find out how they did come in—probably not from confrontation" (Moran 1989, 51). Adds Syndee Brinkman, founder of the National Alliance for Animal Legislation (NAAL), who agrees with the less confrontational but still direct approach, "The important thing is to do something. I don't feel I can allow one person to walk by me flaunting a dead animal" (Moran 1989, 51). In addition to the issue of which tactic is more likely to alienate or help, there is a deep division reflected in such comments concerning the role of moral and rational persuasion in achieving change. The question of the role of moral argument relates to a variety of other issues, especially animal research. (We discuss these conflicts in greater depth in Chapter 8.)

While the anti-fur campaign is very much a grass-roots campaign employing a diversity of approaches and expressive of differing views about how to achieve change, there is widespread agreement that the battle against exploitation of animals for their skins is winnable by appealing to consumers, and that this must be done by replacing the stylish appeal of fur with a sense of moral repugnance at their sight. That battle is being conducted in a variety of ways—by demonstrating where furs are sold, by advertising campaigns, by civil disobedience—in short, by keeping the issue before the public in whatever ways activists can manage.

Increased anti-fur activity has the industry worried, and for good reason. Since 1987 the market has been in serious trouble. Pelt prices worldwide have dropped to as much as half the 1986 price depending on the kind of animal, and finished coats are regularly being marked down as much as 60 to 70 percent to move them off racks. Major furriers, such as Antonovich, Evans, and Fur Vault, have suffered losses in the millions that wiped out their profits from the previous boom years, and many furriers have declared bankruptcy and shut their doors. A number of department chains, such as Nordstrom and Lord & Taylor, have discontinued selling furs altogether. Fur auctions have seen unusually high numbers of pelts unsold (at the end of the 1988–89 season some 500,000 muskrat pelts and 60,000 coyote pelts were unsold and in storage), and a third of those who trapped in the winter of 1987–88 did not bother to purchase licenses again for the 1989–90 season. The average number of pelts taken dropped from 50 to 17, while the total number of animals trapped for fur dropped from 17 million in 1986–87 to just 3.5 million in 1989–90. In Canada the situation is similar: trapping dropped by 55 percent from 1987–88 to 1988–89. In 1989 Canadian wholesale business was down 27 percent, exports dropped 25 percent, and imports fell off 29 percent.

Understandably, activists have come to believe that they are making progress. After all, they have self-consciously targeted the consumer end of the market, and the market is in serious trouble. They suggest that their activism should be credited for falling profits, bankruptcies, and furriers going out of business. In support of this they point to the correlation between the growing numbers joining the picket lines in the years since 1985 and the economic downturn in the fur industry following the 1986–87 season.

On the other hand, industry defenders hold pretty much to the party line that the opposition has had no effect. Explanations of the downturn offered by the industry itself often refer to the October 1987 stock-market crash, ongoing recessions, mild winters, and overproduction in some countries after the very successful 1986–87 season. Retailers who have dumped furs are quick to mention that they do so

for economic reasons, not because they have been in any way persuaded or pressured by animal advocates. Occasionally grudging
credit is given for a limited impact on the market: "The animal rights
activists do have an impact, but only when all other conditions are bad
for the fur industry," as Elliott Miller, a lawyer who handled two furrier bankruptcies, said.[6]

Knowing with any degree of assurance to what extent a variety of
potential causal factors was operative in the fur slump is enormously
difficult. The confidence expressed on both sides seems unwarranted.
It is obviously politically advantageous for each side to make the
claims they do—activists want to encourage the troops (who, after all,
spend spare time, personal resources, and emotional energy protesting), and industry needs to deny any influence so as not to encourage
further protest.

Nonetheless, animal rights activists are probably having some
effect. The importance of image should not be underestimated: in
recent years furs that do not look like fur have become fashionable, so
much so that a *Fur Age Weekly* writer commented, "Many collections
left retailers asking, 'This is fur?' When asked whether the prospect of
protesters confronting her in New York had her concerned, one fur-
owning woman, Catherine Ebersol, said she was not worried. Her
mink-lined raincoat 'is reversible,' she said, 'so I can wear it as a mink,
but I can also hide the fur whenever I feel like it.' She also has a
sheared beaver coat she wears to work: 'It is a very flat fur, not at all
flashy or luxurious,' she said. 'I hope the anti-fur people will think it's
fake'" (*NYT*, 19 November 1989).

Indeed, fake furs (made from synthetic materials) are being promoted as fashionable and humane. J. C. Penney promoted its fake furs
in preference to real ones, explaining in the label that real furs result
from the "inhumane slaughter of animals solely for their skins." A
number of prominent designers, such as Bill Blass, Carolina Herrera,
Oleg Cassini, and Giorgio Armani, have announced they would stop
working with fur: "When Armani introduced his fake fur collection in
Milan last March, he couldn't resist patting himself on the back.
'Thank you, Emporio Armani, for saving our skins,' a voice intoned as
the curtain opened on a menagerie of stuffed animals."[7]

Probably the clearest indicator of the effectiveness of the opposition
is how the fur industry is itself responding. Despite protestations to the
contrary, it is clear that the industry is worried about the potential of the
anti-fur campaign, and its members point out that the European animal

rights movement has already destroyed the market there. (In fact, the most recent blow may have substantial effects in the 1990s: in November 1991 the European Community banned imports of pelts from leghold traps beginning in 1995.) Groups with names George Orwell would be proud of have recently formed with funds contributed by furriers to defend their industry: the Pro-Fur Committee, Fur Industry Mobilization Fund, Fur Farm Animal Welfare Coalition, Fur Bearers Unlimited, Fur Information Council of America. Millions of dollars have been dedicated to an aggressive advertising campaign to counter the animal rights opposition, and additional funds go into spying on the movement to keep tabs on activists and to supply governments with information about "terrorists." When considering claims that the protests are not the source of their difficulties, one has to ask why an industry suffering from a very difficult market would be willing to spend so much to defend against an opponent it regards as impotent?

But more important than how much credit to take is the question of where the current success will lead—What lies ahead? There are those who believe complete victory against furs is just a matter of time. As John Leo wrote in 1989 in *U.S. News & World Report,* "The fur industry is very vulnerable because it is not in a position to mount a serious counterargument . . . the animal rights folks will win this contest fairly quickly, maybe in two or three years."[8] But despite the progress, it would be a serious mistake to claim victory yet, and no one within the movement is doing so. One reason not to be so self-assured of victory is the fact that the industry has been in tough shape before (in the 1960s) and has bounced back, despite opposition from the humane movement.

But perhaps the main reason to worry is that at the same time the market is very bad, the fur industry in the United States is also undergoing some changes that may have profound implications for the anti-fur movement. One is that new markets outside the country are opening up—particularly, Japan, where there is very little in the way of an animal rights movement (though anti-fur protests have occurred there). According to the *New York Times,* Japan has become the second largest market in the world for furs, just behind the United States.[9] A number of companies, including Oscar de la Renta, Wagner Fur, and Springer, Inc., have already made the move to the Japanese market (Clifton 1990, 34). As furriers sell to Japanese customers it will be difficult to hope to have much impact on consumer demand through the kinds of tactics currently employed in the United States.

Second, and perhaps even more ominous, imported fur coats are taking a larger and larger proportion of the American market—up from 30 percent in 1983 to 70 percent in 1989. At the same time, despite the new market in Japan, exports are also diminishing. While the U.S. and Canadian industries are hurting (and the European is all but dead), a new industry is taking shape. Large, well-diversified and "vertically-integrated" multinational corporations are entering the industry, taking advantage of the desperate condition of the existing companies. Jindo, a South Korean corporation, has purchased Fur Vault, which, though it accounts for 10 percent of the U.S. market, had lost over $7 million between 1987 and 1989. But unlike its American competition, Jindo seeks to control the entire process from ranch to garment production to retail sales. In doing so it can cut down some of the risks of oversupply or undersupply, and it can eliminate transportation costs, enabling it to cut prices and compete very well with nonintegrated retailers without losing its profit. Jindo, which currently has something like 3.5 percent of the world fur market, has set a goal of acquiring 10 percent of it.

This development could make the battle much more difficult for the anti-fur campaign. It will be harder to influence conduct on fur farms and retail markets in Asia than it might be in the United States. While there would still be hope of continuing to influence consumer demand here, the large amount of fur sitting in cold storage from the previously bad seasons will ultimately be dumped at lower prices—which may have the effect of creating more demand here when garments are available at much lower prices. So, while progress has been made in the campaign against fur, the American movement will face new and difficult challenges in the coming years.

The Fight against Factory Farming

Agricultural uses of animals constitute the most extensive and extreme exploitation of animals in America today. Thousands of people who have learned of this exploitation (by being exposed to such powerful sources as Singer's *Animal Liberation* or the powerful images of *The Animals Film*, a full-length documentary that graphically exposed the details of a variety of forms of exploitation) have been sufficiently personally affected by what they have learned to become vegetarians or vegans (those who avoid all animal foods, including eggs and dairy products). But the logic of institutional exploitation requires that more change than just the life-styles of movement followers: animal rights advocates first and foremost are calling for an end to the exploitive uses of farm animals. But progress on this issue is difficult.

In Europe some progress has been made on agricultural issues: campaigns to educate consumers and pressure governments to change—and some countries have begun to act—have effected groundbreaking legislation in Sweden, Switzerland, the Netherlands, and, to a lesser extent, Great Britain. In 1981 Switzerland began phasing out battery cages: by 1987 caged birds had to have a minimum of 500 centimeters (197 square inches), and by 1992 traditional cages were to be outlawed and hens must have access to protected, soft-floored nest boxes. In the Netherlands battery cages will have been outlawed by 1994, and access to nest boxes and scratching areas will be mandated, with a minimum of 1,000 square centimeters (394 square inches) per bird. In Sweden battery cages were outlawed in 1988, and cows, pigs, and animals raised for fur must be kept "in as natural an environment as possible." In 1986 the ministers of agriculture of European Community countries agreed to a minimum cage size by 1995 of 450 square centimeters (177 square inches), which is a step in the right direction but not a very significant one (less than one in seven British hens would be affected by this). In 1987 the European Parliament (which has no legislative power) recommended that battery cages be phased out of the EC by 1997 (Singer 1990, 112–13).

Clearly some progress has been made, though there is much to be done even within Europe. Richard Ryder points out that Britain, "strong on ideas and weak on action," has failed to act on changes recommended by the Brambell Committee in the 1960s; the House of Commons Select Committee on Agriculture, which recommended in 1981 that battery cages and veal crates be eliminated; and the government's Farm Animal Welfare Council, which in 1984 and 1985 had recommended changes in slaughtering procedures (Ryder 1989, 265, 267). But British government regulations as of 1987 do at least require that a calf must be able to turn around without difficulty and be fed "sufficient iron to maintain it in full health and vigour" and enough fiber for normal development of the rumen (Singer 1990, 136).

Perhaps the roots of these changes can be traced to the publication in 1964 of Ruth Harrison's *Animal Machines,* which exposed to Britons the brutality of modern farming methods. A year later a British government committee was formed to investigate the issue of agricultural animal welfare. The Brambell Committee issued an important set of recommendations, urging, for example, that debeaking, docking of pigs' tails, and tethering of sows and veal calves all be prohibited by law, but the legislation was never put in place. In general, the committee recommended that every farm animal should have "five freedoms": "In principle we disapprove of a degree of confinement of an animal which necessarily frustrates most of the major activities which make up its natural behavior. . . . An animal should at least have sufficient freedom of movement to be able without difficulty to turn around, groom itself, get up, lie down, and stretch its limbs" (quoted in Singer 1990, 142). It is a rather sad commentary that such a recommendation even needs to be made—but some 25 years later billions of animals raised for food are still deprived of these basic freedoms, especially in the United States, where little significant motion toward reform has occurred.

A number of organizations in Britain took on the project of effecting change. Perhaps the most important is an organization formed in 1967 by former farmer Peter Roberts, called Compassion in World Farming (CIWF). CIWF ran some very effective ads to help create pressure for change. One dramatized the fact that battery hens cannot even spread their wings by showing a hen with spread wings standing over a battery cage—the wings far exceed the limits of the cage. Another group formed in 1971—Chickens Lib—has also maintained pressure for change. Founders Violet Spalding and her daughter Clare Druce made effective use of photographs of fatigued and unhealthy battery hens in their campaign (Ryder 1989, 263–64).

The effort to change farm conditions in Sweden met with very little resistance in the parliament there. Farm organizations appealed to consumers' pocketbooks; they argued that laws requiring cattle to be grazed, that pigs not be tethered or crated, and that the caging of chickens be ended would all mean higher prices at the market. Apparently consumers were willing to pay the price: as Astrid Lindgren, the 80-year-old author of the Pippi Longstocking children's stories and leader of the effort to pass the legislation said, "People are willing to pay a little more to get decent food and treat animals decently. Because if you don't, you don't feel very good inside."[10]

The individuals and organizations tackling factory farming and meat eating in the United States are up against the same difficulties as the European and British groups. Unlike fur or even animal experimentation, the vast majority of people are directly involved in the exploitation of so-called food animals, through their purchase and consumption of them. The social acceptance of meat eating, the view that it is inevitable and proper, together with the invisibility of the animals and the conditions of their treatment clearly pose a formidable challenge. Tactics that have brought success in other areas, such as protests, sit-ins, or direct confrontation, are more likely to meet with ridicule and rejection than with the desired changes in behavior. It is easy to imagine the results of animal activists confronting people eating a chicken leg or a hamburger, as TSU has confronted fur wearers. There is simply not enough social conscience regarding meat eating generally for such tactics to work. As a result, organizations that have devoted themselves primarily to farm-animal issues and vegetarianism have emphasized somewhat different strategies and have focused largely on educational and legislative work. And, rather than take on the entire issue of meat eating and farm-animal abuse at once, the focus of campaigns has been to educate the public about the worst abuses first, encouraging a gradual elimination of the meat habit.

While the major animal rights organizations such as PETA, IDA, and ARM! are critical of factory farming and promote vegetarianism, there are a small number of organizations dedicated specifically to working on factory farming issues, who have taken a leadership role in the campaigns against factory farming. Among the most important groups are the Farm Animal Reform Movement, the Humane Farming Association, and Farm Sanctuary. Some organizations with a focus primarily on health and environmental issues, such as EarthSave, have also played a role.

The first major campaign Farm Animal Reform Movement (FARM) undertook was the Veal Ban Campaign in 1982, and it is partly to FARM's credit that the extremity of the conditions under which veal calves are raised is as well-known among the public as it is today. FARM took out advertisements in newspapers and magazines and created additional publicity by picketing restaurants that serve veal. Within a short time after FARM initiated the campaign a number of larger organizations, including HSUS and the ASPCA, began speaking out against veal farming. FARM's founder and president Alex Hershaft exemplified the use of dramatic tactics to educate during the Veal Ban Campaign by confining himself for 24 hours in a veal crate outside the White House.

Two programs that Hershaft developed and now hopes a larger organization will adopt are "World Farm Animals Day" and "The Great American Meat-Out." World Farm Animals Day came from brainstorming at an Action for Life Conference in 1983, in response to the felt need to find a way to acknowledge farm animals in a way that made people aware of the nature of their sacrifice. The day selected was, appropriately enough, Mohandas Gandhi's birthday, 2 October, in recognition of the fact that Gandhi has probably done more for farm animals than any other individual.

The second annual event FARM initiated, the Great American Meat-Out (20 March, to usher in spring), originated as a response to the proposal of a U.S. Senate resolution to endorse National Meat Week. FARM decided that instead of drawing attention to National Meat Week (which, after all, very few people had ever heard of) by forming a protest, they would counter it by creating a special day on which people would be asked to give up meat—for just a single day (on the model of the highly successful Great American Smoke Out days).

Like FARM, the Humane Farming Association (HFA), formed in 1984 by director Brad Miller, has focused a great deal of energy on education and legislation to improve the plight of veal calves. A California-based group with 60,000 members, HFA wrote the California veal crate bill, which, had it passed, would have required crates to be large enough for the calves to turn around and assume more natural postures. Unfortunately, the bill was not passed, though members of Congress and the public were educated about the cruelty of veal through this campaign, as well as through the many advertisements in such major magazines as *Time* and *Newsweek* and through HFA-sponsored television spots. On 20 June, 1986 HFA sponsored "Night on the Town" protests of veal in 22 cities, where activists picketed restaurants that serve veal and passed out informative leaflets to patrons. This focus on one particularly blatant form of farm-animal abuse, as opposed to meat eating generally, proved to be successful, with many patrons responding with interest.

Farm Sanctuary has continued the campaign against veal, but unlike FARM and HFA it has approached the issue through closer contact with and exposure of the public to farm animals. In 1986 Gene and Lorrie Bauston began visiting livestock auctions where they saw live veal calves and sheep and piglets left for dead, sometimes thrown onto piles of dead animals. Unable to leave them to die, they began to bring them home. Beginning with only an old Volkswagen from which they sold vegetarian hotdogs to help raise money, by 1987 they had opened the doors of Farm Sanctuary. Not only have they documented the abuse of downed animals (their videotape *The Down Side of Livestock Marketing* contains graphic footage of the suffering of animals unable

Alex Hershaft, president of the Farm Animal Reform Movement, protesting veal crates on World Farm Animals Day in front of the White House. *Photo by Louisa Di Pietro*

to walk or too sick to be sold at auction), but they have initiated investigations and campaigns to stop such abuses. As a result of a successful investigation of a pig cruelty case in Kentucky, a pig farmer was ordered out of business because of cruelty to farm animals. Among the many abuses uncovered in this case, pigs had been forced to drink their own urine to sustain themselves and were confined in open pits, unable to escape extremes of heat and cold. This case marked the first time that a farm was closed down because of cruelty to animals.[11] More recently, the Baustons have successfully campaigned to get the Lancaster Stockyards in Pennsylvania to adopt a "no-downer" policy (i.e., outlawing the sale of downed animals) and have held protests at the south St. Paul, Minnesota, Livestock Market, following Becky Sanstedt's publicizing of the abuses there. Eventually, in response to

Gene and Lorrie Bauston, founders of Farm Sanctuary, with Albie and Opie. *Courtesy Farm Sanctuary*

Sanstedt's documentation and the national media coverage generated, this stockyard also agreed to adopt a "no downer" policy.[12]

Located in Rockland, Delaware, Farm Sanctuary is currently home to nearly 400 animals, including chickens, turkeys, ducks, geese, rabbits, sheep, pigs, and cows, and provides tours to the public and a bed and breakfast with vegan cooking. Thanks to the generosity of an organic farmer, the sanctuary spans 175 acres, with 12 large barns. Visitors are greeted by an inquisitive turkey at the gate and are encouraged to rub the bellies of numerous pigs (the pigs themselves do the encouraging). The sanctuary provides a valuable outreach to children and the public generally—a personal interaction with these usually invisible and exploited animals. The Baustons continue to rescue sick and abandoned farm animals and provide veterinary care and intensive, round-the-clock nursing care. After an animal is well it may be adopted out to the public (after a careful screening process), or it spends the rest of its days at the sanctuary.

In addition to directly saving the lives of hundreds of animals, Farm Sanctuary has publicized the plight of farm animals in prominent media stories that have appeared in the *Wall Street Journal* and on National Public Radio, and through public service announcements which have been aired in many major cities throughout the United States. There is also a quarterly newsletter and a growing membership.

The positive image of both farm animals and vegetarianism is also a prominent feature of EarthSave, the vegetarian-environmental organization founded by author John Robbins. Robbins, in line to inherit the Baskin-Robbins chain of ice cream parlors, gave up his inheritance in favor of promoting the health and environmental benefits of a vegan diet. His book, *Diet for a New America* (1987), has educated thousands of people about the myriad health risks of a meat- and dairy-based diet, as well as the connections between meat production, world hunger, and environmental degradation. This integrated approach is important, because many people assume that giving up meat is an unreasonable and possibly dangerous sacrifice. If they come to see vegetarianism as not only ethically and environmentally important but also beneficial to their personal health, they will obviously be more receptive to an alternative diet. As Angela Turner, editor of *New Scientist,* has somewhat cynically commented, "What chickens really need to get the public on their side is a disease which is caused by the battery systems and which is harmful to humans."[13] Robbin's book makes clear that the eggs themselves are harmful, regardless of how they are produced. EarthSave arranges conferences, speakers (Robbins himself is an extremely dynamic and highly sought-after speaker), and distribution of information on these issues. The strength of this approach is evident; those who have come to realize that they are gaining, rather than losing, by becoming vegans, are much more receptive to considering the plight of farm animals, which EarthSave literature also graphically describes. A further strength of the organization is its bridging of animal rights and environmental interests—a much-needed coalition.

What have been the results of the campaigns to end farm-animal suffering? Legislatively, there has been no meaningful improvement in the welfare of farm animals, at either the state or national level. Bills to give veal calves more room, for example, have repeatedly gone down in defeat in response to the powerful agribusiness lobby. On the other hand, the public has been made aware of the issues, and there is evidence that Americans are reducing their consumption of meat, though the role of ethical considerations in these decisions is not altogether clear. Perhaps the case of veal is clearest: consumption of veal is drastically reduced, and in California, according to HFA, the number of major veal-crate operations has dropped from 27 to only three. Public consciousness about veal has clearly been raised. For example, in the 1991 movie *Father of the Bride* the bride refuses to serve veal at her wedding on ethical grounds. This is stated with little explanation, indicating that the film's director had no doubt that the reference would be understood by the public.

The Struggle against Animal Experimentation

The greatness of a nation and its moral progress can be judged by the way its animals are treated. Vivisection is the blackest of all the black crimes that man is at present committing against God and his fair creation.

—Mohandas Gandhi

Animals are not our tasters, and we are not their kings.

—Tom Regan

Campaigns on behalf of laboratory animals are too legion to cover comprehensively; instead we focus on some examples of major issues and campaigns, most of which have had a specific focus and short-range goals, such as ending pound seizure, eliminating product testing, giving students the right to refuse dissection, strengthening existing laws protecting laboratory animals, or focusing upon the abuses of specific laboratories. In addition, numerous organizations seek to end all use of animals in research. These organizations often lend their support to the shorter-range goals, along with their long-term antivivisection campaigns.

Animal Rights and Abolitionism.   The last legislation designed to abolish vivisection entirely was defeated in the 1920s. While sponsoring legislation to make vivisection a crime was an active part of the early American antivivisection movement, the modern opponents of vivisection can no longer expect such sweeping and immediate reforms. Vivisection has become a deeply entrenched feature of modern biomedical science, supported by powerful economic and political forces. Nevertheless, an end to all animal research remains a long-term goal of the animal rights movement, with organizations such as the American Antivivisection Society (AAVS), the New England Antivivisection Society (NEAVS), the National Antivivisection Society (NAVS), and the Physicians' Committee for Responsible Medicine (PCRM) focusing their campaigns on public education, elimination of specific types of vivisection, and developing alternatives. Many other organizations, while campaigning on numerous other fronts as well, work to end vivisection.

Moral opposition to vivisection is as fundamental to the animal rights movement as is vegetarianism, and some features of the two campaigns are similar. In both cases the long-range goal of abolition appears unlikely to be achieved in the near future; banning the killing of animals for food and banning vivisection are not realistic legislative goals at the present time. Thus, in both cases the campaigns focus on elimination of specific forms of abuse and on public education, which will make these goals appear both desirable and achievable in the long run. Furthermore, as the moral argument for vegetarianism has been presented along with the evidence that a meat-based diet is unhealthy and a vegetarian diet is promotive of good health, so the moral argument opposing vivisection has been presented along with objections to the scientific validity of using animals in medical research designed to cure human disease.

Just as there are vegetarians who abjure meat eating purely on health grounds and who are not part of the animal rights movement, there are antivivisectionists who oppose animal research purely on the grounds that it is scientifically invalid. These "scientific antivivisectionists" attempt to influence the public to accept that uses of animals are misguided, and in many cases even fraudulent. For example, the Medical Research Modernization Committee takes this approach. While it takes no position on the moral status of animals, it does raise scientific objections to animal studies—"objections that are as compelling as the animal rights arguments."[14] In an extreme version of this approach, championed by Javier Burgos of Students United Protesting Research on Sentient Subjects (SUPPRESS), the issue of animal rights is explicitly disavowed, with the claim that "true" antivivisectionists focus exclusively on the scientific invalidity of animal research and the ways in which it has damaged human health. This organization has made the film *Hidden Crimes,* in which the injury to human health from use of animals is heavily emphasized, and has produced television ads with the same message.

Such individuals and organizations are no more a part of the animal rights movement than someone who advocates vegetarianism purely on grounds of human health can be considered part of the animal rights movement. Since scientific antivivisectionists base their opposition to vivisection on purely factual considerations, they cannot have the same abolitionist goals as those who base their objections on moral grounds. Frequently their arguments hinge on the disanalogy between humans and other animals, which they claim shows medical research designed to help humans to be invalid. But such an argument cannot rule out the use of animals in research to help other animals of just the same species, nor can it rule out the entirely nonmedical uses of animals designed simply to find out more about animal physiology or behavior.

Nevertheless, the argument that animal research is scientifically flawed or fraudulent and thus unnecessary has played a highly prominent role in antivivisectionist campaigns of organizations that also endorse the ethical stance of animal rights. For example, the AAVS makes available books such as Hans Ruesch's *Slaughter of the Innocent* (1978) and Robert Sharpe's *The Cruel Deception* (1988) through the mail-order sections of its magazine, *AV.* These works focus on the mistakes made through the use of animal research and the important disanalogies between humans and other animals. In Britain the British Union for the Abolition of Vivisection (BUAV), influenced by the work of Dr. Robert Sharpe (who served for a period as their scientific advisor), now promotes the message that vivisection is not only unethical but also bad science. Ruesch's book argues, in addition, that vivisectors are sadistic and mentally ill individuals. In some of the literature popular among the growing community of animal rights activists in the United States, one also finds appeals such as this:

It is clear that this sad cat, with pus and blood oozing from its deliberately inflicted cranial wound, enduring induced convulsions which have no relevance to human epilepsy, is yet another victim of the greed of the grant-hungry pseudoscientists that infect our universities and hospitals.

In a continuous state of terror, behaviorally and socially deprived, and in psychological and physical pain, this monkey has had her eye stolen by ambitious experimenters at U.C. San Francisco, in spite of the differences that exist between all species, and in spite of the fact that the study of naturally occurring eye problems in humans has been—and remains—the only reliable source of information regarding human eye disorders.[15]

The focus on issues concerning medical and scientific validity is motivated by the uncontroversial assumption that most people will not act against their perceived self-interest. Just as they are not likely to give up eating meat if they believe that doing so will harm their health, they are not likely to be opposed to vivisection if they believe that it is crucial in providing life-saving medical knowledge and technology. If they can be convinced that research on animals involves risky extrapolations and in fact holds back medical science, their opposition to vivisection is almost assured.

Because many scientific and medical authorities insist that animal research is vital to medical progress, the battle becomes one of credibility. Here moral and scientific arguments become entwined; the vivisectors' claims for the scientific validity of their practice are challenged in part by attacking these people's motives, credibility, and ethics. As George Bernard Shaw put it, "Anyone who would not hesitate to cut up a dog would not hesitate to lie about it." Thus, the conditions in which animals in laboratories are kept, the suffering they endure, and the very willingness of animal researchers to inflict suffering are often used to challenge the credibility of their claims that animal research is scientifically valid and indispensable.

The haunting pictures of animals immobilized in stereotaxic devices, animals with open and festering wounds and missing eyes and limbs, and animals in tiny barren cages function not only to arouse the horror of the viewer to the suffering of the animal, but to call into question the scientific authority of those who would deliberately inflict such suffering. The politics of science—the greed for recognition and research grant money—also figure into the moral/scientific critique of vivisection. Certainly the fact that other examples of scientific fraud have become well-known to the public must help nurture this suspicion about vivisectors.

To many observers of the movement (e.g., Sperling 1988), the campaign to end vivisection is *the* major focus of the movement and its philosophy. As we have argued, this is a misperception but one that is understandable in light of the history of the movement. The first highly visible animal rights activism at the national level was directed against animal research. The World Day for Laboratory

Animals demonstrations helped galvanize the movement and continue to be the largest and most visible demonstrations for animal rights each year.

World Day for Laboratory Animals. Each year since 1983 activists have held protests throughout the United States and the world during the week of 24 April, the original World Day for Laboratory Animals. The protests were originally organized by Mobilization for Animals (MFA) under the direction of Richard Morgan. MFA began as a task force formed at the 1981 Action for Life and Mobilization for Animal Rights conferences but rapidly outgrew its original charter, drawing together a coalition of over 80 animal rights and animal protection groups on several continents. The 1983 protests were focused upon primate centers in Boston; Madison, Wisconsin; and Davis, California. Their objective was to create the largest, most visible protest activity in the history of animal work in our nation. Michael Giannelli, science advisor to the Fund for Animals, related the protests to the highly visible Silver Spring monkeys and to the growing criticisms of much behavioral research, such as that performed by Harry Harlow: "This is the time to act. We definitely should take advantage of the momentum of PETA's Silver Spring case and recent congressional hearings. Behaviorism and the psychological testing of primates are especially open to criticism, so the focus is particularly well chosen."[16]

The objective was indeed achieved, with thousands turning out at each location for highly organized, peaceful marches and demonstrations. In Madison, Wisconsin, where 5,000 demonstrators were bussed from several states, protesters filled the streets that morning, marching through the University of Wisconsin campus, past the primate center and onto the quad for a day of speeches from scientists and movement leaders as well as music and poetry from celebrities. Attendees of the march recall the reaction of Madison residents, who like the rest of the United States, awoke that day to the surprising strength of the newly coalescing animal rights movement. As the first protesters would pass a house, amused onlookers would smile, then look down the street in disbelief at the endless throng of people. For those in the movement it was perhaps an equally surprising and empowering realization.

The goal of MFA was not abolitionist but rather to achieve whatever improvements were possible for animals in laboratories. MFA

asked for access to information about research, representation on poli-
cy-making boards, on-site inspections of housing, pain relief, and
transportation of experimental subjects, and emphasis on alternatives.
As Paula Van Orden of the Fund for Animals stated, "Compromise
isn't a dirty word. We have to be presented as a varied group. We desperately need to show the politicos that we can work together,
because humane groups are notorious for infighting. It's important
that we pull together on one thing, even though we go our separate
ways afterwards. Then, we can pull together on something else"
(Violin 1982, 9).

In 1984 the World Day protests spread to many more cities, with
fasts, torchlight vigils, effigy burnings, and, in Davis, California, 15
arrests for civil disobedience. Two thousand people gathered at UCLA
on 29 April. Local organizations sponsored many of the rallies and
marches and focused on local lab-animal abuses. Two hundred bill-
board messages against dissection and experimentation were mounted throughout Los Angeles and Orange County, sponsored by
SUPPRESS and SAV (Society against Vivisection). In Berkeley 500
people demonstrated at the University of California campus in protest
of the shoddy care given there to laboratory animals. Major protests
took place in three Florida cities, as well as in Denver, Atlanta,
Chicago, Indianapolis, Cumberland (Indiana), Boston, St. Louis, New
York, Portland (Oregon), Cincinnati, Columbus, Dayton, Pittsburg,
Richmond, and Madison. The ALF also chose April and May for a
series of raids on laboratories in Sacramento, California; Minnesota;
Ontario; and, most notoriously, the University of Pennsylvania Head
Injury Clinic of Thomas Gennarelli.

By 1985 World Day protests had spread to hundreds of cities, with
27 arrested for civil disobedience in Berkeley and Davis. In recent
years World Day has expanded to become an entire week of activism
on behalf of laboratory animals. The protests continue annually
throughout major cities in the United States, Canada, Britain,
Germany. No longer organized by MFA, which itself became bogged
down in political in-fighting, recent World Week protests have been
coordinated by In Defense of Animals. Whereas the goals of the first
organizers of World Day were not immediately abolitionist, the message of these events is abundantly clear. The focus of a particular
march may be psychological research on primates, wound laboratories, or a head injury clinic, but the participants have, as Tom Regan
put it in a recent World Week speech, declared "War on Vivisection."

Animals in the Classroom. Campaigns to end dissection and the use of live animals at science fairs predate the modern animal rights movement, and some notable successes have been achieved in these areas in recent years. In 1969 Christine Stevens and the Animal Welfare Institute (AWI) scored the first significant success in the reform of science fair standards. Their protests concerning the blinding of sparrows at a fair sponsored by the Westinghouse Science Talent Search reached the editorial pages of several publications. As a result, Westinghouse revised its regulations and instituted a ban on the use of vertebrate animals, which remains intact today.[17]

In the early 1980s the Student Action Corps for Animals (SACA) formed to encourage students at all levels to refuse dissection and demand alternatives. In 1987 Jennifer Graham, a 15-year-old high school student from Victorville, California, made national news when she refused dissection and demanded alternatives, insisting that she should not be given a lower grade due to her conscientious refusal. As a result of the publicity surrounding her experience, California passed legislation in 1988 requiring schools to provide alternatives for students up to grade 12 who refuse dissection (though the law allows teachers the final say on whether an alternative is available, as long as the teacher's decision is neither "arbitrary or capricious"). Currently, numerous alternatives—such as computer programs, models, and videotapes—are available for students in the K-12 grade levels. In 1988 Holt, Rinehart & Winston released a new edition of their high school biology lab textbook, which included only one optional invasive use of animals (a frog dissection). The teacher's edition explained the omission of the usual dissection projects found in other texts: "for most students, behavioral observations foster a greater respect for living organisms."[18] The National Science Teacher's Association has declared its preference for such noninvasive alternatives over dissection, as has the National Association of Biology Teachers. Alternatives such as "Visifrog," an interactive computer program which teaches physiology and anatomy, are arguably educationally superior to dissection, since they allow for repetition of identification skills rather than a single, and often traumatic, dissection experience.

The moral urgency of finding alternatives to dissection became much clearer recently, when the world's largest supplier of biological specimens for dissection, Carolina Biological Supply Company, was indicted following an undercover investigation by PETA. Local animal rights activists, such as members of North Carolina Network for

Animals, had been aware for years that the company transported and kept cats in deplorably filthy conditions, that dealers supplying the company stole animals from residents throughout the area or posed as potential pet owners, and that "euthanasia" of animals was often improperly performed. On the basis of the videotaped documentation provided by PETA's undercover investigator, the USDA brought indictments against the company. PETA's investigator witnessed truckloads of cats being gassed with carbon monoxide, with many of them surviving and reviving while their veins were filled with formaldehyde. An investigation of a nearby biological supply company, Ward's, revealed similar abuses.

The struggle over classroom practices has also occurred at the university and even graduate levels. Defenders of vivisection have occasionally appealed to the value of freedom of inquiry (or academic freedom) to defend the practice. Critics have argued, however, that this position is rather hollow, given that it would also imply that principles protecting human research subjects would be unacceptable—a consequence few would be willing to endorse. But the issue of freedom does play an important part in the issue in universities in other ways. For example, in 1987 Dr. Nedim Buyukmihci, a professor of veterinary ophthalmology at the University of California at Davis, offered his students the option of using cadavers or terminally ill animals to learn to perform eye surgery. The university removed Buyukmihci as teacher of the class, but he persisted in informing the students by letter that they should be allowed alternatives if they had ethical reservations to killing animals to learn surgical techniques. Not coincidentally, Buyukmihci, founder of the Association of Veterinarians for Animal Rights, was also an outspoken animal rights advocate and critic of the university's use of pound animals. The university began disciplinary proceedings against Buyukmihci, which could have resulted in his being fired from his tenured position, on such grounds as that he "used his position as a faculty member to attempt to coerce the judgment or conscience of third-year veterinary students" and that he "demonstrated a lack of respect for the opinions of his associates."[19]

In turn, Buyukmihci filed a civil rights lawsuit claiming that his constitutional right to free speech had been violated by the university. In November 1989 he received a preliminary injunction against the university, preventing them from instituting any disciplinary proceedings against him until the case came to trial. Then in August of that year the university settled with Buyukmihci before the case came to trial.

The settlement was entirely in Dr. Buyukmihci's favor and vindicated his claims: the university admitted to liability for their actions, agreed to a permanent injunction against any punitive action based on Buyukmihci's statements about animal rights or student rights, agreed to reinstitute the merit pay he should have received, and agreed to pay him $75,000 in damages and attorney fees. Buyukmihci felt further vindicated around the same time when the veterinary faculty (in response to a threatened lawsuit by two students) instituted the alternatives he had been urging for a number of years.

Consumer Product Testing.   There are a number of claims about which there is little or no disagreement within the animal rights movement. One of these is the claim that "safety" testing products such as cosmetics or household cleansers on animals is unjustified and ought to be immediately discontinued. Whatever disagreements about the use of animals in medical and scientific research may exist do not extend to this area, which is estimated to involve some 20 percent of the 60 to 100 million animals used in laboratories in this country each year.

The best known tests are the LD50 and the Draize tests. The LD50 stands for "Lethal Dose 50%," signifying the quantity of a substance needed to kill 50 percent of the animals to which it is force fed. The test is intended to measure acute toxicity. The Draize is an eye irritancy test; animals (usually rabbits) are restrained in stocks with their eyes forced open, while the substance to be tested is repeatedly dripped into their eyes. The degree of ocular damage is recorded. In the early years of the animal rights movement, producers were able to justify using such tests because various federal agencies either required or encouraged their use. For example, the Food and Drug Administration (FDA), while never explicitly requiring the use of the animal tests that had become standard, has required that each ingredient in a cosmetic be "adequately tested for safety" prior to marketing since 1938 (Mason 1985, 9). If the safety of the product has not been substantiated, a warning label to that effect must be placed on the product. Producers seem to have used toxicity testing, then, in the belief that their products will sell better without a warning label, and also in the belief that use of the standard tests would protect them in the case of suit for injuries by consumers. Because the commonly accepted tests for determining safety within industry have been animal tests since early in this century, the FDA requirement could certainly be interpreted to encourage their use, even if not explicitly mandating any particular test.

The argument against animal testing rests on a few simple grounds: the tests are not considered accurate even within the scientific community (for a variety of reasons animal tests are at best a very crude indicator of human toxicity), they are not necessary for determination of product safety, and the products being tested (e.g., cosmetics) are not important to human well-being or health. Therefore, the immense suffering they cause to animals is clearly unjustifiable. But to have a clear, convincing argument for change is one thing; to achieve that change is another.

From the start, activists were quick to see that the use of these tests is vulnerable, because the companies using them are frequently marketing products that appeal to fashion and image. To associate such products with images of suffering, blinded rabbits would be a powerful tool in the battle to eliminate such tests. But it was really the work of a coalition created by Henry Spira that gave the campaign against product testing its first successes, and thus its momentum. In fact, as the philosophical work of Peter Singer inspired the movement, so did the early example of Henry Spira's successful campaigns.

In a very real sense, the campaign was made possible by the fact that Spira had achieved other successes and therefore had tremendous credibility in the fledgling animal rights movement of the late 1970s. The product testing campaign began in New York, where Spira spearheaded a group of people who, in 1980, created a coalition of 407 animal organizations to end the Draize. Creation of the coalition was itself an enormous feat: not only did the newer, more radical activist organizations join together with some of the older, radical groups (such as the three major antivivisectionist groups—AAVS, NAVS, and NEAVS), but also included within the coalition were a number of the largest and most conservative of the humane associations: HSUS and ASPCA. Clearly, Spira was able to build this coalition because of his track record in the prior two campaigns.

The coalition to end the LD50 and the Draize first attempted a cooperative strategy, approaching Revlon and asking it to fund research for alternatives. Initially, Revlon, Inc., executives provided little encouragement, but a full-page ad in the *New York Times,* revealing the grisly tests to a public largely unaware of cosmetic testing, forced Revlon to reconsider its position. The vice-president who had refused to speak with Spira was fired, and Revlon began to see the wisdom of making a commitment of $750,000 over three years to fund a laboratory to research alternatives to the Draize at Rockefeller University. Shortly thereafter, Avon Products, Inc., agreed to fund a similar program at Johns Hopkins University.

The coalition then turned to the LD50. But instead of going the same route, they reasoned that the real expertise for reducing and replacing animal tests might reside in the corporations themselves rather than in universities. "The universities, after all, are interested in obtaining more money and doing more research. Perhaps that will prompt them to achieve quick successes so that they can boast of their achievements, but then again perhaps it won't. Anyway, we didn't want to be simply unpaid fundraisers for every medical school in the U.S.A." (Spira 1985, 204). Therefore, the coalition approached the Procter & Gamble Co., one of the largest producers of personal care products (which fall under the FDA definition of cosmetics), and asked them to develop an internal plan to reduce and replace animal testing that would be publicized as a model for other corporations. Procter & Gamble consented, published the plan, and agreed to publicize any discoveries of their "Animal Science Task Force." In 1984 Spira was able to point to a number of examples of Procter & Gamble's implementation of this reduction strategy, as well as a number of other major companies that vowed to work to reduce their use of animal tests (Spira 1985, 204–5).

The campaign seemed to be succeeding. A number of leading cosmetics companies had pledged to reduce their usage of animals or help fund the effort to discover alternative, nonanimal tests. But these commitments did not satisfy everyone in the movement, especially PETA, which was becoming a powerful force in the animal rights movement. PETA inaugurated its own Compassion Campaign and was calling for the boycott of companies that still used animal testing. Spira maintained that it was wrong to attack the companies that had shown some movement when there were other areas of industry (such as pharmaceuticals and chemicals) that used extensive testing but had contributed nothing and made no commitment to change.[20] But this argument did not stem the tide of pressure for more immediate change, for a number of reasons. For one thing, while cosmetics firms had done more than any other area of industry to fund alternative research, they were also the only industry that conducted toxicity tests without being required to by law or regulation. Since a number of companies existed that marketed "cruelty-free" products—involving no animal testing—such as Beauty without Cruelty and Aubrey Organics, activists wondered why they should not press corporations for an immediate elimination of all animal testing rather than a commitment to gradual change.

Second, the seriousness of those commitments was questioned. Susan Rich, PETA's Compassion Campaign director, pointed out that the contributions to alternative research were a drop in the bucket in relation to the assets of the corporations in question. Between 1979 and 1986 the combined contribution of corporations in the United States and Britain was reportedly $6 million. The industry spent $1 billion on advertising in 1985 alone. Bristol-Meyers Squibb Co. itself had sales that year of $4.5 billion and spent $250 million on research and development of new products. Yet Bristol-Meyers had contributed just $750,000 to alternative research over five years. The entire 500-member Cosmetic, Toiletry, and Fragrance Association (CTFA), of which Bristol-Meyers is a member, had contributed only $2.5 million to the effort during that time. PETA's Pacheco pointed out that "for every" $30,000 in sales, about a quarter (25 cents) is spent on alternatives (Grunewald 1986, 17).

And lastly, the coalition's campaign also wobbled on its reliance on corporations' own proclamations that they were complying with the reduction program. In 1985 the CTFA claimed that a survey it conducted showed that the use of animals in acute oral toxicity tests (e.g., the LD50 and related tests) had been reduced somewhere between 75 and 90 percent. But use of animals in other toxicity tests—dermal, eye irritancy, inhalation, subacute (involving exposure for three months), and chronic (up to two years)—was not mentioned in the statistics. The suspicion that cosmetics companies were trying to achieve a public relations success without making real changes was further reinforced by the realization that the numbers did not add up to overall decreases, despite the fact that companies had decreased use of certain animals and the numbers of animals in certain tests.

Uses of many kinds of animals (but not rodents until recently) must be reported under the Federal Animal Welfare Act, and so PETA was able to obtain reported figures through the Freedom of Information Act—a source of information that has proved important to animal rights campaigns time and time again. According to PETA's release, in the period 1981–84 Procter & Gamble's overall use of dogs, guinea pigs, hamsters, and rabbits increased from 9,981 to 10,553; the Gillette Co.'s use of guinea pigs, hamsters, rabbits, and primates increased from 1,495 to 4,208; and Bristol Meyers's use of dogs, cats, guinea pigs, hamsters, rabbits, and primates increased from 1,642 to 3,692. Critics charged that companies claiming that they had reduced the use of animals in the LD50 may actually have increased their use in other lethal-dose tests, such as the LD20, LD40, or LD100 (Grunewald 1986, 18).

PETA was not the only organization involved in the breakaway from the coalition's approach. The younger, more radical grass-roots organizations, as well as national groups like PETA and the antivivisection groups, were all calling for immediate cessation of all product testing. In addition to the legislative efforts encouraged by the coalition, the campaign broadened to involve demonstrations, shareholder's resolutions, undercover investigations, and boycotts. Despite the "gains" that had been achieved, Spira's approach was abandoned by most: pressure on cosmetics companies was to be increased on a number of fronts. National groups like In Defense of Animals and Trans-Species Unlimited pushed for the higher-pressure campaign.

Consumers were urged to boycott any company that continued to test on animals. PETA, for example, sends out lists of companies that do and do not test, so consumers can choose "cruelty-free" products and producers. Inviting consumers to vote with their dollars has been an important element of the campaign: in addition to supporting companies that market nonexploitive products and pressuring companies to join their ranks, it also gives individuals something immediate and relatively easy to do to help the effort—a crucial element of any grass-roots campaign.

Undercover investigation—something PETA has been well known for since the Silver Spring case that catapulted them into national prominence—has also played a role. In 1986 release of videotapes of Gillette's cosmetics testing lab in Maryland led Gillette to shut the lab down. They did not cease testing, however, but simply opted to have independent contract labs test for them. PETA's resulting boycott of Gillette had a twist: as Gillette provided a customer satisfaction guarantee, consumers were urged to send Gillette products back for refunds in the "Dump Gillette" campaign. In another investigation, Biosearch, a lab in Philadelphia that did contract work for such companies as Procter & Gamble; Benetton Group, S.P.A.; and Cosmair, Inc., was exposed. A PETA investigator saw "rabbits blinded by bath gel and watched mice drowning in cooking oil," and provided photographs of Biosearch's operation, which were subsequently made into a widely distributed video (PETA Guide 6).

In 1987 PETA led an action at Noxell Corp.'s headquarters that involved civil disobedience—a first for the anti-testing campaign. Nineteen people were arrested for blocking access to the entrance with a banner that said "No Blinding for Beauty." By 1989 Noxell announced it would no longer use the Draize test. Other companies were also announcing that animal testing would cease: Benetton (which had been target of an international boycott), Avon (which had been the subject of an "Avon Killing" campaign), and Revlon all announced an end to animal testing in 1988–89 (PETA Guide 7).

Another strategy used in the latter part of the 1980s was to purchase stock in companies (or identify sympathetic stockholders) and submit resolutions at stockholders' meetings against continuation of animal testing. Interest in this approach was sufficiently broad that in 1988 the Investor Responsibility Research Council, an independent group that provides information to investors on company practices (e.g., doing business with South Africa, labor issues, environmental impact), began including reports of animal testing practices.[21]

On the legislative front, bills relating to animal testing have been introduced at all levels of government since the mid-1980s. In 1985 Congresswoman Barbara Boxer introduced the Humane Products Testing Act, which would require government agencies to discourage use of animal tests. In April 1987 hope for more rapid progress was made when the FDA finally agreed to take a number of measures aimed at discouraging the use of the LD50: including statements in the Federal Register against use of the LD50, removing references to the LD50 and incorporating nonanimal tests in guideline test protocols, meetings with industry representatives, and continuation of its own internal policy of not using the test.[22] Critics continued to insist that the FDA was interested in maintaining the status quo and was pretty much powerless to compel the cosmetics industry to do much of anything—even submit data from their safety testing, as was revealed in congressional hearings in September 1988. Representative Ron Wyden, chair of the committee conducting the hearings, commented, "FDA's existing authority to regulate cosmetics is no better than a toothless pit bull guarding a multimillion dollar mansion."[23]

Also in 1987 a bill to prohibit the use of acute toxicity and eye-irritancy tests in Maryland passed both houses of the state legislature and was expected to be signed by the governor, but it died when differences between the house and senate versions of the bill could not be ironed out in the joint Judicial Committee.[24] In 1990 the city of Boston passed a resolution asking the state of Massachusetts to ban cosmetics testing.[25]

The state that has most raised activists' hopes for successful legislation on this issue is undoubtedly California. In 1989 state Assemblyman Jack O'Connell introduced AB 2461, a measure that would ban the use of the Draize and other eye- and skin-irritancy tests for cosmetics and household cleaner uses within California. The bill passed both houses of the state legislature in 1990 but was vetoed by then-Governor George Deukmejian. When Deukmejian was succeeded by Pete Wilson, the coalition that worked on AB 2461 reintroduced a slightly weaker version of the bill in the 1991 session. In June 1991 the bill cleared the state Assembly and was about to be introduced in the Senate when the state budget stalemate put all other legislation on hold. At one point the majority that had previously supported the bill seemed threatened by politics having nothing to do with the bill or its intent, when a senator decided to link the bill to abortion, because the bill did not explicitly rule out use of human fetal tissue as an alternative to the use of the Draize. After the budget stalemate was resolved the bill passed the senate, only to be vetoed by Governor Wilson.

Though there have been stunning victories for activists in the product testing campaign, there has also been considerable resistance. In 1989 In Defense of Animals (IDA) targeted Procter & Gamble specifically for boycott and demonstrations at Procter & Gamble facilities and at stores marketing its products. Though there are many companies still testing, Procter & Gamble was singled out for three reasons: it continued, apparently even increased, its animal testing; in June of 1989 it sent out a memo to other companies urging formation of an industry coalition to promote animal testing (proposing a $17.5 million budget for three years); and it had opposed the California Draize Ban Bill, all despite its alleged commitment to reduction and elimination in favor of alternatives. In 1993 the Procter & Gamble boycott was still continuing.

And Procter & Gamble has not been alone in resisting change. Some companies have apparently decided to dig in and fight a public relations campaign. In explanation of a 20 percent surcharge on CTFA dues, President Edward Kavanaugh wrote, "Animal rights fanatics threaten the very heart of our compact with consumers—*assurance of product safety* today, *safe innovations* for tomorrow. The industry needs the ammunition to mount an aggressive and targeted program designed to present our position to legislators and public opinion shapers before it is too late." And a number of companies that have stopped testing have done so grudgingly (Avon) or only as a "moratorium" (Mary Kay Cosmetics, Inc., and Amway Corp.).[26]

The 1980s brought tremendous advances for animals in product testing. The early campaign showed that coalitions of diverse animal groups could be built and could achieve certain kinds of results. While these were not what everyone wanted, they constituted progress toward the ultimate goal of total cessation of animal toxicity testing. At the same time, the more confrontational approach of pressure from public exposure, boycott, and protest were also demonstrated to be effective in convincing a number of companies that animal testing was more costly than it was worth to them: it was easier to be a good guy than be the target of continued negative publicity. The results of both approaches are important: serious research into alternatives to animals commenced. Some credit the campaign against animal testing for creating in vitro testing, a new field of scientific inquiry. And a growing number of companies conduct no animal testing. Some have come into business to take advantage of the growing cruelty-free market, while others have decided to eliminate their testing. In both respects activists have learned that a well-coordinated campaign that taps into the enormous economic power of consumers and targets carefully selected opponents can bring about change. Nonetheless, as the Procter & Gamble example shows, the campaign to end animal testing of even the most frivolous products has not been won by animal advocates yet, despite the gains made.

Pound Seizure.   Ever since medical students found their unwilling subjects in the streets of London and the Battersea Home for Dogs defiantly proclaimed none of its charges would go for research, "pound seizure" has been an emotionally charged political pressure point for both opponents and proponents of research. The term "pound seizure" itself reflects the violation of animal welfare territory: researchers seizing dogs and cats from shelters that were supposed to be a safe haven for lost or abandoned animals. Some states have laws that *require* publicly owned shelters to make shelter animals available to research; some leave this decision up to municipalities; and in others the use of animals from pounds is simply prohibited. Animal rights activists oppose all but the last arrangement.

Dog being dragged from an animal shelter onto a truck to be transported to a medical laboratory. *Courtesy Last Chance for Animals*

There are two common reactions to using dogs and cats from shelters for research. Some people think it logical to use unwanted animals for a good purpose—after all, if they are going to die anyway, why breed more animals for research while "wasting" these? Others find the prospect of such animals being sold to research labs horrible, even if they are not opposed in general to animal research. Few people find the prospect of their own pet winding up in a laboratory acceptable, even if they can no longer keep their pet. These two fundamental responses are appealed to by each side in pound seizure battles, though the real issues are much more complex.

From a scientific perspective, whether animals obtained from shelters are good research subjects, and whether it is "cost-effective" to use them, depend on what specifically is being done with the animals. For many purposes, pound animals make poor research subjects. It is sometimes argued that the use of pound animals is desirable and even essential, since human beings are also "mixed" (i.e., of heterogeneous genetic backgrounds). Given this, it would seem that using only highly uniform purpose-bred animals would not give an accurate picture of how humans might react to some procedure or medicine. This argument is not convincing, however, as it confuses diverse origins with unknown origins. Animals obtained from shelters may well be purebreds and not at all heterogeneous in background. In fact, researchers prefer to buy purebreds that are available at pounds, such as labrador retrievers or beagles. Lack of knowledge about pound animals' age, temperament, and disease and vaccination histories introduce many unknown variables into experiments, thus undermining their validity. From the point of view of experimental control, it makes no more sense to use pound animals in experimental studies than it does to use wild rats obtained from the city dump. It is precisely this sort of concern that has led the National Institutes of Health to abandon the use of pound and "random source" animals.

From a superficial economic point of view, it may appear to be cheaper to use pound animals, since the initial purchase cost (at anywhere from $25 to $200 per animal) is lower than for purpose-bred cats and dogs ($500 or more). But as Raymond Zinn of the NIH has noted, such comparisons fail to take into account the expensive conditioning that pound animals generally must undergo before they can be introduced into an experiment.[27] Conditioning involves holding the animals for up to two months to determine whether they are diseased, treatment for parasitism and other problems they may have, vaccinations, and "debarking," so that they cannot bark or cry and make a disturbance. Furthermore, owing to the variability in these animals, larger numbers must be used in order to obtain significant results, and a higher mortality rate can be expected (Rowan 1984). In research involving the use of surgery rooms, anesthesia and expensive personnel, the costs of using a larger number of animals can easily outweigh the lower initial purchase price of the animals.

Nevertheless, there are contexts in which all of these factors are unimportant, such as when animals are used for nonrecovery surgery in order to try out new procedures, to perfect manual dexterity, or in training and demonstration. In such cases the unknown history of the animal may be irrelevant, for it need only survive a short time, and be killed at the conclusion of the session. Thus, it is important to make a distinction between research using pound animals—which generally involves studying the effects of treatments over some period of time and introduces all the above-discussed problems—and the use of pound animals in various nonrecovery procedures.

Not only are such nonrecovery uses of pound animals scientifically more acceptable, but they would appear to be less objectionable from the point of view of animal welfare, for it is hard to see why it should make any difference, at least from an animal's perspective, whether it dies from a painless injection at the shelter or dies without ever recovering consciousness from a single surgical procedure in a laboratory. In principle, it would appear to be unreasonable to argue against such uses of pound animals.

Here, unfortunately, the issue of trust enters the picture. If assurances were offered by the research community that pound animals were to be used only for nonrecovery procedures under complete anesthesia, the animal welfare and animal rights communities simply would not believe them. Part of this lack of trust has to do with the general abhorrence for those who conduct research on animals, whether or not this is merited. But, beyond any general suspicion concerning the moral character of vivisectors, the research community has not proven reliable in this regard. Cases of animals being operated on without adequate anesthesia have been repeatedly discovered, and cases of animals being put to uses other than those promised have also surfaced. For example, the Indian government stopped the export to the United States of rhesus monkeys from that country after discovering that they were being used for purposes other than those for which they had agreed to export them—development of vaccines and biomedical research. In fact, many were being used in military radiation experiments.

Those defending uses of pound animals have promulgated false claims on numerous occasions. When the voters of San Bernardino, California, were presented with a choice regarding pound seizure, the argument supporting the practice (printed in the official voter's pamphlet) claimed that "research is painless by law" and that "pets are never used" by research, despite the fact that both claims are well-known to be false. Thus, animal advocates consider it difficult to accept guarantees that an animal released from a shelter to a laboratory will meet a painless and rapid death.

This issue of trust is further complicated by the fact that a second source of "random source" dogs and cats is through the theft of pets by unscrupulous animal dealers or "bunchers." Such individuals steal untold numbers of pets each year and sell the animals to laboratories.

Sometimes they answer "free pet" ads posing as prospective owners. Dog theft rings exist throughout the country and are extremely difficult to catch. One organization, Action 81, has devoted itself exclusively to this issue. Recently, Last Chance for Animals was instrumental in doing the undercover work that led to the arrest of a kennel operator in southern California. Barbara Ruggiero had been selling to research animals she had obtained under the false pretense of taking them in to be placed in good homes. Despite LCA's documenting of the case and persuading the police to make an arrest, ultimately leading to Ruggiero's conviction, crimes such as animal theft are low law-enforcement priorities, and the complicity of researchers in not demanding a strict accounting for the origins of all animals purchased further exacerbates the problem, as well as the ire of animal activists.

As this issue of pet theft reveals, the pound seizure debate involves issues quite unrelated to the question of the scientific validity or cost-effectiveness of using pound animals. Another argument offered against pound seizure concerns its effects on animal control efforts. When pound animals are used for research in an area, not only is pet theft a problem, but animal control is adversely affected as well.[28] People who find they can no longer keep an animal, or who find a stray, are less likely to surrender it to a shelter knowing that it may be sold to research. They generally hope the animal will be adopted or at least meet with a painless death. When given a choice, only a small fraction of people turning animals into shelters will voluntarily surrender them for research purposes.[29] Rather than taking the animal to a shelter where pound seizure is in force, they may dump it in the hopes that it can survive or that someone else will take it. This drives up the cost of animal control as more animals roam the streets and must be collected by animal-control personnel. The community image of shelters selling to research suffers, and fewer people come to adopt animals. Those who do come sometimes find a poorer selection, since researchers will compete with the public for the most adoptable animals, as docile, healthy animals make good research subjects, and feral, vicious, or sick animals do not. These sorts of considerations have led the American Association of Humane Administrators to oppose selling pound animals to research.

Of course, in addition to scientific and pragmatic considerations, there are fundamental ethical issues surrounding pound seizure. Even supposing that some research on animals can be morally justified, is it ethical to take those animals that have come to trust human beings and subject them to painful experiments? Is it ethical to exploit the misfortune of abandoned and lost animals, which in many cases have already suffered physical and emotional stress? It is the view of the animal rights and animal welfare movements that pet overpopulation and the suffering it causes is a national disgrace, rather than a resource that ought to be exploited. On the other hand, is it justifiable to breed animals specifically for research when there are animals already in existence that could be used? Is not the use of purpose-bred animals on equal moral footing with that of pound animals? If so, it would seem that fighting to end the use of animals simply because they come from a particular source is a kind of special pleading.

Such ethical dilemmas show that pound seizure issues are related to broader issues regarding animal research, and these issues divide animal welfarists from animal rightists. Animal welfarists do not generally reject all uses of animals for research, nor do they regard rats, pigs, and other less-favored animals as requiring the same protection as pet dogs and cats require. Animal rightists regard all such animals as having value and rights, and they generally oppose all animal research. Thus, while animal rights activists and animal welfarists can agree in their opposition to pound seizure, they do not necessarily agree on the alternatives to it, such as the use of purpose-bred dogs or other species. As a result they disagree over the scope of the problem and the strategies for fighting it. The seeds of these disagreements have flowered into difficulties in the campaigns to end pound seizure, as we shall see.

Between 1979 and 1981 the Metcalf-Hatch Act was repealed, and pound seizure was prohibited in Connecticut, Wisconsin, and Los Angeles. These early successes of the newly invigorated animal rights movement alarmed the research community. In response to this trend, the research community mounted a counteroffensive, forming the National Association for Biomedical Research (NABR) through merger of the NSMR and the Association for Biomedical Research, and the Foundation for Biomedical Research (FBR), which has been an active opponent of animal rights. Attempts to prohibit pound seizure statewide in California in 1982–84 were defeated twice owing to the efforts of the well-financed California Biomedical Research Association (CBRA) and the University of California, which spent over $200,000 to defeat the campaign (Giannelli 1986, 11, 12).

With such heavy opposition, the formation of a coalition of animal rights and animal welfare groups to fight pound seizure seemed appropriate. Furthermore, opposition to pound seizure is an issue on which animal welfarists and animal rightists agree. Under the direction of activist Michael Giannelli, the National Coalition to Protect Our Pets ("Pro Pets"), a coalition of 11 sponsoring organizations with many additional supporters, was formed in 1985. Sponsoring organizations included AAVS, AHA, ASPCA, the Fund for Animals, HSUS, the MSPCA, Michigan Humane Society, NAVS, and NEAVS. These organizations were committed to financial support and entitled to one vote each. In addition, 300 organizations publicly declared their support for the goals and policy statement of Pro Pets: to seek legislation banning the sale of animals to research at the national, state, and local levels.

Internal difficulties sapped the effectiveness of Pro Pets from its beginning. One of the original charter groups, ISAR, withdrew support, and issues such as whether to advocate substitution of "purposebred" animals for pound animals led to irreconcilable differences. These differences reflect the fundamental ideological and strategic differences between humane organizations, which seek to reform and regulate animal experimentation, and animal rights organizations, which seek abolition.

The ideological differences between animal welfare and animal rights contingents fighting pound seizure are also reflected in the differences in strategic approach advocated by the two sorts of groups. This is not limited to members of the Pro Pets coalition but resurfaces in pound seizure battles wherever they occur. The battle over the San Bernardino city animal shelter illustrates this conflict quite well. At a time when other shelter sources of dogs and cats in southern California were drying up, the shelter in San Bernardino supplied hundreds of dogs to research institutions such as Loma Linda University, City of Hope, Cedar's Sinai, and the Jerry Pettis Veterans Administration Hospital. The shelter was the target of civil disobedience and protest, with members of Last Chance for Animals scaling the roof and chaining themselves together in front of the office doors in August 1985. The protests finally led the city council to call for a public referendum on whether to continue the sales. The local Humane Society of San Bernardino Valley worked together with Pro Pets on the campaign, sponsoring debates, newspaper and radio ads, and mass mailings. The animal rights groups, including Action for Animals and Last Chance for Animals, conducted a campaign of their own, unable to agree with Pro Pets and the more conservative Humane Society on policies and tactics. They also ran advertisements, went door to door soliciting votes, made phone calls to voters, and sponsored a benefit concert. The disjointed efforts of the two anti–pound seizure contingents converted many voters but ultimately failed, as the referendum was lost by 231 votes (less than a single percentage point). The failure of the referendum in San Bernardino, and a similar failure in Mendocino County, put an end to Pro Pets. Nevertheless, the fight to end pound seizure has continued at all levels. In 1988 the National Stop Pound Seizure Coalition declared 1 December National Stop Pound Seizure Day and held a rally outside the Los Angeles County Board of Supervisors meeting (though the city of Los Angeles had prohibited pound seizure in 1981, the county had not). In a subsequent vote, pound seizure has ended in Los Angeles County. At the national level, the Pet Protection Act (H.R. 778)—supported by Pro Pets—would have all but ended pound seizure (by restricting NIH funds to uses of animals obtained from breeders) but was defeated after a campaign by NABR to convince legislators that labs should not bear the onus of determining the origins of test animals.[30]

In 1988 another bill, the Pet Theft Act, was introduced to make sellers responsible for documenting the source of the animals they were selling. Though the bill had wide support among animal rights and animal welfare groups, it was opposed not only by NABR but by two animal groups, ISAR and ASPCA. The split in the animal rights community had its source in differing interpretations of the bill. ISAR and the ASPCA maintained that the bill could be interpreted to implicitly endorse pound seizure. Others pointed out that the Congressional Legislative Counsel had a different opinion. The bill died in 1989 but was reintroduced with some altered language in 1990. Still opposed by the ASPCA and ISAR, it finally passed in November 1990.[31]

While a national prohibition on pound seizure has failed to materialize, local victories against pound seizure have occurred. Fourteen states have banned pound seizure, and many localities have as well. Where coalitions failed, the determined efforts of animal activists over time have put an end to pound seizure in San Bernardino. Margo Tannenbaum, Last Chance for Animals, and a few determined San Bernardino activists succeeded in convincing the city council to end the practice on 1 July 1991. The victory is a lesson in persistence: activists had been rescuing individual dogs from research for five years by adopting and placing each one before researchers could show up to claim it. Furthermore, activists worked at every level, from the mayor's office to the streets, where hundreds threatened civil disobedience. Ultimately, the council voted with its pocketbook. Making animals available was costly to the city, and—owing to activists' efforts—the city was making no money on sales to research. The resolution to suspend sales to research was clinched, however, by the Pet Theft Act requirement that dealers selling to research (including animal shelters) hold animals for five days. This implied much greater costs for the city (which would have had to build additional facilities to house animals for longer periods) if it wished to continue to make animals available to researchers.

The campaigns to end pound seizure provide an example of the ideological splits between animal welfare and animal rights groups that make building effective coalitions difficult. These differences are important philosophical and ideological differences, going much deeper than the personality conflicts that sometimes affect the cohesiveness of the movement. Their resolution may be crucial in bringing an end to pound seizure.

At a much broader level, the vicissitudes of the campaign to end pound seizure point to a crucial issue for the movement: the ability to work effectively with animal welfare and other groups. The story that began this chapter—the campaign to end the Canadian seal hunt—is a case of many organizations working successfully together. The story with which we end this chapter illustrates a different pattern with a less successful result.

Solving the Pet Overpopulation Problem

For many years leaders in the humane community have pointed out that there is a dark side even to the keeping of pets. Each year millions of dogs and cats are killed for no other reason than that they are homeless. The killing of these animals is called "euthanasia," but this is a misleading euphemism because "euthanasia" means a good or merciful death, one that is in the interest of the animal. The killing we are referring to here is performed as an overpopulation measure, not because the individual animals are sick or injured and would be better off dead. It is ironic that we kill the most favored of all animals in our society—pets—simply because we are not willing to take measures needed to prevent unwanted births.

In recent years the humane and animal rights communities have begun working together on the pet overpopulation problem. As we have seen, much of the attention of animal rights activists has been given to the kinds of hidden institutional exploitation that traditional humane societies did not address, such as factory farming and vivisection, yet in the last few years a consensus has been building that activists from both communities could profitably work together to achieve solutions to the shameful pet overpopulation problem. In the early years, animal rights activists may have wanted to distance themselves more from these kinds of concerns out of a felt need to create a clear ideological distinction, but in the late 1980s animal rights people began turning their attention to these problems also. It was natural that they would do so: clearly the situation is tied up with the very attitudes and values (that animals are objects for human use, and when they have no use, they are disposable) that the animal rights movement is attempting to alter.

It was also natural that animal rights people would enter the discussion, because despite the efforts of the humane community, the problem was not lessening. In fact, shelter killing, though unpleasant and personally difficult, had become an assumed fact of humane work. As Edward Duvin—who has written a series of jarring articles on the subject—put it,

How could it be . . . that those entrusted with the well-being of shelter animals weren't shouting the unadulterated truth about this slaughter from every street corner? How could they ever hope to end the killing without the public understanding the full magnitude and sheer horror of this tragedy?

Yes, most humane societies had education and spay/neuter programs, but they carefully tiptoed through the tulips so as not to "offend" anyone, fearful that public support—financial and otherwise—would be jeopardized. Moreover, denial mechanisms played a major role, as killing the vast majority of homeless shelter animals is difficult enough to face privately—much less publicly.[32]

Duvin goes on to implore humane societies to get out of the killing business: "give the needles to animal control agencies and devote all your energy to waging a relentless war on breeding" (Duvin 1992, 20).

The idea of a "war on breeding" is the common thread in the new approach to this problem. The older approaches—education, encouraging spaying and neutering, and the like—have not worked. Trying to get at the problem by reducing the numbers being born is clearly a good idea. Perhaps the problem was not being solved, however, because the humane society programs were voluntary, and because, as Duvin pointed out, the community as a whole had not been forced to face the problem and take responsibility for it. In the late 1980s the Peninsula Humane Society in San Mateo County, led at the time by Kim Sturla, decided to promote a more aggressive approach. They worked to introduce legislation in the county aimed at reducing the numbers of cats and dogs reproduced in the area by restricting breeding. The idea was to achieve zero population growth. To do this, the legislation called for a six-month moratorium on breeding, and then for breeding to be limited (in a way to be worked out by a task force) as long as there were more animals available in the shelters than there were homes for them.

The San Mateo ordinance passed after an intense public battle that pitted animal activists against dog and cat breeders. Undoubtedly, the fact that the Peninsula Humane Society made sure that the public was aware of the real cost of overpopulation by dramatically euthanizing several healthy animals in front of television cameras made a difference in convincing the board of supervisors to pass the ordinance.[33]

After the success in San Mateo, Kim Sturla went to work with the Fund for Animals, heading up a project to help other organizations and communities develop similar ordinances. Passage of the San Mateo ordinance produced a fair amount of media coverage—perhaps because of the aggressive tactics of the Peninsula Humane Society—and so Sturla's advice has been in demand. A number of organizations around the country have been working to introduce similar legislation locally.

Unfortunately, just how successful the San Mateo ordinance will be in the long run remains to be seen. While the objectives of the ordinance are unassailable, it was passed in a compromise form that left most of the important decisions about implementation to the task force that was to be appointed later, rather than including criteria for permissable breeding within the ordinance itself. Those who opposed the ordinance (specifically those who breed animals for profit) made sure that they had control of the task force. As a result, breeding is only limited to those who can afford to pay a small fee for a special license. Nonetheless, San Mateo represents a hope for new possibilities of success in animal activism for a number of reasons. For one thing, it represents a good opportunity for animal rights organizations and humane societies to work cooperatively. And for another, it represents an area in which there is some hope that meaningful legislation on behalf of animal interests may be achievable in the not too distant future.

Chapter Five

The Dialogue and the Dance: The Opposition

Opponents of animal rights come in many shapes and sizes: some are unconvinced by the philosophical arguments against speciesism; some recognize that animal rights advocates are motivated by a sense of compassion and justice, though they may disagree with the philosophical critique of speciesism. Beyond the healthy debate that animal rights philosophy has engendered, it is not surprising that some people consider activism on behalf of animals—whatever the tactics—as threatening to the special place humans have reserved for themselves in the universe.

Consequently, it should come as no surprise that there is more than a merely philosophical opposition to the animal rights movement: there is an organized response that wields considerable political and financial power. Much of the opposition consists of forces in place long before the movement existed: individuals and corporations with a vested interest in the continued exploitation of animals. The majority of Americans eat meat, and millions love leather boots, fur coats, rodeos, and hunting. Giant corporations have an interest in opposing the movement: the meat, egg, and dairy industries; fur industries; biomedical industries; pet industries; entertainment industries (horse racing, dog racing, circuses, rodeos); cosmetic and pharmaceutical industries; and hunting and fishing interests. Before the modern animal rights movement gained its current visibility, these corporations and interests already had reached the hearts and minds of the

American public, and their influence is a significant part of the explanation for the commitment of Americans to animal products. One might argue that most of these industries simply exist in order to supply natural demands of people, but this argument ignores the vast energy that has gone into creating and perpetuating these demands and interests. Children are not born with a desire for fur or leather or a love of hunting, and many children are upset to learn the origins of meat. Attitudes toward animals and animal products are obviously the result of a complex combination of cultural tradition, parental influence, and conditioning through school, peers, and the media.

Brief Profiles of the Opposition

To help readers understand the opposition to animal rights, we will take a brief look at some of those preexisting opponents and what they were doing before the modern animal rights movement came into being; then we will examine these segments' responses to the increasing visibility and effectiveness of the animal rights movement.

Beef, Egg, and Dairy Councils.   Long before the public had heard of animal rights, the meat and dairy industries were spending millions of dollars a year to assure a continued strong market for their products. The National Dairy Council was formed in 1915 for the purpose of "educating the public about the importance of drinking milk and consuming dairy products."[1] The council provides workshops in most major cities to train teachers in their version of nutrition and spends enormous amounts of money on classroom materials, television advertising, and billboards promoting dairy products. The schools have become so accustomed to relying on the dairy council that, when Congress began the "National Nutritional Education Training Program" in 1977 to educate children, teachers, and school cafeteria personnel about good nutrition, most states simply used the additional federal money to buy more Dairy Council supplies.[2]

In similar fashion the National Livestock and Meat Board makes it a point to "reach the children of the land at an early age" and "prepare them for a lifetime of meat eating." Educational materials distributed to schools throughout the United States assure children of the importance of eating meat and drinking milk. The "four basic food groups" are, in fact, an invention of these economic lobbies. The manager of the California Beef Council stated that at least half of the public schools in the state receive the Beef Council's "consumer information" program. More than 1,000 teachers are sent "beef teaching manuals, lesson plans, charts, and other material" (Robbins 1987, 126). This literature not only emphasizes the importance of eating meat but paints a rosy picture of the lives of farm animals. Pictures of chickens in barnyards or old-fashioned barns, cows grazing in green pastures, and pigs smiling all the way to being "made into eating meat" grace the pages of the coloring books and brochures.

Quite independent of the animal rights movement, however, the beef and dairy industries have come in for hard times in recent years, owing to the mounting evidence that the high fat and cholesterol content in meat and dairy products is unhealthful, and that the claimed benefits of these foods in the form of protein can easily be obtained from vegetable sources. As the medical journal *Lancet* long ago reported, "Formerly, vegetable proteins were classified as second-class, and regarded as inferior to first-class proteins of animal origin, but this distinction has now been generally discarded."[3]

The idea that good health requires large amounts of protein has also been discarded, and in fact large amounts of protein are linked to osteoporosis. Numerous studies have shown that the more protein taken in, the more calcium lost (Robbins 1987, 191). Even more damaging to the animal food industries has been the strong evidence that animal products lead to heart disease, stroke, numerous forms of cancer, and other diseases. A study conducted by Loma Linda University involving 24,000 people found the heart disease mortality rates for milk- and egg-consuming vegetarians to be only one-third that of meat eaters. Pure vegetarians (people who consume no animal products, also called "vegans") had only one-tenth the heart disease death rate of meat eaters (Robbins 1987, 215). In fact, the consensus has become overwhelming in recent years that the fat and cholesterol in animal products causes heart disease, with everyone from the surgeon general (1979) to the USDA and HHS (1980) agreeing. The evidence regarding strokes and cancer is also very strong (Robbins 1987, 208, 217), and exposés linking meat consumption to salmonella poisoning, ingestion of pesticide residues, growth hormones, and PCBs have all contributed to the negative meat image. An example of such an exposé is Orville Schell's 1984 book, *Modern Meat*, which documents many harmful legal and illegal substances now fed to cattle, as well as the connection between meat eating and the production of drug-resistant bacteria.

All of this evidence of the unhealthfulness of animal products has put the meat, egg, and dairy industries in a position quite similar to that of the tobacco industry, and, as John Robbins has pointed out, these industries have had a similar response (218). Just as the tobacco industry has paid researchers to do studies and publish results suggesting that the evidence linking smoking to lung cancer is equivocal, so the meat, egg, and dairy industries have hired researchers to issue reports affirming the healthfulness of their products. Of the six studies in the medical literature that fail to show a rise in blood cholesterol level with the consumption of eggs, five were sponsored by various egg lobbies, and the funding of the sixth was not identified (Robbins 1987, 223).

These organizations have also put together deceptive advertising campaigns, attempting to portray their products as low in fat. In one such ad the servings depicted were only three ounces (average servings are twice this), and the fat had been removed using a surgical scalpel. For this advertisement the California Beef Council received the annual award for the year's most deceptive and misleading advertising from the Center for Science in the Public Interest. The California Milk Producers promoted milk with advertisements claiming "Everybody Needs Milk" until the Federal Trade Commission took legal steps toward prosecuting them for "false, misleading, and deceptive" advertising. Similarly, when the National Commission on Egg Nutrition took out an advertisement stating, "There is absolutely no scientific evidence that eating eggs, even in quantity, will increase the risk of a heart attack," the FTC, spurred into action by complaints from the American Heart Association, filed a formal complaint for misleading and deceptive advertising. The egg industry has also run ads suggesting that cholesterol is an essential dietary nutrient but have had to discontinue these ads under court order (Robbins 1987, 221, 226).

In addition to being attacked on health grounds, the meat industry in particular has come under attack due to the environmental destructiveness of raising beef. It is now well known that the rain forests in South America are being devastated in part to provide cattle grazing to supply beef to the fast food industry (Robbins 1987, 364). Overgrazing on public lands in the United States also has deleterious effects, and feedlot runoff is implicated in much pollution of streams, lakes, and aquifers (Mason and Singer 1980, 84–88). And in drought-stricken California, raising of beef has come under fire. According to some sources, it takes 2,500 gallons of water to produce a single pound of meat (Robbins 1987, 367).

While all of the attacks on the meat, egg, and dairy industries have put them on the defensive, they have also prepared them well for the onslaught of charges from animal rights activists. The lobbying mechanisms, public relations firms, and school contacts were in place long before the animal rights movement began to grow in the 1970s. These groups represent formidable and effective foes of those seeking changes for animals.

Hunting Lobbies. Hunting has been controversial in the United States for more than a century, and those supporting hunting have developed powerful lobbies and government support over time. Indeed, the National Rifle Association (NRA), which is both pro-gun and pro-hunting, is the wealthiest lobbying organization in the country. In addition, federal and state agencies designed to manage and protect wilderness are heavily pro-hunting, because in many states such agencies receive their financial support from the sale of hunting and fishing licenses. This financial relationship has allowed hunters to claim credit as conservationists, while their influence leads them to manipulate habitat and "wilderness management" to suit their needs.[4]

Hunters have long maintained that their activity is not only consistent with principles of conservation but actually promotes the health and well-being of the wilderness and the various species of animals that dwell therein. They argue that by killing off the excess numbers of animals, they preserve the balance of nature, and that if they did not perform this valuable function the animals would overpopulate, leading to degradation of the environment and starvation of animals. Hunters have long claimed that their view of wildlife is scientific, while those who oppose hunting are characterized as sentimental anthropomorphizers. Hunters have historically had friends in high places, ever since President Theodore Roosevelt, a renowned big-game hunter and the first "environmental president," went on the offensive against naturalists such as Thomas Seton who opposed hunting. Roosevelt, who was crucial in establishing national parks and promoting conservation, viewed animals as resources and objects and regarded those who saw them as individuals as sentimental anthropomorphizers.[5]

The battle over the role of hunting in wilderness "management" continues today. Given that most Americans are committed at some level to the concept of conservation, hunters, who constitute a small minority, have had to convince the public of the benign and beneficial influence of hunting. Through numerous agencies and organizations, this message has been repeatedly and effectively communicated. For example, the North American Wildlife Foundation states that "the majority of the funds that support [wildlife conservation] come from the so-called consumptive users of wildlife—the hunters and anglers. For the most part, the non-hunting taxpayer who enjoys bird watching or other nonconsumptive uses of wildlife gets essentially a free ride in the pursuit of his hobby" (Baker 1990, 175).

To understand the power of the pro-hunting lobby, it is important to recognize the economic relationships between hunters and hunting groups and the government agencies that oversee parks and wildlife. According to sports magazines and organizations, hunters are responsible for preserving and protecting the wilderness, since the revenues from hunting and fishing licenses fund the management of these areas through the various government bureaus, such as state departments of fish and game. As a result of this economic relationship, however, these government agencies "manage" wilderness in order to maximize "game" species such as deer or quail. Far from protecting the wilderness, these bureaus spend large sums of taxpayer dollars to manipulate wilderness areas for the benefit of hunters. They plant browse for deer, acquire winter deer parks, and breed and stock areas with species such as the pheasant, which are not even native to the United States. Fish and wildlife bureaus in the United States spent only 3 percent of their funds on nongame animals during 1978, for example, even though these species comprised 90 percent of the animals under their supervision. In 1988 they spent 90 percent of their funds on game species. The fish and wildlife service is clearly serving the interests of the hunters, but the vast majority of the funds (90 percent) come not from hunters but from general tax revenues.[6]

The wildlife that has increased, however, has been game species, at the expense of many other endangered species. According to Jasper Carlton of the Biodiversity Legal Foundation, 3,000 to 6,000 species of vertebrates, invertebrates, and plants warrant listing under the Endangered Species Act, and the United States is losing species at a rate comparable to that of tropical Brazil. But the state and federal wildlife agencies have failed to formulate recovery plans or even list many species as endangered. These agencies are too busy promoting hunting and "managing" the hunts in order to ensure their own continued financial support. Repeatedly, forest service and fish and game agencies allow hunting even of species that are clearly endangered, such as the Florida black bear and panther. They do this because they want the revenue generated by hunting licenses.[7]

These agencies must also spend a good deal of time and money to ensure that more hunting licenses will be purchased in the future. Hunting has been on the decline in the United States, and this is unacceptable to the financial well-being of these agencies. Their solution is to promote hunting. In a 1982 issue of *The Environment* (a publication of the New York State Department of Environmental Conservation), for example, the most urgent priority on a list of public education plans is an effort to reach young people by introducing them to hunting and fishing. For many years this same agency has sponsored an annual essay contest titled "Hunting Is Conservation" for youngsters in grades five through eight (Baker 1985, 227). In 1980 the U.S. Fish and Wildlife Service granted $52,000 in taxpayer dollars to organized hunters in Virginia with the option to grant an additional $200,000 per year over the following five years for "Operation Respect." The object of this project was to convince schoolchildren that game management is a sound practice. Included in the curriculum are courses in hunting techniques, trapping and archery, and children are warned about the biological fallacies in the Walt Disney movie *Bambi* and told that, in real life, Bambi's shooting would be a sound management practice (Baker 1985, 228).

Educational campaigns such as these have made many people believe that hunting keeps numbers of animals such as deer in check, preventing them from starving and overbrowsing habitat. In fact, the manipulations of state and federal agencies at the behest of hunters keeps populations of deer artificially high in order to maintain the "maximum sustainable yield" for the hunters. Nonhuman predators, such as coyotes and wolves, that would compete with hunters for "game" species are also eliminated by these agencies, which only further upsets natural ecological balance. A textbook in wildlife management featuring a picture of a man aiming a high-powered rifle from the cockpit of a helicopter states, "When coyotes or wolves are to be reduced for the benefit of wild ungulates, aerial shooting is usually the technique of choice." Deer populations are artificially increased in various ways—including the clear-cutting of forests—with resultant destruction of nongame habitat (Baker 1985, 41, 111). Meanwhile, wildlife ecologists, and even those who promote hunting, know that deer populations do not need to be "managed" through hunting. According to the standard reference work on the subject, *White-Tailed Deer Management and Ecology*, "Most wildlife biologists and managers can point to situations where deer populations have not been hunted yet do not fluctuate greatly nor cause damage to vegetation. Certainly deer reach overpopulation in some park situations, but the surprising thing is how many parks containing deer populations have no problem" (Pacelle 1991, 18).

Nevertheless, the prohunting position of those who work for Fish and Game and and other wilderness management agencies is perpetuated among those who will manage parks and wilderness in the future. Students of "wildlife science" at universities are indoctrinated in classes into the wisdom of hunting (Baker, 1985, 40).

The hunting lobby has staunch supporters in every state legislature, in Congress, and in the White House. These lobbies assure that hunters will be allowed access to public parks and wilderness areas and that programs promoting hunting and maximizing the number of living targets available for hunters will be funded. While the NRA claims to support conservation and wilderness, its official lobbying position is quite revealing: "We believe that without some legitimate, overriding environmental interest, the NRA will support the expansion of designated wilderness only when hunting opportunities and access are preserved and the continuation of sound wildlife management practices are ensured."[8]

In other words, the NRA is only for wilderness preservation when it will promote the special interest hunters have in living targets. In fact, hunters have in some cases joined the mining and timber industries in blocking wilderness areas from federal protection. For example, the NRA and the National Wildlife Fund (a pro-hunter organization, despite the impression created by its name) joined the mining, oil, and timber industries in successfully blocking protection of 100 million acres of Alaskan lands under the Alaskan National Interests Conservation Act. Their opposition to protection was based on the fact that the plan to turn the area over to the National Park Service would have made the area off limits to hunting.[9]

As the previous example illustrates, the pro-hunting lobby often disguises itself in the form of organizations that claim to be focused on conservation, such as National Wildlife Fund. Many of its 4.5 million members are unaware of its pro-hunting bias and are nonhunters. Other such organizations include the Wilderness Society, the National Audubon Society, the Wildlife Conservation Fund of America, the Wildlife Legislative Fund of America, and the Izaak Walton League. Even the World Wildlife Fund, which has been successful in stopping the poaching of endangered species around the world, endorses hunting in some situations (Pacelle 1988, 7–9).

The Biomedical Establishment. The biomedical establishment has a long history of dealing with antivivisectionists, itself having developed in response to nineteenth-century antivivisectionism. While the American Medical Association has been most visible in countering antivivisectionism, many other groups representing diverse interests promote animal research. Universities and private laboratories that perform the research, the pharmaceutical industries and a wide variety of companies invested in product testing are all natural opponents of animal rights. Like the meat and hunting interests, these industries influence government through lobbying groups, such as the National Association for Biomedical Research, which lobbies on behalf of the Charles River Breeding Laboratories, the world's largest supplier of laboratory animals (*Agenda*, July–August 1984, 10). Government agencies—such as the National Institutes of Health, the National Science Foundation, and the National Institutes of Mental Health—also support animal research, quite literally, by funding it (to the tune of approximately $7 billion per year). Military researchers wound, burn, and irradiate thousands of animals every year. Since animal research has long been a backbone of psychological research, the American Psychological Association is also a proponent. Agribusiness, already an opponent of animal rights for obvious reasons, also supports the research industry that has made the genetic manipulations of farm animals and factory farming itself feasible. "Ag" schools are bastions of farm-animal research, as are veterinary schools, which routinely use animals obtained from shelters to teach students various procedures.

The "medical-industrial complex" presents a formidable adversary of animal rights. As with the meat, dairy, and hunting interests, the research industry finds its way into the classroom via science fairs and biology-class dissection.

The Current Backlash

Any social movement that successfully challenges the status quo and the vested interests of those in power will meet with resistance. This resistance comes both directly from those challenged (e.g., white supremacists attacking civil rights workers) and via government infiltration and sabotage (e.g., the FBI campaign against domestic opponents of U.S. policy in Central America during the 1980s). Of course, it is helpful to be able to cast the challenge as a threat to important values that most people accept unquestioningly. Thus, it is not surprising that the animal rights movement is characterized by defenders of the status quo as constituting a threat to freedom—in the marketplace, in the search for truth, even in our personal lives. Furthermore, it should be no surprise that its detractors are anxious to closely associate the animal rights philosophy with the more radical and controversial activities of the Animal Liberation Front.

To the extent that the success of a campaign or movement for social reform can be measured in terms of the strength of the resistance it faces, the animal rights movement has been successful, and the ALF has been uniquely successful. The FBI, the American Medical Association, the NIH, the American Farm Bureau, and numerous organizations that profit from animal use are expending a good deal of energy and money to put the ALF out of business and to discredit the animal rights movement as a whole. Indeed, there are organizations, such as the National Association for Biomedical Research, the Incurably Ill for Animal Research (iiFAR), and the California Biomedical Research Association whose sole purpose is to attack the animal rights movement and to defend animal research.

It is important to point out that these various organizations and law-enforcement bodies have two related yet distinct goals. Obviously, law-enforcement agencies seek to capture and convict those who have broken laws, and laboratories and factory farms wish to avoid being raided. There is also the much broader interest that the state, the corporate structure, and many segments of society have in preventing the animal rights movement from achieving its goals, whether or not its tactics are legal. As with other campaigns waged by the FBI and other organizations, the objective is often stated in terms of law enforcement, while in fact a broader goal of protecting vested interests in the status quo is actively pursued.

While the strategies for achieving this end are various, a popular method is to portray the ALF as a violent, terrorist organization; to associate other animal rights groups with this image; and thus to alienate the general public and the less radical elements from the "radical hard core" of the movement. When the "radical fringe" of the movement has been isolated, the broad base of concern for animals can be shifted from the demand for animal rights and an end to exploitive institutions to the call for "animal welfare" and "protection," a much less threatening prospect to those who wish to continue to use animals as they are used today.

In the case of the AMA, these goals and strategies are a matter of public record. In response to the perceived threat of animal rights activism and the ALF in particular, the AMA developed and distributed to its members an Action Plan in June 1989. The plan is quite explicit in its goals:

To defeat the animal rights movement, one has to peel away the outermost layers of support and isolate the hardcore activists from the general public and shrink the size of the sympathizers. This can be done by *exploiting the differences* that already exist over goals and tactics—*especially the use of violence*. The extreme goals and tactics of the hardcore activists must be exposed fully for the public to see. . . .

The hardcore types and the activists will not alter their views. They are dedicated. The sympathizers however are soft and the general public is up for grabs. These people can be scared away if they come to see the violent tactics of the movement as dangerous and counterproductive. . . .

The animal activist movement must be shown to be not only anti-science but also a) responsible for violent and illegal acts that endanger life and property and b) a threat to the public's freedom of choice.

In its lengthy "Statement of the Problem," the Action Plan goes on to define other goals, including taking the humane treatment issue away from the animal activists by showing that the research community supports humane treatment of lab animals and promoting the benefits of biomedical research. This section of the plan concludes that "implementation of the plan will require a major financial commitment from many sources. The AMA will sustain its commitment for whatever length of time it takes to turn the tide of this public issue."

This is not surprising in light of the history of the antivivisection movement and organized medicine's response to it. In fact, it is not an unusual response to those who challenge the corporate status quo in any way (Glick). But the proposed scale of this assault is impressive. Included in the plan section "General Strategy," the following tactics (among others) are suggested: develop legal challenges to activists' efforts; mobilize physicians and federation of medicine with AMA in the lead role; distribute the AMA White Paper ("Use of Animals in Biomedical Research: The Challenge and Response") through community service organizations, schools, libraries; develop brochures, videotapes, public forums, public television programs; develop school modules; organize writing campaigns for popular magazines; pay entertainment personalities to advocate biomedical research; place ads in major market magazines, buses, trains, and museums; develop public service announcements; use public opinion polls to monitor public opinion; and develop a Physicians' Speakers Bureau.

Many of these programs are well on their way, though it is unknown how much money the AMA has actually committed to these efforts. For example, the California Biomedical Research Association offers scholarships and cash prizes to high school students who write winning essays on "Why Are Animals Used in Biomedical Research?" The flyer, distributed to high schools throughout California during 1990, offers $500 for winning essays and states that its purpose is to "increase public awareness of the benefits of biomedical research." A June 1990 *Reader's Digest* article exemplifies the kind of advocacy called for by the AMA: "The 'Animal Rights' War on Medicine." The author, John Hubble, paints animal researchers such as Edward Taub (the researcher charged with multiple counts of cruelty in the Silver Spring monkeys case) as blameless victims of extremist attacks and animal rightists as uncaring of the severe damage they are doing to medical research. Hubble targets such moderate organizations as HSUS for being antivivisectionist and for publishing an editorial by animal rights proponent Tom Regan endorsing civil disobedience for the cause.[10] Lest there be any doubt about the intent of the piece, Hubble concludes with a section of steps to take to "Stop the Fanatics," including advice to contact Incurably Ill for Animal Research (iiFAR) to find out which humane societies have not been taken over by "extremists" before making contributions. The article also suggests opposing legislation to regulate research, and supporting legislation to make ALF raids federal crimes.

Also in June 1990—which, perhaps not coincidentally, was the month in which thousands of animal rights activists marched on Washington (an event well publicized a year in advance)—*Scientific American* published an article about the response of the medical community to the threat of animal rights activism. The article reported that the Foundation for Biomedical Research (FBR) had prepared a series of advertisements for television. One features former Surgeon General C. Everett Koop explaining what the *Physician's Desk Reference* is, as he rips out its pages. "Without animal research, this book would make very light reading," says Koop holding the empty bookbinding.[11] The same article notes that researchers are staging counterdemonstrations, spearheaded by organizations such as NABR. Thirty-one states currently have such organizations. And just days before the March for

Animal Rights, Louis Sullivan, Secretary of Health and Human Services, made headlines by labeling the entire animal rights movement as terrorist. West Coast activists had by then become accustomed to the label: nearly two years earlier California Attorney General John Van de Kamp listed the ALF one of the three most active terrorist organizations in the state, along with neo-Nazi groups and the Jewish Defense League.

Pharmaceutical companies have also joined in active opposition to the movement. Ciba-Geigy produced the glossy booklet "Portraits of a Partnership for Life: The Remarkable Story of Research, Animals, and Man." The foreword, by Koop, explains the need for the booklet: "The biomedical research community has been harassed in recent years by animal rights groups trying to suppress necessary research by eliminating the use of animals in research. Research projects by brilliant scientists have been stopped, and facilities at leading institutions have been vandalized by proponents of animal rights." The 48-page booklet offers several testimonials from people who say they owe their lives to medical research, such as Robin Ford, a transplant patient who "credits her survival to miracles in medical treatments." True to the spirit of the AMA Action Plan, "Portraits" portrays animal rights advocates as groups that "often support or carry out illegal break-ins and vandalism."[12]

The ideological agenda of the AMA and other groups opposing the animal rights movement includes not only the vilification of the movement but attempts to redefine the terms of the debate. Repeatedly, campaigns to improve the conditions of animals are recast by the opposition as crucial choices between human and animal benefits. Just as the biomedical community has attempted to make questions about the use of animals in biomedical research appear to be attacks on sick children, the fur industry has attempted to transform the issue of wearing fur from the issue of cruelty to that of freedom of choice. Billboards declaring that "America Means Freedom to Wear Fur" appeared in southeastern Pennsylvania and central New Jersey in the fall of 1989.[13] Afraid of being isolated as providing an unnecessary luxury, the fur industry strives to associate itself with more deeply entrenched uses of animals for food and research. Thus, they have attempted to divert criticism from the fur issue to animal rights philosophy in general, suggesting that objection to fur is a slippery slope to vegetarianism and abolishing medical research. The NRA characterizes hunting (as well as gun ownership in general) as a freedom of choice issue, and pro-hunting lobbies characterize killing animals as wildlife management, predicting attacks from mountain lions and outbreaks of rabies and lyme disease in the event that hunting is curtailed. No organization is more blatant in capitalizing on the "us vs. animals" tactic than Putting People First, whose leader, Bob Wewer, has accused Patricia Feral of Friends of Animals of favoring letting rabid dogs attack children and claiming (just after the Gulf War) that U.S. Representative Barbara Boxer of California "opposes medical research to aid America's fighting men and women" (*Agenda*, April 1991, 36).

The Massachusetts Farm Bureau used this tactic to particular advantage in fighting reforms in veal crate laws. In 1988 Citizens to End Animal Suffering and Exploitation (CEASE) succeeded in placing a statewide referendum on factory farming issues on the ballot. Specifically, Question 3 would have prohibited veal-calf confinement, suffocation of unwanted chicks in hatcheries, and unduly painful methods of castration and dehorning. Initial polls indicated public support for Question 3 was favorable, with 55 percent of voters favoring and only 22 percent opposing it. But the Massachusetts Farm Bureau created the Committee to Save the Family Farm and hired a public relations firm that focused on a doleful-eyed farmer who worried that he wouldn't have a farm to leave to his son if Question 3 was approved. The Committee to Save the Family Farm outspent its opponents by 20 to 1, and Question 3 was defeated. Phil Maggitti argues that the most ominous development in this case—and perhaps in the whole panoply of attacks against the animal rights movement—is the media's frequent willingness to aid and abet the counterattackers.

"The kindest thing the media said about Question 3 was that it was 'misguided,'" reported *Harrowsmith* magazine; "more typical were editorials calling the measure a 'con job' and a 'booby prize bill.'" The *Boston Herald* declared that the sponsors of Question 3 were "extremist 'nuts and berries' types," and the *Taunton Daily Gazette* concluded that "CEASE is comprised of militant vegetarians determined to outlaw the eating of meat" (all quoted in Maggitti 1990, 19). CEASE President Mark Sommer found that "one of the greatest frustrations of the campaign was the disinformation that the Farm Bureau put out about us and the willingness of the media to accept it as fact. As a journalist I was absolutely appalled by how little effort most reporters put into their articles."

The lack of vigilance in the media and the willingness of the media to allow government and big business to define the issues and provide the content of the news is unfortunately well documented, and is not at all peculiar to reporting about the animal rights movement. According to Maggitti, a "journalist" (reportedly paid to speak on animal rights to scientific groups) wrote in a *Washingtonian* article that Alex Pacheco had admitted in court to staging photographs of monkeys in restraining devices in the Silver Spring monkeys case. According to Roger Galvin, prosecutor in the case, there is simply no reference in the transcripts to any staged photographs. PETA is suing her for making defamatory and malicious statements (Maggitti 1990, 19).

What makes such cases ominous for the movement is that the opposition has vast financial resources available to promote their perspective. Without an independent and vigilant press, the public perception of any controversial issue such as animal rights is in the hands of those who have the most money. Without investigative journalism, those opposed to the movement can easily portray the image of violent animal activists simply by announcing that it is true and issuing press statements. An example of just this kind of manipulation occurred on 5 October 1990, when the AMA held a news conference in which prominent researchers assailed the animal rights movement as violent, describing bomb threats and hate mail they had received. One researcher, Richard C. Van Sluyters, claimed that he had been the target of a bombing in which one person had been killed. The article merely relays Van Sluyters's comments without question and places this little gem at the article's end, almost as an afterthought.[14] When we contacted the press office at the University of California at Berkeley (where Van Sluyters is employed), the office said it knew nothing of such an incident, and Van Sluyters himself failed to return our phone calls attempting to pursue the story. No such attack or victim is mentioned in any source that we could locate independent of this *New York Times* article, which simply reports the statements made at the AMA press conference without investigating their accuracy.

In another case United Press International ran a story attributing the murder of Hyram Kitchen, dean of the University of Tennessee College of Veterinary Medicine, to "animal rights extremists" who it said promised to "kill a dean a month" for the next 12 months.[15] Subsequent investigation revealed no link to the animal rights community, and that the original report was based upon "conversations with colleagues of Kitchen about threats they had received."

In addition to the mainstream media, industry employs its own spokespeople and literature to defend further against criticism from animal rights advocates. As a large proportion of veal is purchased by restaurants, Eric Fleck recently "set the record straight" to the restaurant business in the *Nation's Restaurant News.* According to Fleck, critics are well intentioned but misinformed about the real purposes of veal-confinement systems: "To ensure the health and safety of special-fed veal calves, each one is given an individual stall. That allows it to interact with others without having to compete for the proper amounts of feed and rest. . . . But the fact is the individual stall system has generated the most sensationalized attacks on veal by a small but vocal group of activists. . . . The veal industry has always responded to improvements recommended by animal scientists.[16]

Apparently Fleck was promoting the same line as a brochure (called "The Truth about Veal") produced by the Veal Committee of the National Livestock and Meat Board, which is hardly surprising, as Fleck is both a veal grower and chairman of the Meat Board's Veal Committee. According to the Humane Farming Association, the Federal Trade Commission has been investigating charges HFA made in 1991 that the Meat Board engaged in false and deceptive advertising in distributing this brochure.

Government officials and agencies have often lent their support to animal industries as well. As veal confinement was receiving adverse publicity, in 1981 U.S. Secretary of Agriculture John Block funded a number of studies of calf, hog, and poultry confinement. By April 1984 the results were in, but no public release of the documents was made. Instead, the USDA provided a one and a half page "Interpretive Summary," which referred to veal calves as "dairy calves." Nevertheless, animal advocates learned that a copy of the unedited summary of the veal studies had been leaked to the American Veal Association at least two months earlier, apparently to allow them time to prepare their defense, as the findings were rather negative. Had representatives of the veal industry not published the summary themselves in *The Vealer,* the bad news might have gone unnoticed. The summary of the veal studies stated that "calves require some degree of exercise to prevent lameness and chronic stress. Relationships were indicated between increasing degree of constraint, increasing stress and decreased disease resistance. The results indicate that long-term chronic close confinement can have adverse effects on the overall productivity of calves by inducing physiological changes associated with stress. The results also indicate that calves have a drive for social interaction and exploration as well as locomotion" (*Agenda*, July–August 1984, 11). Among other things, one has to ask why a government agency would fund studies and then suppress the results unless it had some interests to defend aside from the truth concerning farm animal welfare.

The fur industry has also attempted to prevent the "antis" (as industry spokespeople refer to their opposition) from having any effect on business, and it has also coordinated the effort industrywide. In April 1985 the first cooperative effort of the fur trade was formed, when approximately $82,000 in seed money was provided by 20 retailers to a new group, Fur Is for Life, Inc. (FIFL), which formulated a two-phase campaign against animal rights activism: phase 1 included a national public relations campaign, advertising that played on the idea of animal activists being terrorists, literature and training sessions for retailers; phase 2 was to include promotional advertising themes. In one of the FIFL-produced ads a photograph of a man wearing glasses and a hood (presumably the attire of the ALF), menacing the viewer with a hatchet, appears above the text, which reads,

Meet the World's Newest Terrorist

This man spray paints fur garments and slashes them with razors. He throws bags of human waste through store windows. He steals animals used for vital medical research.

He calls himself an "animal rights activist." But his actions are those of a terrorist. Someone who will strike out at innocent people. Anytime. Without warning.

In January 1987 FIFL changed its name to Fur Retailers Information Council (FRIC) because "the old one caused confusion." FRIC subsequently changed its name again to Fur Information Council of America (FICA), leading Merritt Clifton, *The Animals' Agenda*'s news editor, to speculate that the reason was that the acronym FRIC sounded a bit too much like a euphemistic vulgarity. According to Carol Wynne, FICA's executive director, the group's original name had been selected because of its association with the ad campaign emphasizing that "a fur will last a lifetime," but the name as well as the strategy of attacking opponents as terrorists ended when the organization realized it was receiving bad advice from its public relations firm. Since the demise of FIFL, the organization has realigned the campaign to emphasize the positive and attempt to limit the visibility of the "antis."

But how could the fur industry limit the visibility of the "antis"? After all, animal activism was gaining more and more publicity during the 1980s. One way was to pressure media not to cover anti-fur demonstrations or accept anti-fur advertising. Mass media such as television networks, major newspapers, and national magazines are often unwilling to accept advertising that is "too controversial," which can sometimes be read as "contrary to the interests of our other advertisers." This approach has worked at times. The Connecticut group Friends of Animals (FoA) produced a costly television commercial only to find that the major networks would not run it for fear of "controversy." In addition to their reluctance to become embroiled in controversial issues, much of the mass media in fact promotes such exploitation of animals as fur trapping and ranching. The awarding of furs as prizes on television game shows and in beauty pageants are obvious examples. As Patrice Greanville pointed out, "It is through the respectable 'society' and 'style' columns of the nation's major newspapers, and through the multitude of fur ads they accept, that furs receive the final stamp of social approval."[17]

The strategy of limiting the visibility of critics is part of a larger goal: to eliminate debate on the topic of furs—a debate FRIC thought counterproductive to promoting furs. It is better to create a positive image of a product than to take on critics directly, especially when your position is indefensible. Thus, fur promoters rarely agree to debate the issue publicly—on one occasion a national television talk show ("The Larry King Show") could not find anyone to agree to appear on behalf of the fur industry. The public debate seen in response to the recent attempt to ban furs from Aspen, Colorado, was an exception—a fur retailer debated on ABC's "Nightline." Generally, fur promoters regard debating as a lost cause, because any time the issue is given a hearing, the public becomes aware of the suffering that goes into the production of furs. In short, people begin to associate furs with the living, feeling animals they are made from, and this tends to threaten sales. Even the U.S. Department of Justice (to which FRIC supplied information on anti-fur activism) advises fur industry representatives to refuse to debate, though why our government would find it appropriate to take sides on this question ought to give citizens pause. In a "confidential" memo released by FRIC to retailers, Joseph Morris, Office of Liaison Services of the USDA, says, "Don't give these groups credibility by publicly responding to their misleading information. . . . The public in England believed that the anti's [*sic*] had a legitimate point of view so they were willing to accept violence as a means to an end" (*Agenda*, April 1988, 28–29).

The close relationship between the fur industry and the government is reinforced by statements made by Rick Parsons (FRIC's director) in *Fur Age Weekly*, that FRIC's purpose was "to assist law enforcement agencies with information about the internal operations of animal rights organizations." In its drive to identify "terrorists," FRIC has had demonstrations photographed and requested furriers to supply names, addresses, and photos of local animal activists to match them (*Agenda*, November 1988, 32).

Of course, it is not enough for public relations people to know the strategy: they had to disseminate it to trappers, fur farmers, and the entire industry if it was to be effective. So, for example, the magazine *The Trapper* gave this advice in the article "How to Talk about Fur Farming":

Do not show mink being skinned or killed or allow pictures of your pelting operation. Do not demonstrate neck breakers or other killing devices. Do not offer or allow interviewers the opportunity to take photos of mink in pens. If the interviewer insists on a photo, bring a mink to them while they wait outside and away from the pens. Do not allow zoom-in or close-up shots of the animals as this will portray the animal as cute, lovable, cuddly and adorable to the urban viewers. The reason you can give to avoid the situation described above could be that you are afraid that strangers and unusual commotion will disturb and upset your animals. Don't try to handle a media interview on your own, without any help. We cannot afford bad publicity of any kind.[18]

It is not always possible to avoid debate on wearing furs, however. Animal advocates have persisted in protests and appeals to consumers with sufficient regularity (especially each autumn, when fur sales traditionally pick up) that they could not be ignored. A 1988 Gallup poll concluded that the threat is serious, and so it became necessary to find a response more convincing than silence. There are a number of related themes in the fur industry's response to its critics. Apparently it found out from research that regardless of attitudes to fur, 80 percent of the public thinks whether or not to wear it should be up to the individual, especially given that choice is an important issue to many women. Thus an ad campaign promoting fur as a question of individual choice was hatched. A typical ad along these lines shows a woman, ⌐lad in fur, holding a child. The caption says: "Some people are opposed to a very basic luxury: Your freedom of choice."

Another approach from furriers attacks more directly: not by providing justifications for fur garments—still considered a losing proposition—but by attacking the opponents of fur. Clearly the idea is to move the issue away from furs and focus instead on the philosophy and tactics of animal rights advocates. This approach attempts to create fears that opposition to fur must bring with it a vastly changed life-style: vegetarianism, refusal to use medicines tested on animals, and much more. In 1990 FICA ran this ad on Fur-Free Friday: "The people who say today is Fur Free Friday said yesterday was Turkey Free Thanksgiving."

Those intent on stopping animal liberators have also worked to make laws dealing with such acts more harsh. In the fall of 1989 bills were introduced into Congress to make breaking into laboratories and agricultural facilities a federal crime. HR-3270, introduced to the House by Texas Democrat Charles Stenholm, was supported by 200 co-sponsors, including almost everyone on the Agriculture Committee and its Research Subcommittee. A similar bill, S-727, aimed at serious acts such as burglary and limited to research labs, was approved by the Senate on a voice vote in 1990. According to *Congressional Quarterly*, hundreds of farm and research groups backed this legislation, headed by the National Association for Biomedical Research.[19] Versions of the research break-in bill have been enacted in 11 states since 1988. NABR has also successfully lobbied against enforcement of the Federal Animal Welfare Act: rules to enforce the 1985 amendments to the act were delayed until 1990, and some have only recently been published, partly because NABR's allies generated thousands of letters to the USDA.

Hunters—particularly the NRA—have also pursued legislative recourse in the attempt to make hunt saboteur activities illegal. In recent years, over half the states have enacted "hunter harassment statutes" that make it a crime to interfere with or harass hunters. These laws' constitutionality, however, was successfully challenged in Connecticut, when Francelle Dorman, an activist who had been charged under the law for talking to hunters, filed a suit in federal court seeking a declaration that the statute was unconstitutional, even though charges had been dropped against her. The federal appeals court held that the Connecticut law was a regulation of speech based on its content, because it only targeted speech opposed to hunting and was thus unconstitutional.[20]

Lawsuits are another weapon of the opposition. When PETA released a videotape showing Las Vegas performer Bobby Berosini beating the orangutans used in his act, the Stardust Hotel sued PETA for defaming Berosini's character. The suit asked for $80 million in damages. During the five-week trial Judge Myron Leavitt, who, according to the *Los Angels Times*, had personal ties to the Stardust Hotel, repeatedly denied PETA the right to present eyewitnesses to Berosini's use of a metal bar to routinely strike the orangutans, while permitting Berosini to perform his act for the jurors at the beginning of the trial. According to PETA, Berosini's attorneys were allowed to stray from discussion of the beatings, distracting the jury with characterizations of PETA as "wild-eyed east coast cockroach worshippers." Kenneth Gould of the Yerkes Regional Primate Center, who has passed on "surplus" orangutans to Berosini from the center for years, testified that he did not think orangutans are capable of psychological suffering and that Berosini's two- by three-foot solid-metal cages were "fine."[21] The jury found in favor of Berosini, ordering PETA to pay Berosini $2.25 million in damages and assessing Ottavio Gesmundo, the dancer who made the secret tape of Berosini beating the orangutans, $750,000. The award was reduced by the judge, but PETA is still appealing the decision.

Another lawsuit has succeeded in eliminating one of the most effective anti-fur organizations in England. Lynx, which had waged highly successful advertising campaigns against the fur industry since 1985, published an exposé of a fur farm in its newsletter in 1989. Subsequently, Lynx was sued for libel, and it lost. Though advised that it had many excellent grounds for appeal, Lynx lacked funds to proceed with further litigation. Lynx co-founder Mark Glover (who personally faced bankrupcy as a result of the suit) stated afterwards, "It is a very great disappointment on a number of levels—not the least of which was the almost total lack of support that Lynx received from other animal groups around the globe. The final irony was to witness an RSPCA inspector offering evidence on behalf of the fur farm—a practice that *that* organization is theoretically opposed to on moral grounds."[22]

Opponents of the animal rights movement are not content to limit themselves merely to the power of the pen, press, and law, though these are powerful tools. Infiltration, sabotage, and agent provocateurs are all part of the war against the movement. Perhaps the most chilling story to date is the saga of Fran Trutt, the one positively identified "terrorist" in the movement. On 11 February 1988 Fran Trutt was arrested in Norwalk, Connecticut, and charged with placing a 12-inch radio-controlled pipe bomb near the parking space of Leon Hirsch, chairman of U.S. Surgical Corporation. Hirsch had won the longtime enmity of animal rights activists for extensive use of dogs in training company salespeople to implant surgical staples, even though the technique could be shown as well without living animals. Trutt, who had participated in demonstrations condemning Hirsch's use of dogs, was the subject of media exposés as an example of the fanatical and violent wing of the animal rights movement. The full story of how she came to place the bomb on that fateful day is less well known.

Marc Mead, the man who drove Trutt and the bomb to the scene of the crime, was upset by publicity that appeared to suggest he was an accomplice. In early January 1988 Mead delivered a press release to the *Westport News* explaining that he was really a hero, since he and the authorities had carefully staged the entire episode, assuring that no damage or injury would occur. The ensuing investigation revealed that Hirsch had employed a man named Jan Reber of Perceptions International to arrange the entire event. Reber had in turn hired Mary Lou Sapone as an agent provocateur to incite Trutt to obtain and plant the bomb.

According to Trutt, Sapone told her shortly after they met that Hirsch ought to be "blown from here to kingdom come" and offered to pay for the bomb. That Sapone also attempted to enlist Merritt Clifton of *The Animal's Agenda* in the U.S. Surgical bombing lends credence to Trutt's story. Clifton apparently told her that this was a "half-assed, stupid idea," and the matter ended there. Sapone apparently also infiltrated Earth First!, as she was listed as its Connecticut representative when founder Dave Foreman was arrested in May 1989 at the culmination of an 18-month FBI investigation.[23]

On 17 April 1990 Trutt accepted a plea bargain, pleading "no contest" to charges she tried to murder Hirsch. The arrangement was a blow to some in the movement, since they had hoped that the full story of Trutt's entrapment would receive widespread publicity during the trial. Nevertheless, the taped conversations between Sapone and Trutt aired during the pretrial hearings do reportedly implicate Sapone. Reber continues to profit from the backlash against the movement, publishing the *Animal Rights Reporter*, a magazine designed to give information about the movement to those intent on fighting it (at a hefty subscription price that puts it out of range of most within the movement). The *Animal Rights Reporter* denies any connection with Perceptions International, though they do seem to share office space.

The Trutt case is highly unusual in having implicated an animal activist in an attempted violent act, but there is no evidence that Trutt acted on behalf of or at the behest of any organization. At the 1989 Summit for the Animals, an annual event that brings together representatives from the most important national animal rights organizations, the more than 60 representatives present unanimously adopted a resolution that condemned the use of violence against any animals, human or nonhuman (Regan 1990, 24). The major animal rights organizations have made it clear that they do not endorse any violent activities, and those advocating violence would almost certainly be identified as infiltrators, outsiders, or of questionable mental stability. Whatever the interpretation of such proposals, animal rights activists clearly recognize them as detrimental to their cause.

As any movement grows, however, some violent or unstable people will inevitably be attracted into it. These people may gain satisfaction from violence or its threat, or may resort to it out of frustration at the slow pace of change. A number of prominent animal researchers have reported receiving death threats over the telephone and other personal harassment. Not all of these reports can be written off as manipulation of the media by the research establishment. As deplorable as such actions are, it is important to recognize that they represent the frustrated and misguided acts of individuals. Whether the animal rights movement is itself violent ought not to be measured by the actions of such individuals. By this criterion, every social and political movement in history would undoubtedly have to be classified as violent. The question is whether violence is part of the philosophy, goals, or strategies of organizations. Clearly it is not.

Given that advocates of animal rights are motivated by moral concerns that are not apparently self-interested, it is useful for the opposition to find any means it can of discrediting the integrity of the movement. Infiltration of groups, provocation, and harassment of activists is not rare, and is undoubtedly on the rise. The first few ALF raids provoked acknowledgment of serious problems in the treatment of laboratory animals. Thomas Gennarelli's head-injury laboratory was shut down after a four-day sit-in at the Department of Health and Human Services. HHS Secretary Margaret Heckler is purported to have called the NIH to cancel Gennarelli's funding after watching only a few minute's worth of the tapes taken from the lab. Heckler's successor, Louis Sullivan, was vocal in his belief that the animal rights movement is a "terrorist" movement. In the wake of the City of Hope (Duarte, California, 1984) raid, USDA investigators discovered many Federal Animal Welfare Act violations and fined City of Hope $11,000.

But reaction to more recent raids has been quite different. No acknowledgment of problems to be corrected has arisen in raids on the University of Oregon, the University of Arizona, Loma Linda University, the University of California at Riverside, or the University of California at Irvine. Instead, activists are being questioned and, in some cases, jailed for refusing to cooperate in investigations of the ALF raids and the animal rights movement.[24]

Since 1987 three grand-jury investigations into the ALF and the animal rights movement have taken place in California. Dozens of activists have been subpoenaed, and some of them have been intimidated into cooperation. In grand-jury investigations information is often solicited about individuals regardless of whether there is any evidence or reason to think they are implicated in crimes. Immunity from prosecution is sometimes given—regardless of whether it is requested—and then failure to answer questions can lead to contempt charges. This is precisely what happened to Debra Young when the grand jury convened in Sacramento to investigate the University of California at Davis fire. In August 1990, after refusing to give the names of her associates in the animal rights movement, Young, a 35-year-old nurse herself in poor health, was jailed. After two days Young was released having agreed to cooperate.[25]

Young's capitulation is unusual, however. In a number of cases activists have refused to cooperate with the grand juries and have served jail time without reversing their decisions not to answer the questions. On 31 October 1990, 37-year-old Henry Hutto was jailed for refusing to answer questions in the same grand jury investigation. Hutto was placed in solitary confinement and kept in jail for 45 days. As a vegan, Hutto was unwilling to eat most prison food and was denied alternative food cooked by friends and relatives. He lost nearly 20 pounds but maintained his silence.[26]

The most recent case of an activist being jailed for refusing to speak to the grand jury is that of 27-year-old Jonathan Paul. Paul's stay in jail is also the longest to date. Though not apparently a suspect in the case, he was subpoenaed in November 1992 in connection with an investigation of a break-in at Washington State University in Pullman. After refusing to identify other activists from photos placed before him, Paul was found in contempt. Hoping to coerce him to testify, he was placed in the Spokane County Jail, where he remained for five months. He was finally released on 9 April 1993, the court having concluded that he would never testify.[27]

Crescenzo Vellucci, a reporter for the *Sacramento Bee* and longtime activist, had formed a legal defense fund, the National Foundation for Animal Law (NFAL), to help defray the legal fees of individuals who might be involved in the investigation. Vellucci was arrested on 12 October 1990 and charged with four felony counts of burglary, conspiracy, theft, and criminal mischief in connection with an ALF raid at the University of Oregon. Bail was initially set at $200,000, and he remained in jail, unable to raise the money. The charges against Vellucci and the other activists were eventually dropped, but not before he lost the job he had held for many years as a journalist. During the investigation, activists claimed that their telephones were tapped and their homes broken into. By the time the investigation had concluded, a dozen activists had been called to testify, some cooperating and others refusing. As of this writing, no charges have been filed against anyone for the Davis fire. Vellucci has charged that his arrest was part of the wave of McCarthyistic harassment by the government against animal activists.

According to Vellucci, a six-month investigation by NFAL has uncovered a secret nationwide campaign—conducted by government agencies, possibly acting in concert with animal industries—to undermine animal rights organizations and activists. Vellucci claims that the effort has been highly successful, with numerous infiltrators having penetrated the movement, turning over information to the FBI and spreading disinformation campaigns designed to turn activists against each other (Vellucci 1991, 50). He warns that most activists do not yet realize what has happened and mistakenly attribute disruptions and factional fighting to "personality conflicts."

Vellucci claims that four infiltrators have been identified recently in California and Oregon. In one case, Vellucci claims an infiltrator who posed as a sincere enviornmental and animal rights activist for nearly a decade has informed on at least 15 activists. In another case the alleged infiltrator had been active in prominent California animal causes in the 1980s (1991, 52). When infiltration is as deep and long-standing as these cases represent, the distrust and confusion generated by such revelations is far-reaching. Vellucci and his wife, Sheila Laracy, recently found themselves the target of attack from other activists, and they believe these attacks have been orchestrated by infiltrators (1991, 53). Activists must stand up for each other, according to Vellucci, and denounce infiltrators. But the power of infiltration as a tool of those who wish to undermine a social movement should not be underestimated—after all, who are the loyal activists and who are the infiltrators?

Recently a manuscript entitled "Killing People to Save Animals," authored under the pen name Screaming Wolf, surfaced in northern California. As its title indicates, the text argues that the animal rights movement should endorse violent means in order to achieve its goals. Even though the manuscript was being circulated by a longtime activist, movement representatives were quick to disavow it and disassociate themselves from its call for violence. *The Animals' Voice* refused to run advertisements for the book, and activists have condemned the manuscript and those responsible for it. In an article for *The Animal's Agenda* Tom Regan characterized the book as a clear case of provocative literature, in the tradition of *The Protocols of the Elders of Zion*, an anti-Semitic forgery supposedly revealing secret plans of Jewish leaders to control government, finance, and the media.

Clearly the opposition to the animal rights movement constitutes a significant force. Whether "Killing People to Save Animals" is part of an effort to undermine the momentum the young movement has achieved is difficult to know, but clearly there is a pattern of such activities. How activists respond to such challenges will severely test their character and determination.

To this point we have detailed the story of the animal rights movement: its historical roots in the humane and antivivisection movements of the nineteenth century, the emergence in the 1970s and 1980s of an organized effort to achieve the goals of the animal rights movement, and the opposition that this effort has drawn forth. Like other social movements, the animal rights movement is animated by ideas. It is not surprising, therefore, that the emergence of a new breed of activism on behalf of animals in the 1970s corresponded to a period of philosophical reflection about the moral status of animals. While it may seem unlikely that the finer details of philosophical debates play a very large role in the thinking of most activists or their opponents, that there is a rethinking of the role of animals in our morality has been of the utmost significance in this movement. Indeed, it is not just the broad sweep of philosophical change but also some of the differences of detail that are taking center stage in determining the future direction of the movement. It is to the ideas that capture this rethinking of our obligations to animals that we must now turn.

Chapter Six

A Movement of Ideas: Philosophies of Animal Rights

In this chapter we present the major ideas behind this new activism: the philosophies of animal rights. These ideas represent some of the main attempts to work out a coherent answer to the question of the moral status of animals. In light of the fact that philosophical conceptions of morality are not uniform in contemporary thought, it should come as no surprise that there are different schools of thought concerning the role of animals, even among those who think that traditional thinking about the place of animals must be challenged and rejected. This chapter outlines the ideas of six of the major thinkers in the animal rights movement, as well as the criticisms raised against these ideas. In addition, we consider the extent to which the arguments and conclusions of these philosophers are those espoused by activists.

Peter Singer: Liberating Animals

Peter Singer's *Animal Liberation* has had a profound influence; many activists refer to this book as a turning point in their thinking about animals and in their lives generally. It is largely as a result of Singer's pioneering work, together with that of Tom Regan, that questions about the treatment of animals have become a serious topic of discussion today, within both moral philosophy and American society. Of course others have raised serious questions about our relations

Australian philosopher Peter Singer, author of *Animal Liberation*. *Courtesy Bert van Dijk, NL*

with animals, especially in the English tradition (Singer, though Australian, did his graduate work at Oxford University, where he was influenced by others to take up issues concerning animals),[1] but the contemporary scene is much more profoundly influenced by Singer than by his predecessors. Perhaps the influence of *Animal Liberation* is to be traced to Singer's success in bringing philosophical argument about the moral status of animals to bear in a straightforward way on factual information about the treatment of animals in modern farms and laboratories. When juxtaposed with a hard look at self-interested human bias, the facts (of which most people remained happily ignorant) lead to some startling questions and conclusions about our cherished institutions and personal habits.

Sexism, Racism, and Speciesism. Singer sees the fundamental issue as a question of whether the interests of nonhuman animals should be considered similarly or differently from the way we consider human interests. This is a question of the moral status of animals: Are they to be equal members of our moral community, deserving of concern for their interests, or should they be accorded some lesser status (e.g., viewed primarily as means to our ends)? Singer's considered position is that there is no rational basis for distinguishing interests along species lines; rather, we should be concerned morally about anyone who has the capacity to suffer or enjoy. Were we to take the interests of nonhuman animals seriously, this would constitute a "liberation" for animals analogous to the two great liberation movements of recent decades in the United States: that of blacks and women.

Singer develops his argument for liberating animals by explicitly considering these analogies to women's and black liberation. The simple point to be made about discrimination against blacks and women is that it involves making distinctions along lines that are morally irrelevant to the question at hand. For example, whether or not someone is qualified to rent housing is a function of such things as his or her ability to pay the rent, to be a good neighbor, and to respect the landlord's property. To bring a person's race or sex into consideration in such a decision is to consider an irrelevant factor. Race and sex simply have no bearing on the qualities that are relevant to justifying granting or denying housing to someone. Considering race or sex here would make equals unequal.

But "equality" in this important sense does not mean that sexism and racism are wrong simply because they falsely assume that men are different from women and blacks are different from whites. At a deeper level, the lesson to be learned from sexism and racism is not that we are really all alike in abilities or inclinations. Singer allows that differences beyond those culturally produced may emerge. Nonetheless, this does not disturb the commitment to equality. The real meaning of equality is not *descriptive* but rather *prescriptive*—a commitment to equality does not imply that no factual differences can be found between individuals who are nonetheless equals. Crucial in the commitment to equality is the belief that such differences (whether racial, sexual, religious, related to intelligence, appearance, etc.) are morally irrelevant to how we should treat other human beings: each human being deserves to have his or her interests taken into account and given the same weight as the like interests of any other human being.

The English philosopher Jeremy Bentham (1748–1832) expressed this idea concisely: "Each to count for one, and none to count for more than one" (Singer 1990, 5). This is the basis for finding sexism and racism objectionable: such biases discount the interests of some in favor of others, not because of the nature of those interests but solely because they are the interests of a less favored group. Bringing in the irrelevancies of race or sex is not just an intellectual error: it is invidious discrimination that injures people deeply and unjustly. When we reflect on the *reason* that sexism and racism are wrong, we see that a similar attitude toward the interests of nonhuman animals is equally indefensible. If animals other than humans *have* interests, can there be any unbiased justification for ignoring them in considering what to do? To give preference to the interests of a being solely because it belongs to one's own species is analogous to preferring the fulfillment of interests of members of one's own race or sex. As the latter preferences are racist and sexist, so Singer (following Richard Ryder) calls the former "speciesist." The basic thrust of Singer's critique of our current treatment of animals is that it is profoundly speciesistic and thus cannot be made consistent with sound moral principles.

Equal Consideration and Equal Treatment.   Fundamental to a proper understanding of Singer's position is a distinction he makes between *equal consideration* and *equal treatment*. A moment's reflection shows that commitment to treating all humans as equals does not mean that we must treat each human in exactly the same way: good reasons can be found to treat people differently according to differences in their needs, abilities, preferences, and situations. For example, few would think that equality implies that even two-year-olds ought to have the right to vote or access to postgraduate education. They simply do not have exactly the same interests as others who may vote or seek postgraduate degrees. Yet this does not mean that the interests they do have are any less important than the interests of those who can do such things. Thus, the commitment to equality—to avoiding racism, sexism, or speciesism—does not imply that we must treat all exactly alike.

While pigs may have some interest in the outcome of a presidential election (because they will be affected by the agricultural policies of the candidates), they have no interest in voting, as they cannot understand the options being posed. So there is no moral error in denying them the vote, though this does not release those who can vote from considering the pigs' interests in the way they vote. Furthermore, insofar as we are comparing interests that are *dissimilar*, it does not follow that we must treat two individuals in the same way in order to give their interests equal consideration. Not all interests are equally compelling, as when one person on a date may desire casual sex and the other may not. In such a situation it would be wrong to think that an unbiased evaluation of the competing interests makes it a standoff, for the important interest humans have in determining for themselves whether they share intimate relations with others is clearly more important than the desire to have sexual encounters. Similarly, the desire to live is more important than the desire to enjoy the taste of meat. Not all interests are equal, nor are all equally important to the individual holding them.

The Significance of Suffering and Enjoyment.   Singer argues that a morally enlightened view would include serious consideration of the interests of other animals in addition to human beings. But which kinds of animals? The answer is straightforward: all those who are "sentient"—that is, those capable of suffering or enjoying. A few words must be said about Singer's choice of the capacity to suffer or enjoy as the demarcation between those who are of moral concern and those who are not. Even though rose bushes, for example, may be injured by our actions (by failing to water them, by crowding them too closely together, or by simply uprooting them), to do so is not of moral concern in the same way that injuring a squirrel, pig, or human is. As Singer points out, all the kinds of evidence we might employ to determine whether someone suffers or enjoys—the nature of their nervous system, kinds of behavior they engage in, and the evolutionary usefulness of pain to the organism—are lacking in the case of plants and even some animals, and so the only reasonable conclusion is that they simply lack the capacity to suffer or enjoy (Singer 1990, 235).

This division is a morally significant one. While it may be difficult to know exactly which organisms fall on which side of the line, it is clear that mammals, fish, birds, and reptiles share these capacities, while rosebushes, cacti, and elm trees lack them. How far along the evolutionary scale we must go before reasonably attributing the capacity to suffer or enjoy is a difficult question. Singer suggests that mollusks—with the exception of octopi—are possibly lacking in the capacity to suffer. While it is true that a completely worked out ethic must say something about how to draw this line, inability to draw it precisely will not diminish the challenge to our current treatment of animals whose sentience is not in question. As we shall see, not much in Singer's case for liberating animals hinges on drawing this line very precisely, and it would be mistaken (or, worse, an evasion of the serious issues) to worry too much about such line drawing.

Why should the presence or absence of the capacity to suffer or enjoy determine whether a being is an object of moral concern? Singer has two reasons for this. In the first place, his moral perspective places the promotion of interests as fundamental. Unfortunately, he does not enter into a discussion of the meanings of "interest." Nonetheless, certain things are clear from his discussion about the intended meaning of this term. Singer uses the example of a stone being kicked: while we might alter or even destroy a stone, we could not possibly affect its *welfare* in any way, no matter what we do to it. For example, we speak of compulsory education as being in the interest of the compelled children, meaning that their welfare is positively affected by education (even taking into account the negative factor of compulsion). This example should also make it clear that by "interest" Singer does not mean simply those things the individual in question *takes an interest in* (i.e., is curious about, desirous of, or otherwise takes a positive attitude toward). The satisfaction of desires or preferences may frequently be in our interest, but interests are not limited to being the object of positive attitudes. Some children would prefer not to be in school at all. It is presumably true that decent education is nonetheless in their interest.

Singer's view might be expressed this way: what is in one's interest is always a state of affairs that positively affects one's welfare. The question now becomes, How do we know whether an individual has interests in this sense or not? Singer's answer is that the capacity to suffer or enjoy is both a necessary and sufficient condition of the possession of interests: proposed actions that affect one who cannot suffer or enjoy cannot damage that individual's welfare. Thus, the capacity to suffer or enjoy makes one an object of moral concern because it provides one with interests that deserve to be taken into account when we consider what actions to pursue.

The importance of suffering on Singer's view is not limited to physical pain. We may think of the sensations one endures when one has a headache or a sprained ankle as paradigm cases of suffering, but nothing in Singer's account commits him to holding that this is the only kind of suffering. In the human case this is obvious: we can suffer emotionally (as in grief, disillusionment, or terror) or experience the frustration of plans gone awry, hopes smashed, and dreams evaporated. None of this can be explained in terms of painful sensations. Nor need this complexity be taken to distinguish humans entirely from nonhumans. Different kinds of animals may also suffer in ways not reducible to unpleasant sensations: examples include loss of those who are socially meaningful, frustration of desires, and stress at the tedium that insufficiently stimulating environments provide. A wealth of ethological data support this.[2] While it may be difficult to say exactly how close the experience of another species is to our own in such cases, it is clear that nonhumans are not limited in the ways they may suffer to physical pain.

Speciesism and Utilitarianism. The second way that suffering and enjoyment become important in Singer's view is due to the particular moral theory he adopts. Singer's moral outlook (explained more fully in publications other than *Animal Liberation*) is a form of "utilitarianism," specifically a form of utilitarianism known as "act utilitarianism." Act utilitarians hold that among the alternative actions available to an agent that alternative which is likely to provide the greatest balance of good over bad consequences is the morally correct one.[3] Some commentators have written as if Singer's argument for animal liberation were out and out utilitarian, depending for its correctness on the highly controversial utilitarian moral theory. Before discussing the respects in which Singer is drawn into the debate about the form and correctness of utilitarianism, it is important to note the aspects of his argument in *Animal Liberation* that are not dependent on this particular moral theory, for it is our contention that much of significance in Singer's case for animal liberation survives any attack on his utilitarianism.[4]

One of the more powerful aspects of *Animal Liberation* is the presentation of the unpleasant facts of our treatment of animals. Two areas Singer gives considerable attention to are science and agriculture. His decision to focus on these areas is well justified, for it is here that some of the most extensive, yet also most hidden exploitation of animals occurs. It is also in these areas that each of us is implicated in these institutional practices: through taxes, consumer demands for safety and new medical technologies in the case of scientific research, and personal, albeit indirect, involvement through our dietary habits in the case of intensive farming. A clear utilitarian argument can be mounted against much that occurs in laboratories and factory farms. The Draize test serves as a clear example. In this test samples of potentially toxic substances are placed in the eyes of rabbits without opportunity to rinse or otherwise rid themselves of the foreign substance. The results are then observed over a period of three to four days. One of the primary uses of the Draize test is to test new cosmetic products, such as eyeshadows. Clearly the interests served by testing new cosmetic products can hardly outweigh the interests of animals damaged by the Draize test, especially in light of the fact that many cosmetic alternatives exist at present. Thus a moratorium on such testing would not restrict the availability of such products (which many consider to be somewhat frivolous in the first place) but only prevent the introduction of new products that used animal tests. We could have cosmetics and avoid the suffering caused by their testing with little sacrifice. In fact, many products exist in this and other areas in which testing is done that have been safely used for years even though no initial animal tests were run. Some manufacturers now see a market in conscientious consumers anxious to purchase products free of animal exploitation, so-called cruelty-free products. Because a moratorium on testing need not prevent the introduction of new products, a utilitarian should agree that continuation of the testing is morally wrong.

Yet a careful reading of *Animal Liberation* shows that Singer also presents an important objection to the current treatment of animals that is not based on a utilitarian calculation but expressed in terms of demanding that we avoid speciesism. For example, he suggests the following rule of thumb for determining the justifiability of scientific research using animals: an experiment using a nonhuman animal is justifiable only if the same experiment would be justifiable if performed on a human being at a similar or lesser level of mental ability who had no prospect for mental development (i.e., a severely retarded or brain-damaged individual) (81–85).

Singer's point is that if we object morally to the same experiment performed on a similarly situated human subject—that is, one incapable of suffering in any different ways or to any greater extent than the proposed animal subjects—then the experiment must be morally objectionable when performed on animal subjects. To deny this is to embrace speciesism, for it shows an unabashed, unjustified preference for humans merely because they are members of your own species.

The interests of the proposed subjects are simply denied equal consideration because of their species, not because the interests in question are different or the damage to their interests is less.

A recent program to harvest organs from anancephalic human babies (begun in 1987 at Loma Linda University in California) provides a good example of what Singer is speaking about here. Anancephalic babies are born without portions of brain and skull, and they usually die at birth or shortly thereafter. Even if they do not die, their prospects for a "normal human life" are nil. The program's intent was to find parents who would volunteer to have their doomed anancephalic babies placed on life-support systems to prolong their lives until recipients could be found for their healthy organs. Because these infants lack consciousness and the ability to suffer, keeping them alive would not seem to harm them in any way. Following a number of failed attempts at harvesting such organs, Loma Linda University announced that the program was being phased out not because it was a medical failure but because of ethical reservations about the program. Perhaps the most significant reservation expressed was the ethical difficulty of crossing into "uncharted territory by prolonging life not for the benefit of the patient but for the sole purpose of harvesting organs."[5] Yet researchers at the same university made headlines just a few years earlier by attempting a heart transplant from a healthy baboon (Baby Gabriel) to a human infant (Baby Fae). That program was not suspended for ethical reasons; in fact, public statements have been made by Loma Linda that the trans-species transplants will continue at a later date, once further study makes them more likely to succeed (Baby Fae survived only 21 days). But to continue the program that exploits healthy, intelligent animals for their organs and discontinue one that did not damage the interests of infants who had no potential to develop mentally because of concerns about "prolonging life . . . for the sole purpose of harvesting organs" is a clear case of speciesism.

Objections to Singer's Philosophy

Utilitarianism and Killing.   Much of what Singer argues appeals to the demand that we avoid speciesism. Nonetheless, his moral framework is utilitarian, and it is to this side of his thought that we must now turn. Act utilitarianism, as we have noted, urges that correct action is achieved by selecting the alternative that promotes the greatest balance of good over bad results. But what counts as good or bad results? One classical form of utilitarianism, "hedonistic utilitarianism," developed by Jeremy Bentham and John Stuart Mill (1806–73), maintains that it is pleasure (or enjoyment) and pain (or suffering) that we should account most fundamentally good and bad, respectively. In *Animal Liberation* Singer seems to share this position, giving pride of place to concern about the unmitigated suffering imposed on animals every day. For example, when speaking of the conditions under which animals are reared in factory farms, he returns time after time to the suffering that such conditions impose on the animals we eat: the consequences of stress from overcrowded housing, the boredom of artificial and understimulating environments, the frustration of natural instincts that such environments produce, and the pain of mutilations such as castration and debeaking. Singer goes so far as to say that "the conclusions that are argued for in this book flow from the principle of minimizing suffering alone" (21).

Thus the immorality of factory farming can be shown independently of the fact that the animals we eat must be slaughtered in order that we may do so (though Singer is careful to point out that slaughter as currently practiced also produces a significant amount of suffering). Even if it turned out that killing animals for such a purpose was not strictly wrong in itself (as long as it was done painlessly to animals who had been reared humanely), Singer thinks that the case against factory farming—and even the case for vegetarianism—is still quite strong. Thus, from the perspective of a utilitarianism that focuses entirely on experiential states in accounting for right or wrong action, we can see quite readily why much of what we do to animals today is morally unacceptable. But problems arise for Singer's account when he turns to the question of the wrongness of killing animals:

To avoid speciesism we must allow that beings which are similar in all relevant respects have a similar right to life—and mere membership in our own biological species cannot be a morally relevant criterion for this right. Within these limits we could still hold that, for instance, it is worse to kill a normal adult human, with a capacity for self-awareness, and the ability to plan for the future and have meaningful relations with others, than it is to kill a mouse, which presumably does not share all of these characteristics; or we might appeal to the close family or other personal ties which humans have but mice do not have to the same degree; or we might think that it is the consequences for other humans, who will be put in fear of their own lives, that makes the crucial difference; or we might think it is some combination of these factors, or other factors altogether. . . . I conclude, then, that a rejection of speciesism does not imply that all lives are of equal worth. (18–20)

Clearly this passage urges the case for similar rights to life for similarly endowed organisms from the point of view of avoiding speciesism, not primarily from a utilitarian consideration. The principle of equality urges us to remain consistent: where no relevant differences exist, then that treatment—those rights appropriate for one species—are also appropriate for others. Such arguments take us only so far, however, for they do not tell us what kind of treatment or rights are appropriate in either case. For that we need more, and it is here that a utilitarian perspective provides answers. Many commentators, however, are concerned about how adequate those answers are when it comes to accounting for the wrongness of killing, even in the human case. Generally speaking, there have been three kinds of objection to Singer's position: (a) the concern that a hedonistic act utilitarian cannot find a sufficient foothold to explain the evil of death (either for humans or animals), (b) the related concern that utilitarianism implies that there is nothing wrong with considering animal (and possibly human) lives replaceable, and (c) the concern that it sanctions a homocentric (and thus speciesistic) view of the value of nonhuman life. Sorting out such issues, abstract as they may seem, is central to understanding the philosophical debate about what constitutes a position that promises genuinely to ground and defend rights for animals.

Can utilitarians focusing on pleasure and pain explain the wrongness of killing? The least difficult kind of case for utilitarians is when killing involves suffering—the actual death may be painful, and fear or even terror may occur additionally—but these factors do not seem sufficient to account for what is most centrally wrong in killing someone. This becomes apparent when we consider that none of these experiential elements are strictly necessary for killing to occur. Critics have often highlighted this by posing cases in which the victim presumably would be murdered in his or her sleep, thus eliminating the elements of fear or painful sensation surrounding the death. Furthermore, one is also asked to suppose that the victim is either unknown (e.g., a hermit or orphan) or someone that most others would prefer dead to eliminate appeal to the unhappiness of others who may be aware of the death in explaining why killing is wrong. It is clearly possible to describe cases in which the wrongness of killing someone cannot reside in anyone's unpleasant experiences, and so the classical hedonistic utilitarian seems to have difficulty explaining why killing an unwitting victim would be wrong.

Another concern about utilitarian accounts of the wrongness of killing concerns the question of replaceability. Critics often charge that, given a hedonistic utilitarian perspective, it is not particularly important who experiences pleasure and pain, so much as how much pleasure and pain there is in the world. Thus, hedonistic utilitarianism might sanction the killing of individuals insofar as they are replaceable by other individuals who will experience comparable or even better balances of pleasure over pain. In fact, one defense of sport hunting is built on the notion that the replaceability of animals is a virtue. Robert Loftin argues that the fact of replaceability of "game" animals makes protection of the areas in which wildlife reside possible, since it is the hunters who provide for its preservation (through license fees, political pressure, etc.). As hunters would not work and pay to preserve wilderness if they could not hunt, the replaceability of animals seems essential to preservation of wilderness.[6] To see animals as thus replaceable is a consequence of utilitarianism that Singer would surely be hesitant to endorse.

Singer's response to these problems has been to accept that a full account of what is wrong with killing cannot be based entirely on hedonistic utilitarianism: the view must be expanded to focus additionally on the satisfaction or frustration of desires and preferences as well as pleasure and pain as goods and evils. In general this makes sense, for we consider it a loss for someone not to have what he or she prefers, even if the person is not aware of that fact (and thus experiences no pain at the loss). It is simply worse not to get what one wants than to get it. This view helps to explain why death may be a loss for someone, even though she is in no position to feel or acknowledge the loss. Thus killing one who desires to live is wrong on this view, whether or not that individual knows she is going to die.

The inclusion of preferences allows Singer the following maneuver in response to the killing objection: for organisms capable of the desire to continue living (which implies a certain self-awareness), killing would be wrong because it would frustrate this important preference. For organisms lacking the requisite mental sophistication to form such a desire, painless killing is not wrong. Thus, Singer's solution is to accept that some animals who have interests may nonetheless lack an interest in living per se, and thus killing them is not wrong.

Michael Lockwood has pointed out that there is an even stronger response available to Singer. Death is an evil not simply because it frustrates the desire to continue living but also because it frustrates most of the major desires an individual may have. It would follow that even if one lacked the capacity to form a desire to go on living, other long-term desires might be sufficiently frustrated to account for the wrongness of killing some animals who are not sufficiently self-aware to form the desire to continue living. To die prematurely would frustrate these other desires and thus is contrary to their interests, whether they know it or not. On the other hand, those who lack a capacity to form long-term desires in general would not have a significant interest in living per se on this account.[7]

Singer believes that the move to a combination of hedonistic and preference utilitarianism deals with the replacement objection, for the individual animal whose preference to live is frustrated cannot simply be considered replaceable without loss by another animal with a comparable pleasure-to-pain ratio. In replacing one with another a net loss occurs, since the preference of the first is still frustrated even if the preference of the second to live is now being satisfied. Unfortunately, a view that emphasizes satisfaction of preferences is just as susceptible to replaceability arguments such as Loftin's as one emphasizing experiential states. Even though more is lost when an individual with preferences is killed, more can be gained by the introduction of comparable replacements. There just does not seem to be any good reason to think that the newly introduced preferences (which presumably would not have existed without the act of replacement) cannot counterbalance the frustration of the killed animal's preferences—for example, if an individual is replaced by another with greater prospects of satisfaction.

It seems, then, that Singer has trouble explaining why killing is wrong. As he points out, even if replaceability were morally justifiable according to utilitarianism, that would not justify such practices as factory farming, since it is questionable whether introducing an animal into the world with the prospects typical of contemporary farm animals is doing that animal much of a favor in the first place. Nevertheless, this has seemed to some critics (such as Tom Regan) to constitute a weakness in the philosophical position Singer appeals to in explaining the wrongness of our treatment of animals, and thus leaves a Singerian in a difficult position.

Utilitarianism, Justice, and Abolition.   A further and very general problem with act utilitarianism is that actions we might in general regard as immoral and unjust can be justified if they produce the best overall consequences. Suppose, for example, that an angry mob of people threatens to burn down an entire neighborhood of innocent individuals in retaliation for some perceived wrong committed by one resident of the neighborhood. No one knows who the guilty party is, but by framing and punishing one innocent person, the mob can be quieted and many innocent lives can be saved. Should the magistrate in charge frame an innocent individual and allow the mob to execute him? Intuitively, this would seem unjust, but if it saves the lives of many other people, utilitarianism appears to permit—or perhaps even require—this course of action.[8] Similarly, if one or a few animals could be sacrificed in the test of a vaccine to save thousands of (human or animal) lives, then utilitarian reasoning would require that the few animals be sacrificed. The negative utility of their pain and loss of life would be far outweighed by the positive benefits accruing to the thousands who benefited. Thus, Singer's utilitarianism cannot be used to argue for the abolition of animal research.[9]

Singer is quick to point out that in reality scientific research on animals does not produce more good consequences than bad, and thus the vast majority of it can be ruled out on these grounds. But it is an important general feature of Singer's utilitarian approach to ethical questions that it does not allow for the sort of categorical conclusions that many animal rights activists advocate. If one wishes to advocate the total abolition of animal research, the raising and killing of animals for food, and the use of animals in myriad other ways, the utilitarian approach is not the route to take. Of course, others may consider this more compromising feature of utilitarian ethics a virtue rather than a vice.

Empirical Disagreements.   In general, Singer's conclusions about the vast changes that ought to be made in our treatment of animals are based on calculations regarding the consequences (in terms of preferences, pleasure, and pain) of the status quo as opposed to available alternatives. Some critics have maintained that the calculations would really come out differently. For example, R. G. Frey argues that the consequences of giving up meat eating would be much worse overall than the current situation. He argues that severe economic consequences would result from abandoning meat consumption, and he disagrees with Singer about the mental states that can be plausibly attributed to animals.[10] Anyone who disagrees with Singer about animals' abilities to suffer pain and experience pleasure, or to have preferences, will come up with different conclusions regarding the consequences of our current treatment of animals and the correct course of action. In general, utilitarian judgments about the justifiability of actions are sensitive to empirical assumptions, which utilitarians would generally consider an advantage of their theory.

Singer's arguments rely on a scientific understanding of the nature of animals—particularly on accepted precepts of modern biology, psychology, and evolutionary theory. Those who take exception to this perspective disagree with not only his utilitarian calculations but also arguments to the effect that species boundaries are not morally relevant. Those holding a Christian creationist perspective, in particular, may find Singer's arguments against speciesism unconvincing.

Tom Regan: The Case for Animal Rights

The publication of Tom Regan's *The Case for Animal Rights*, like that of Singer's *Animal Liberation*, marked a major advance in the philosophy of the animal rights movement. Singer's work galvanized the movement, bringing before the public's eye the exploitation of animals and showing it to be of a piece with the worst forms of human exploitation. Regan's work showed that a powerful case could be made for the rights of animals from an entirely different moral perspective—one that takes the notion of rights much more literally and seriously than did Singer. Regan's book provided an unprecedented scholarly treatment of the philosophical as well as the ethical issues that the question of animal rights enjoins, and it brought the discussion to a new level of serious attention within scholarly circles.

Though Regan intended to reach a wide audience with *The Case for Animal Rights*, it is made difficult for most lay readers by the detailed philosophical argumentation. No doubt the philosophical difficulty of the book accounts for the fact that it is not as widely referred to by activists as is Singer's book, even though the conclusions Regan draws are much more in accord with many activists' views than those of Singer. Regan is not only rigorous but uncompromising and radical in his conclusions. He argues for the total abolition of the use of animals in science, the total dissolution of commercial animal agriculture, and the total elimination of commercial and sport hunting and trap-

American philosopher Tom Regan, author of *The Case for Animal Rights. Photo by Bryan Regan*

ping. The entire framework of thought that views animals as resources must be replaced by one that understands animals' inherent worth and respects that worth by according them equal moral status with human beings. *The Case for Animal Rights* establishes that such radical views can be consistently and rationally defended and are not the emotional outpourings of a few "extremists." Thus, the book has been influential in establishing an uncompromising and unapologetic tenor in the scholarly defense of animal rights, as well as in the animal liberation movement itself.

The Mental Complexity of Animals.   Those who would deny that animals have moral worth generally begin from assumptions about the mental status of animals, arguing from various mental deficiencies of animals, such as their lack of awareness, beliefs, and language, to conclusions about their lack of moral standing. Those who would attribute feelings, beliefs, and preferences to animals are often accused of being unscientific and anthropomorphic. Regan argues, on the contrary, that those who attribute a complex mental life to animals have the weight of evidence on their side. He marshalls diverse scientific evidence as well as philosophical argument in support of the complexity of animal consciousness. He maintains that at least some animals do share with humans many of the mental capacities they have historically been claimed to lack, and he argues that the capacities these animals do lack are not relevant to their moral value. More specifically, he argues that adult mammals, one year of age and older, are "subjects of a life" and that such individuals have an inherent value. Given their inherent value, they have rights we must respect.

In choosing to restrict his argument to adult mammals, Regan is not claiming that all other species of animals fail to have rights; rather, he is determined to make the case where it is strongest, for those animals who most clearly have the mental complexity requisite for having rights. Whether a case can be made for other sorts of animals remains an open question, as does the issue of whether it is possible to argue for the rights of animals or other beings or entities without appeal to mental life.

The idea that animals are entirely without consciousness has a venerable history. Descartes argued that animals are mere machines, and even to this day talk of animal consciousness is decried in many circles as "unscientific." Some scientists who use animals in experimental procedures still prefer to speak of "aversive responses," such as the "writhing response," rather than directly attributing pain to animals. Regan argues that evidence from a number of independent domains supports animal awareness, and the cumulative weight of these separate arguments makes it virtually certain that animals are conscious. First, Regan observes that our common sense, as well as our language, attributes awareness to animals, and we need to be given some compelling reasons for abandoning common sense.

When we examine Descartes's arguments, however, we find no such compelling reasons, only deep conceptual problems. Descartes claimed that the seat of consciousness is the immaterial soul, and only humans have such souls. This "dualism" of soul and body is notoriously unscientific. Because souls are immaterial they are beyond the reach of scientific observation, and there is no way of explaining how an immaterial soul lacking in mass or physical energy can causally interact with a material body. Thus, as Regan points out, the most straightforward connections, such as the feeling of pain as the result of stepping on a tack, are mysterious on the Cartesian view. In contrast, the view that consciousness has emerged in the course of evolution owing to its adaptiveness, and exists in many species, is in accordance with evolutionary theory and with our understanding of the physiological basis of consciousness. Because this physiology is a shared feature of both humans and animals, attributing consciousness to animals is far more parsimonious than denying it. Regan cites diverse evidence, including the work of ethologist Donald Griffin in showing how a naturalistic explanation of the emergence of consciousness and thought cannot restrict these mental processes to Homo sapiens. Finally, attributing consciousness to animals gives us the most reasonable account of animal behavior, just as it gives us the most reasonable account of human behavior. Taken together, the cumulative evidence of common sense, evolutionary theory, physiology, and behavior establishes beyond reasonable doubt that mammals are indeed conscious.

Having established that mammals are conscious, Regan explores the nature and complexity of animal awareness. Normal adult mammalian animals have beliefs, desires, a grasp of the future, and a sense of themselves. They have preferences and the ability to act on these preferences. Furthermore, we can know, at least in a general way, about the beliefs and desires of many animals. The argument that establishes the consciousness of animals similarly supports these claims. Attributing beliefs and desires to animals allows us to predict and explain their behavior. One example of the sort of evidence Regan appeals to is the work of D. O. Hebb, a well-respected experimental psychologist. Attempts by Hebb and his associates to describe primate behavior without reference to mental states proved disastrous, while making use of such attributions allowed these scientists to handle reliably the animals and predict their behavior.[11]

The weight of evidence is in favor of attributing a complex mental life to nonhuman mammalian species. Modern psychology studies complex cognitive processes of concept learning, memory, and goal-directed behavior in mammalian species from rats and mice to primates. Because the best of modern science—including biology, ethology, cognitive psychology, and sociobiology—attributes these complex mental states to mammalian species, it is most reasonable to conclude that these animals possess these attributes.

Animal Welfare.   Having established that mammals have a complex mental life, Regan sets out to establish a notion of animal welfare that takes the facts about animal awareness and thought seriously, since historically the notion of animal welfare has suffered from the failure to grasp both these facts and their implications. This has led to thinking that the most crucial components in assuring the welfare of animals were avoidance of pain and suffering. Thus, it was assumed that it is not whether animals are killed that is important but simply that they are killed painlessly. Because animals have no concept of death and do not know what humans have in store for them, killing them will not hurt them. Analogously, if an animal has never known freedom, has never known the ordinary social life of species of its type, then it is not deprived in being kept in captivity, as long as its basic physical needs are met. Broadly, this might be called the philosophy of "what you don't know, can't hurt you."

Regan points out that for beings with beliefs, desires, preferences, and goals, this notion of welfare is woefully inadequate. Such individuals have autonomy in the sense that they are able to initiate action to satisfy their desires and preferences. Individuals capable of such action take satisfaction in reaching their goals "by their own lights." When we remove from someone the possibility of satisfying her goals we reduce her autonomy, and this is a harm. For example, if a bright young woman is reduced to the condition of a contented imbecile by painless injections of debilitating drugs, then she is significantly harmed, even though she does not suffer. Similarly, a captive wolf who is fed by his keeper has his desire for food satisfied but is deprived of the satisfaction of hunting for it (92). It is part of our concept of "the good life" that individuals have the opportunity to pursue and attain their goals, not merely that they have their basic needs satisfied. There is no reason not to extend this idea to the case of those animals, which, like us, have autonomy. Thus, it is possible to harm such beings, not merely through infliction of pain but through denying them the opportunity to pursue their goals. As Regan puts it, "There are more ways to harm than simply to hurt. Not all harms hurt, just as not all hurts harm" (97).

The implications of this distinction between infliction and deprivation for our treatment of animals are many. Animals in factory farms and those born in zoos have never known any alternative but are nevertheless harmed through their deprivation. Death itself is clearly a severe deprivation for beings with goals and preferences, since death forecloses all possibility for future satisfaction of goals. We recognize that, even for small children who have not as yet formulated goals and do not yet understand the concept of death, death is a severe deprivation. Thus, it is not necessary to have a concept of death but merely to be the sort of being who has, or will soon have, preferences and goals in order to be the sort of individual who is harmed by death. Thus, untimely death is not consistent with providing for the basic welfare of such beings, whether they be human or nonhuman mammals. Raising animals, however "humanely," and killing them is not consistent with their welfare. Painlessly killing unwanted dogs and cats is not consistent with their welfare and does not deserve the label "euthanasia," since that term implies not merely a painless death but one that is in the interests of the individual killed. Thus, concludes Regan, if we are to genuinely respect the welfare of such autonomous beings, we must cease killing them and depriving them of opportunities for the fulfillment of their goals.

Like Singer, Regan insists on a much expanded notion of animal welfare, which rules out the possibility of keeping animals in laboratories and zoos and on factory farms and fur farms while nevertheless respecting their welfare. Unlike Singer, however, Regan argues that the harm of death must be viewed in light of the inherent value of individuals and not simply in terms of the preferences and possibilities for satisfaction that death forecloses. To appreciate this point we must turn to Regan's ethical theory.

Refutation of Alternative Approaches.   Regan details a very general theory of rights, which accounts for our duties to others, be they humans or animals. In having propounded such a theory, Regan is unique among philosophers defending animal rights. The theory takes a very strong stand on the value of animal lives and the rights of animals, and this view develops out of a series of critiques in which Regan argues that views according a lesser status to animals have deficiencies that only the stronger position can rectify. Thus, in giving an account of Regan's theory, we must begin by explaining Regan's objections to weaker accounts of the moral status of animals.

Regan divides the theories he critiques broadly into direct and indirect duty views. According to indirect duty views, it is only moral agents—those capable of moral judgment and action—whose lives have value and who are thus of direct moral concern. Moral agents include all normal adult human beings. If you are reading this book, for example, you are most likely a moral agent. Moral patients are those individuals who, owing to mental limitations, are incapable of moral deliberation. Infants and small children and some retarded or senile persons, as well as nonhuman animals, would generally be classed as moral patients. According to indirect duty views, such individuals are only indirectly relevant to morally correct action in that moral agents may care about them and morally correct action needs to take into account what moral agents care about. We have a duty not to beat or kill our neighbor's dog, but this is a duty we owe to our neighbor, not to the dog. On the other hand, if no one at all were to care about what happens to a moral patient, then we would have no duty at all to the individual. (Society can take an interest in individuals by making laws against killing them. The indirect duty view would explain what is wrong with killing an abandoned and unwanted infant by pointing out that society as a whole takes an interest in such infants. If society were to change its mind about this, then killing unwanted infants would no longer be wrong.)

Regan argues that all such indirect duty views suffer from moral arbitrariness and fail to accord with our reflective intuitions. Certainly in the case of a small child we do not believe that we would have no duties with respect to it simply because no moral agents happen to have an interest in it. Nor do we believe that it would be acceptable to perform painful experiments on small children or the mentally enfeebled if it so happened that no moral agents objected to this practice. Torturing dogs for trivial reasons would be morally acceptable on the indirect duty view as long as no moral agent were adversely affected. But our intuitions tell us that the harm done to such individuals is a wrong, whether or not any moral agent happens to care. When it comes to moral patients, we have clear intuitions of the wrongness of causing them suffering, of killing them, or of depriving them of opportunities to pursue their basic needs.

These intuitions can be concisely formulated in what Regan calls the "harm principle": that we have a direct, prima facie duty not to harm individuals (187). The duty is prima facie in that it can in some circumstances be overridden (we have the right to kill in self-defense, for example), and it is direct in the sense that we owe it to the individuals themselves. Their lives have value, quite independently of what moral agents think about them. This principle cannot be nonarbitrarily restricted to moral agents. Not only do our reflective intuitions tell us this, but having established that many moral patients have a welfare and can be harmed just as moral agents can consistency requires that the principle be extended to them as well. Moral patients have the same characteristics that give value to the lives of moral agents. Consequently, both human and nonhuman moral patients deserve direct moral consideration.

But what is the nature of the direct moral consideration owed to moral patients? Even moral theories that grant that we owe direct moral consideration to animals generally deny that animals possess rights. Regan endeavors to show that such direct duty views are inadequate and that moral patients must be accorded rights. He examines two prominent views: act utilitarianism and one he dubs the "cruelty-kindness" view.

The cruelty-kindness view is not so much a philosophical position as it is the position of common sense; it is the view that cruelty toward animals is wrong, and that animals ought to be treated with kindness. This view has been the predominant one in the humane movement, and Regan's analysis of its inadequacies adds to our understanding of the difference between that movement and the animal rights movement. As Regan points out, cruelty and kindness refer to states of mind. Cruel people either enjoy inflicting suffering or fail to feel appropriate sympathy for those they cause to suffer. Kind people have good motives and intentions, and their actions exhibit their goodness as people. The person who feeds stray cats is kind; the researcher who drips oven cleaner in a rabbit's eye day after day without a thought for the suffering produced is cruel. But these concepts of cruelty and kindness are fundamentally defective as an analysis of our duties to animals.

First, in focusing on states of mind, these concepts fail to focus on the actions themselves. The little old lady who feeds the cats may be kind, but by promoting the breeding of a colony of unhealthy, feral cats she may promote greater suffering than if she had done nothing at all, and thus do what is wrong. Her intention to do good does not in itself make her action correct. Second, kindness, like charity, is not something that anyone can be owed. It is kind to rescue homeless cats, dogs, or humans, but it is not one's duty to do so. Thus, the cruelty-kindness view fails to tell us what we owe to animals, and reliance on it as foundation for our relations with animals leads to unhappy results. For example, one of the humane movement's major failings is its tendency to focus precisely on actions that are "above and beyond the call of duty" while ignoring a wide variety of types of suffering and exploitation, especially the suffering of farm and laboratory animals.

The second direct duty approach Regan considers is utilitarianism, and here he finds himself at odds with Singer. The extent to which

Singer's arguments in *Animal Liberation* depend on utilitarian assumptions is controversial, but, as we have argued, it does seem that Singer's argument against speciesism is independent of utilitarian considerations. In any case, Regan finds a number of serious difficulties in the utilitarian approach. As noted earlier, utilitarian theory distinguishes between equal consideration (of interests, preferences, or pleasures/pains) and equal treatment. Each individual's interests must be given equal consideration, but in deciding how to treat individuals, one must take into account the aggregate consequences for all concerned. Critics of utilitarianism argue that this leaves open the possibility that some individuals may be exploited if doing so will yield the best aggregate outcome for all concerned. Thus, Regan points out the possibility of secret killings being justified and of other gross injustices. In particular, he argues that utilitarianism cannot obviously rule out the continuance of factory farming or even mandate individuals to become conscientious vegetarians, for it could turn out that the aggregate interests of all concerned would tip the scales in favor of the continuance of factory farming (if, for example, ending this practice could be shown to be likely to lead to an economic collapse and subsequent massive suffering). Furthermore, if only a few persons are vegetarians, so that their actions have no effect on the number of animals killed, then there is no effect of being a vegetarian, so there is no obligation to become one. Thus, utilitarianism does not succeed in securing any specific and direct duties to animals. Our duty is to maximize good outcomes, and this may in some cases be accomplished at the expense of individuals.

Utilitarians may take exception, however, to the terms in which Regan makes his case here. One important question for a utilitarian would be whether conditions are actually such that the aggregate interests do tip the scales in favor of factory farming. As Singer and others have maintained, when we factor in the interests of the billions of animals consumed annually in the United States alone, this seems rather unlikely. This points up the fact that Regan's objection to utilitarianism here is based, at least in part, on an assumption utilitarians do not share: that what a moral theory *could* permit or require (e.g., under vastly altered circumstances) is relevant to its acceptability. In fact, utilitarians would argue that this responsiveness of their theory to changing world conditions is a strength rather than a weakness of a moral theory.

Regan identifies a number of sources of difficulty in utilitarian theory, but the one most central in understanding his view is the idea that individuals are not in themselves valuable but are mere "receptacles" of value. According to Regan, in viewing pleasures or preference satisfactions as of fundamental value, utilitarians view the individuals who contain more or less of these things as without value, as mere receptacles. Because it is not individuals themselves who possess value, individuals can be replaced (as in the example of the secretly murdered hermit) and should be replaced, if in doing so we can bring about a greater aggregate of good. Aggregate goods can be achieved in ways that violate the fundamental interests of individuals, and it is for this reason that utilitarianism has fundamental problems in guaranteeing justice. Regan argues that it is basic to the principle of justice that individuals all be given their due. Because utilitarianism does not guarantee this basic justice principle, Regan rejects utilitarianism as fundamentally inadequate, and offers his own account, to which we now turn.

Inherent Value and Rights.   Regan argues that if we are to avoid the problems confronting utilitarianism, we must recognize that in addition to the value attached to the experiences individuals have, individuals themselves have *inherent value*. This means that their lives have value independent of their effects on or relations to anyone else and independent of the value of their experiences. If someone has little prospect for fulfillment of preferences or pleasurable experiences, they are nevertheless valuable and cannot be replaced. Furthermore, whether or not anyone else values an individual is irrelevant to the inherent value of that individual. Thus, the killing of individuals with inherent value is wrong and cannot be justified by appeal to the aggregate of good consequences it might bring about.

How do we know that we, as moral agents, or anyone else has such inherent value? When we reflect on our lives we recognize that, given our consciousness, goals, desires, preferences, memories, fears, and expectations, our lives have value to us. In short, our being "subjects of a life" is what gives our lives inherent value. But then consistency requires that we recognize that other beings who are subjects of a life also have inherent value for precisely the same reason. Since Regan has already established that (at least) mammals also are subjects of a life, it follows that their lives, too, have inherent value.

Furthermore, all those who have inherent value have it equally. Regan argues that perfectionist theories of justice—those viewing individuals with certain virtues (intelligence, artistic talent, etc.) as being more valuable than others with lesser abilities—are morally pernicious because they provide the foundation for highly inegalitarian social relationships, including slavery and rigid caste systems. Intuitively, we do not think that the life of a retarded person is to be given less value than the life of someone who is not retarded. Nor do we think that the life of a genius is to be valued over that of others. Thus, those who have inherent value must all have it equally.

This idea of equal inherent value is essential to Regan's view, since it is the basis for claims to rights. The connection is through a principle of justice that Regan calls the "respect principle": we are to treat those individuals who have inherent value in ways that respect their inherent value (248). From this principle can be derived the harm principle mentioned earlier, since it can be shown that respecting inherent value entails avoiding causing harm. Moral rights are, in Regan's view, valid claims against other individuals—claims to treatment owed as a matter of direct duty by these individuals. The basic moral right possessed by all subjects of a life is the right to respectful treatment.

Given that subjects of a life have moral rights, Regan argues, we should bring it about that these rights are institutionalized as legal rights. This means not merely that such individuals deserve to have their interests considered among many other factors but that these individuals be treated with respect and protected from harm. For example, human beings in the United States have a legal right not to be used coercively in medicine—as organ, bone-marrow, or even blood donors. Even if many lives could be saved by coercing citizens into such activities, their basic rights not to participate in such activities must be respected. Similarly, Regan's theory calls for an end to the use of animals in medical research, irrespective of the greater good for humans or animals such use might produce. It calls for an end to the raising and killing of animals for food, regardless of whether it could be done painlessly and whether it led to good or bad aggregate consequences. Reform of these institutions is not enough, given the rights view, any more than a reform of the institution of slavery would have been enough to give blacks their due. This is the full force of Regan's categorical abolitionism: the duty to do away with institutions that violate the rights of individuals is fundamental, not contingent on the consequences of doing so.

Criticisms of Regan's View

The Case for Animal Rights is a highly theoretical work, and as such it is open to criticisms of the general moral framework within which it is embedded. Philosophers differ over the nature and usefulness of concepts such as "inherent value," and many utilitarians are suspicious of the concept of moral rights itself (Jeremy Bentham, a major figure in the development of utilitarian theory, called moral rights "nonsense on stilts"). Regan believes that moral theory must be grounded in our carefully examined "reflective intuitions," whereas utilitarians such as Singer view intuition as unreliable. What is highly relevant here is whether Regan has offered a foundation for the complete abolition of institutions such as animal research and rearing animals to be killed and eaten. These are the stated goals of many in the animal rights movement, and Regan claims to provide a philosophical justification for them. If there are questions about whether his theory genuinely does lead to abolitionist conclusions, it is important to examine them.

If a moral theory shuns consideration of consequences in determining what is right, then it must offer some other principled way of resolving situations in which moral claims come into conflict. Regan's principles for resolving cases where rights conflict raise the most pressing problems for his theory. Regan's critics have argued that he cannot both uphold these principles and maintain his strict abolitionism. Recall that Regan objects to utilitarianism on the grounds that in bringing about the best aggregate outcome the fundamental rights of individuals may be overridden. In situations in which the rights of individuals conflict and cannot all be respected, this means that if we must choose to violate the most fundamental interests of the few or the trivial interests of the many, we may be obligated to do the former. Regan derives principles of conflict resolution that avoid this kind of injustice from the harm principle. In particular, when harms are not comparable, the worse-off principle applies: "When we must decide to override the rights of the many or the rights of the few who are innocent, and when the harm faced by the few would make them worse-off than any of the many would be if any other option were chosen, then we ought to override the rights of the many" (308).

Regan offers the following illustration. Imagine that there are four humans and a dog stranded in a lifeboat, but there is not enough room for them all. Unless one goes overboard, all will perish. Given Regan's views about the equal inherent value of all subjects of a life, one might think that he would suggest drawing straws. Instead he argues that it is the dog that must be thrown overboard, for the harm of death is a function of the opportunities for satisfaction it forecloses, and, prima facie, the death of any human would be a greater loss (since humans live longer and have a wider variety of experiences than dogs) and thus a greater harm than would be the death of a dog (324). As a result, the worse-off principle dictates that it is the dog who must be tossed overboard.

One might well raise a question regarding the obviousness of the choice of the dog in such a case. It is easy to imagine cases in which humans, owing to age, illness, or mental enfeeblement, would have less to lose through death than a normal healthy young dog. But Regan would not object and is careful to say that there is only a prima facie case in favor of the humans. The real difficulty emerges when Regan raises the question of what should be done when the choice is between a few humans and *any number of dogs*. Assuming that death is a worse harm for any of the humans than it is for any of the dogs, then the worse-off principle says we ought to sacrifice any number (no matter how great) of dogs to save any number (no matter how few) of humans. The decision to sacrifice the dogs rather than the humans is quite independent of any question of how many individuals, dogs or human, are involved (Regan and Singer, 1985).

Singer has argued that Regan cannot maintain both his strict abolitionist position regarding scientific uses of animals and his commitment to the worse-off principle, for imagine that we modify the lifeboat example as follows. Both dogs and humans are threatened with a fatal disease, but there is a vaccine that might prevent it. The vaccine may itself have fatal side effects, so before administering it, it is rational to test it on some individuals. Singer argues that in this case too, the worse-off principle will pick out the dogs, given that death is less of a harm for them than for humans. And it will continue to pick out dogs, even if it would be necessary to test very large numbers of dogs, but only a few humans, in order to ensure the safety of the vaccine. Because aggregations of harms are disallowed by the worse-off principle, thousands or even millions of dogs could be tested, even if the testing of very few humans would have sufficed.

There is no doubt that Regan's worse-off principle implies that, where conflicts arise and someone will be harmed no matter what we do, that we should direct harm to those who will be least harmed, whether those individuals are human or nonhuman. One defense of Regan against this criticism has noted that the worse-off principle, as a principle of conflict resolution, is designed to handle *exceptional cases*—that is, it tells us how to deal with the unforeseen and unavoidable. Principles of conflict resolution are not designed to create institutions—legally and socially sanctioned practices, such as factory farming, public education, or animal research—that violate the basic rights of individuals. The requirement that rights holders be respected is inconsistent with such institutions.

It is currently illegal to test a vaccine on an unconsenting person or to draw blood from someone against his will, even though we might be able to save lives by doing so. In other words, there is no institution sanctioning such taking of blood without consent. Nor would the worse-off principle sanction the creation of such an institution, as it would violate the rights of those from whom blood was coercively drawn. And for precisely the same reason the worse-off principle cannot condone the institution of animal research or any institution that violates the respect owed to rights holders. If we accept that Regan's principles of conflict resolution are meant to apply to exceptional cases (such as lifeboats) rather than to creation of institutions, and that animal research and agriculture are not exceptional, lifeboat-type cases, then Regan's theory remains abolitionist.[12]

Steve Sapontzis: Appeal to Common Moral Traditions

Another contemporary American philosopher, Steve F. Sapontzis, has developed an argument for liberating animals that is rather different from either Singer's or Regan's approach. Sapontzis rejects the possibility of developing a systematic moral theory that would do justice to common moral beliefs and practice. Instead, he attempts to develop an understanding of the complexity of actual moral practice, which is neither exclusively utilitarian nor rights-based but contains elements of both. That Sapontzis is able to mount a strong argument for liberating animals in light of an understanding of our common moral traditions adds an importantly different dimension to the animal liberation literature.

The argument that animals' interests may ethically be sacrificed in research, farming, hunting and elsewhere is often based on the premise that human beings are a form of life morally superior to animals. One of the recurrent themes in Sapontzis's work is his effort to show that such an assumption is both unreasonable and, even if defensible, will not support the weight it is asked to bear. He attacks the belief in superiority from a number of angles, but perhaps two stand out as most important. First, the assumption that human rationality and intelligence automatically make us superior is questionable. In the first part of *Morals, Reason, and Animals* (1987) Sapontzis makes a sustained attack on the common interpretation of Western morality that gives pride of place to reason in the moral life. The point of this attack is not to offer a replacement—to substitute pure sentiment or the elimination of civilized inhibitions—for reason in morality but to undermine the distortion of actual moral practice by those who elevate reason beyond its actual importance.

The belief that rationality makes us superior might mean a number of things: it may mean that our superior ability to control and dominate by means of reason is what makes us superior. But if that is its meaning, then the suggestion is simply that we are justified in dominating others because we have the ability to do so. When put so bluntly, it is evident that this approach is nothing more than the "might makes right" philosophy we so rightly reject. Another interpretation is that our capacity to engage in reasoning is crucial to being moral agents, but Sapontzis argues that even those who act merely from sentiment can be virtuous agents. Yet another interpretation might give us some hope in the accomplishments of genius (such as Einstein or Mozart) that surely only human rationality can produce and appreciate. But an overall assessment of the value of the rationality that produces and appreciates such genius must also look to its other consequences: for example, to the damage as well as the good we do to the environment we must live in. In the long run, the threat of human intelligence to all the species on this planet may be far greater than any contributions it has made.

The other side of the attack on the belief in human superiority is methodological. By what tests should we decide such a question? What are the criteria of moral superiority? How would we meaningfully evaluate capacities for fulfillment across species lines? In his essay "Utilitarianism" John Stuart Mill maintained that some forms of life are qualitatively superior to others: "Better to be Socrates dissatisfied than a pig satisfied!" But this is a point of view that expresses rather than justifies human bias: we cannot enjoy the life of a pig, dog, or bird. As Mill pointed out, to evaluate competently the superiority of one form of experience over another one must have had exposure to both.

Thus, to pronounce human experience superior to that of a bird, dog, or pig in an unbiased way requires a judge who can experience all these forms of life. But there simply is no such person. As a result, the claim that humans derive moral superiority from this or that characteristic are methodologically flawed.

Sapontzis assembles a series of arguments undermining the claim that humans are morally superior to other species. But even if the claim to superiority did turn out to bear the weight of scrutiny, before it could be used to justify the consumption of animals in science, agriculture, and elsewhere we would have to examine a further assumption: that superiors are justified in routinely promoting their interests at the expense of inferiors. On the face of it, this assumption is not supported by our actual moral practice (which includes many counterexamples of special responsibilities of "superiors" to protect their "inferiors," such as the duty of parents to protect the interests of children) or by Kantian[13] or utilitarian moral theories. In fact, Sapontzis points out that the elimination of such hierarchical thinking is itself a mark of moral progress. The elimination of feudalism, slavery, aristocracies of birth, and sexual and racial exploitation all have in common the rejection of supposed "natural hierarchies" in favor of presumptions of equality. Animal liberation represents a continuation of that progression.

Animals as Moral Agents.   One of the main arguments against considering animals worthy of moral consideration is based on the claim that they are not moral agents. To be a moral agent, it is claimed, one must achieve the level of rationality typical of normal human adults. Therefore, animals (who lack this degree of rationality) do not deserve moral consideration. Such an argument might appeal to the implicit premise that those who cannot act as moral agents are not owed any moral consideration because they cannot fulfill the moral duties required for society's reciprocal relations.

Regan responds to this point by arguing that moral agents are not the only individuals owed moral consideration; moral patients are also morally considerable. One of the distinctive features of Sapontzis's philosophy is his departure from the standard response to this challenge. Sapontzis holds that the agency arguments do not exclude all species of nonhuman animals from membership in the moral community; rather, some animals do act as moral agents.

There can be no doubt that in many cases animals' actions are appropriately described as correct or good: they sometimes aid those in distress, defend their young, and warn others of impending danger. But is it appropriate to consider nonhumans as moral *agents*? Sapontzis identifies two reasons that have been offered to refuse to consider such acts virtuous. The first is that only those who can "act for the right reason" can be said to act morally (as opposed to merely acting in accord with what is moral), and, second, only those who act freely are moral agents.

The "acting for the right reason" objection goes astray, Sapontzis contends, by confusing recognizing and being committed to a moral value with the ability to formulate an abstract principle encapsulating that value. Running these two things together has the consequence that virtue is reserved for those capable of philosophizing about their action, which would have the implication that many people we former-ly regarded as virtuous are not all that virtuous after all. For example, the inarticulate hero who rushes into a burning building to save a child but who later can say very little about his action other than "I couldn't just let her die in there" is surely a moral agent. Sapontzis cor-rectly points out that all that is needed to act for the right reason is the ability to recognize and respond to what is morally significant in the situation, and this ability is not reserved exclusively for those who can articulate what is distinctive about the recognized value.

Perhaps our reluctance to grant that animals can be virtuous agents reflects the view that animal actions are the result of instinct or condi-tioning, whereas human action is free. In this view it is open to humans to select among a number of alternative actions, whereas non-human animals' actions are always conditioned responses or merely instinctive behavior. But this view enshrines misconceptions about the nature of animal and human behavior. We think of instincts as inflexi-ble, mechanical behavior that the animal engages in blindly, but this is only one end of a continuum of kinds of instinctive behavior. At the other end are instincts that are quite flexible, unmechanical, and open. A mother bear, as a mother human, instinctively cares for its offspring, but it does so in ways neither mechanical nor programmed, as they require sensitivity to the offspring's needs and the available resources. Clearly there is a difference between "hard-wired" mechanical behavior and that of a bear pulling its cub back from dangerous rapids—an action responsive to the situation's changing conditions. As long as an action involves recognition of and response to what is morally significant in the situation, the fact that the action is instinctive will make no difference.

Sapontzis concludes, then, that not only humans but at least some animals are capable of virtuous action. He is careful to note one important difference between human and animal agency, however. Humans are not only capable of virtuous action but also of striving to live according to ideals. We attempt to remake ourselves and each other in light of our notions of what a morally good life would be. It is only in the pursuit of ideals that the capacity for rational reflection plays a crucial role. Consequently there is a kind of moral life unavailable to nonhuman animals because of their lack of rationality. But the fact that only rational beings can recognize how virtuous action contributes to achieving an ideal world does not mean that animals are incapable of acting virtuously, nor does it diminish the value of their simpler virtuous action.

Liberating Animals.   It might be thought that animal liberation is simply an exaggeration of the traditional anti-cruelty view. Sapontzis makes it clear that this is a serious misunderstanding. Animal liberation represents a significant break with the underlying assumption of the anti-cruelty view that animals may be regarded as resources for human consumption, limiting moral concern to the humane handling and processing of those resources. Animal liberation means "putting an end to the routine sacrifice of animal interests for human benefit, even where the sacrifice is executed humanely."[15] This idea, Sapontzis correctly urges, is at the heart of the animal liberation movement.

Sapontzis's contention that the fundamental concern of animal liberationists is the routine, avoidable sacrifice of others' interests implies that concerns such as "where to draw the line" miss the mark. Sapontzis's view of interests diverges slightly from the account we suggested for Singer, as Sapontzis maintains that someone has an interest in something if and only if that thing affects (will affect, would affect) his or her *feelings* of well-being (including pleasure and pain, feeling fit or ill, elation or depression, feelings of fulfillment or frustration, etc.) (74). But the implication in this context is the same: plants and cockroaches qualify for liberation only if there is good reason (which there is not) to think they have interests in this sense. Most importantly, deciding where to draw the line has no bearing on whether the consumption of animals in hunting and trapping, rodeos, agriculture, and science is morally acceptable or not, and consequently Sapontzis points out that worrying about such matters may simply be a way of avoiding doing something about the real issues.

Animal Liberation and Equality. Animal liberation means an end to routine, avoidable sacrifice of animals' interests, where "animal" is to be understood as *sentient* animal. But the demand for liberation is not absolute: even human interests must occasionally be sacrificed, and we have developed principles that help us in situations of conflict. Sapontzis's claim is that liberating animals would mean ensuring that their interests are not sacrificed, except where principles that would justify sacrifice of human interests would also apply.

Does this mean that Sapontzis thinks humans and animals are equal? As Singer and Regan suggest, if we interpret this to mean they would have all the same rights, the answer is no. Because not all animal species have the same interests humans do, protection of their interests does not require their having all the same rights.

It is natural to ask whether liberating animals implies that we should consider animals' rights to have equal *priority* with the rights of humans. This seems to cause problems for advocates of animal rights. On the face of it, if human life is more valuable than animal life, then we ought to give priority to the rights of humans over animals. Consequently, the rights of animals (e.g., the right to life) seems a less serious matter. Although we have already seen that Sapontzis attacks the claim that humans are, as a species, superior to other animal forms, his response to the question of priority of rights brings out an important dimension of ethical reflection that is often overlooked, and so is worth considering in detail here. The thrust of his discussion of priority is that one can maintain (as Singer, for example, does) that human life is more valuable than animal life without giving up the central concerns of animal liberation. Sapontzis has worked out an interesting defense of this claim.

Morality includes at least two kinds of principles. *Ordinary principles* give us a sense of the major features of the terrain: they establish what is valuable, what interests deserve how much protection, and so forth. *Auxiliary principles* are invoked to settle conflicts and deal with emergency situations unresolved by ordinary principles. For example, the principle that we should help those in distress establishes a broad value but says nothing about how to choose when only some of those in distress can be helped. For that we must invoke auxiliary principles—such as to protect the weakest, the innocent, those to whom we have special obligations (e.g., our children), or those who make the greatest contribution to society. We saw an example of an auxiliary principle in Regan's worse-off principle. Thus, priority principles—principles determining how to set priorities where rights or interests come into conflict—are one type of auxiliary principle.

The question that arises when we recognize both ordinary and auxiliary principles is how they relate. Sometimes people argue as if we were able to infer what ordinary principles we should be committed to from a knowledge of the auxiliary principles we accept. But this would be a mistake. Suppose we believe that we should always help those who are weaker in preference to those who are stronger (on the assumption that the stronger are less in need of assistance or more likely to survive even when they do). Surely we cannot infer from this auxiliary principle that the strong have less of a right to life than the weak, and that consequently it would be acceptable to sacrifice their lives for the less-pressing interests of the weaker. Thus, we cannot legitimately infer from auxiliary principles what ordinary principles should be.[14]

This point is relevant to the question of animal liberation because the belief that animal liberation means we must give equal priority to animals is based on the assumption that our choice of auxiliary principles dictates the ordinary principles we should accept. But as we have just seen, such an inference is unsound. Thus, recognizing that human life ought to be preserved in preference to animal life in many (though not necessarily all) situations where conflict arises will not justify us in *routinely and avoidably* sacrificing animals' most basic interests where no serious conflict exists. Deciding to save the life of a human infant rather than that of a calf if we were forced to choose between them tells us nothing about the acceptability of keeping calves in tiny veal crates and on liquid diets, in anticipation of killing and eating them.

In clarifying the main goal of liberating animals Sapontzis has made a significant contribution to understanding responses to this goal. Challenges—philosophical or otherwise—to liberating animals should be judged in terms of whether they distort or ignore the central aim of eliminating the routine and avoidable sacrifice of animals' interests. Many of them seem to misunderstand or trivialize the concerns of those who would liberate animals. As John Stuart Mill said, the first response to revolution is ridicule, but, typically, ridicule fails to come to grips with what is important and worthwhile in the object of ridicule.

Why Liberate Animals?   Sapontzis maintains that there are, broadly speaking, three kinds of reason for judging liberating animals the morally right thing to do. In line with his rejection of monolithic moral theories, Sapontzis identifies three broad goals of traditional morality and argues that liberating animals is the right thing to do because it helps advance each goal. The goals relate to suffering and enjoyment, fairness, and, finally, moral character.

Sapontzis argues that one major reason for liberating animals is "reducing the amount of suffering in life and otherwise making life more enjoyable and fulfilling" (Sapontzis 1987, 96). Two points must be understood before this argument can be fully clear. First, we should not understand this goal narrowly—for example, suffering should be understood to include not only such things as physical trauma, pain, disease, and stress but also the loss of something valuable (e.g., the possibility of a fulfilling life). And, second, to determine how to arrive at this goal we must be careful to consider the right alternatives. The real comparison needed is not between the amount of suffering and enjoyment in the world with animals being consumed (the status quo) and the same world minus the consumption of animals. As Sapontzis points out, vegetarians, for example, do not simply eat what is left over when meat is removed from a traditional omnivorous diet:

Our way of life following the liberation of animals would not be one in which a giant hole had been cut; rather it would be a way of life in which there would sooner or later be substitutions most everywhere there had been excisions. It is the consequential value of such a way of life—theirs as well as ours—that must (morally) be compared with the consequential value of our contemporary, animal consuming way of life to determine the moral superiority here of animal liberation or continued animal consumption. (98)

While no precise measurement of the amount of suffering and fulfillment that alternative courses of action promise is possible, there are some clear indications that liberating animals would be demanded by a serious commitment to this goal. For one thing, the mere weight of numbers makes it clear that the routine sacrifice of animals' interests produces tremendous suffering and loss. In the United States alone, some four to five billion animals (not including fish) are raised annually in factory farms and consumed for food, and many more suffer and die in laboratories (estimates range between 20 and 100 million), die from hunting and trapping (hundreds of millions), or die as unwanted pets in animal "shelters" (20 to 30 million). This means that whatever enjoyment or improvement the average American derives from consuming animals comes at the cost of something like 25 animals per year.

While some (e.g., Frey) have tried to argue that the economic dislocations that would result from conversion to vegetarianism would produce rather serious consequences that must be figured into such comparisons, such arguments are not compelling. For one thing, a rapid conversion from our current consumption of animals to liberating them is extremely unlikely. And, furthermore, many substitutes would be developed, thus creating new employment and economic opportunities for those who had previously been involved in processing animals, as well as opportunities for consumer satisfaction. And, finally, as Sapontzis points out, "We would have to place an extraordinary price on the enjoyment and fulfillment we receive from consuming animals to believe that whatever loss would be involved in switching to animal substitutes would not be more than outweighed by eliminating the stress and frustration of billions . . . of animals annually" (99). That is, we would have to place an extraordinarily high value on satisfaction of human desires and a correspondingly low value on the frustration of fundamental animal interests to believe this was even a close comparison.

The second major reason for liberating animals is to ensure that available goods, opportunities, rewards, and punishments are distributed fairly. Sapontzis argues that our treatment of animals exhibits a pattern of unfairness throughout: we eject them from their homes in expanding our own territory; we take healthy, innocent animals and subject them to painful, debilitating, and fatal diseases in order to cure our ills and to continue enjoying unhealthy life-styles (e.g., smoking and drinking alcohol); and we crowd them into factory farms so we can have abundant, inexpensive meat. Clearly such treatment is highly discriminatory. Though human beings have been (and in some places still are) treated in some of these ways, we consider our refusal to treat people so exploitively as a mark of our own moral progress toward making the world a fair place to live. Liberating animals would be yet another step in the direction of attaining this goal.

Sapontzis maintains that one of the main goals of morality is "developing moral character, so that actions will be based more on compassion, respect, courage and other moral virtues" (89). Liberating animals would clearly help to develop moral character, for example by making morality a more pervasive way of life. Many uses of animals are currently considered outside the sphere of morality; most people simply do not experience the choice between eating animals and eating something else as a *moral* choice. Liberating animals would make it clear to us that such choices do in fact raise significant moral questions and thus help to make morality a more pervasive way of life.

This is a valuable point, and it seems correct to say that taking animals' interests more seriously would provide more opportunities to develop one's moral character than expanding the realm of moral concern in other directions—such as to include toys or furniture. For, given their capacities to experience suffering and pleasure, animals can in fact be the beneficiaries of our virtuous behavior toward them.

What is not so clear, however, is the extent to which this provides an independent reason for liberating animals. Unless we had some reason to think that animals are appropriate objects of moral concern (reasons which Sapontzis' other arguments provide), it would be difficult to see that we would really be developing moral character in a desirable way by attending to the treatment of animals. Perhaps this point could be developed into an independent reason for liberating animals by explaining the sense in which the characteristics which are developed through greater sensitivity to animals are natural extensions of virtues, which seems to be the direction Sapontzis is moving on this point.

Marginal Cases.   The claim that animals' interests deserve moral consideration is sometimes met with the objection that only those who can meet a reciprocity requirement are owed moral respect. One common move in response to this objection is to point out that there are certain "marginal cases" (e.g., infants, the severely retarded, the brain-damaged) who it would be unreasonable to maintain are any more capable of being able to fulfill reciprocal duties than are nonhuman animals. Yet our common morality accords their interests with the same protection as those capable of reciprocity. Therefore, reciprocity cannot be considered a necessary condition of being morally considerable.

Sapontzis's recognition of the central importance of concerns with fairness in respect to animals leads him to a different analysis of the "argument from marginal cases." He maintains that this argument misses the fact that the reciprocity objection expresses an important moral insight that must be dealt with, and as a consequence the argument fails to explain adequately what can be said on behalf of animals.

According to Sapontzis, the reciprocity argument expresses the commonsensical idea that if we expect other individuals to respect our rights, it is only reasonable to respect theirs as well. After all, respecting someone's rights may call for some sacrifice (e.g., of liberty), and so this seems the only fair approach. Sapontzis maintains that responding to this idea by pointing out the counterexamples of people whose interests we would protect even if they lacked the ability to respect our rights misses the mark, because the reciprocity requirement could be revised to handle such cases, or else the marginal cases "might be considered 'honorary rights-holders' out of deference for the feelings of species affinity that most all of us share" (141). Invoking such a solution to the problem would be an example of using an auxiliary principle, and, as we have seen, our auxiliary principles do not dictate the content of our ordinary principles.

The issue that must be confronted in respect to the intuitive appeal of the reciprocity argument is what to say about situations that involve disparity of power. If reciprocity were a necessary condition for having moral rights, then the weak—being unable to interfere with the strong's satisfaction of their interests—would not have rights. But this shows that the reciprocity requirement must, despite its intuitive appeal, be rejected. As Sapontzis states, "One of the basic purposes of moral rights is to protect the weak against the strong, so that the weak can have a fair chance of fulfilling their interests" (142). The way to balance the appeal of the reciprocity requirement with this objection is to develop a conception of moral rights that demands reciprocity of those *capable* of giving it (i.e., those roughly equal in power), so that unfair advantages do not arise. At the same time, those already at a disadvantage (the weak) should not be permitted to be exploited by the strong, and so reciprocity cannot be expected in situations of disparate power. Clearly our dealings with animals generally fall under the category of the strong dealing with the weak, and thus it is wrong to demand that animals can have moral rights only if they are capable of respecting our rights (143).

Practical Implications.   Having argued at some length that three major goals of our common moral tradition all lead to the conclusion that liberating animals is the morally right thing to do, it comes as little surprise that Sapontzis takes exception to many of the ways in which we currently use animals. As he points out, "Animals are the most extensively and thoroughly exploited group on earth. Consequently, liberating animals would have the largest impact on our lives of any moral reform movement to date" (197).

Sapontzis is careful to note that, strictly speaking, animal liberation might not require that we be vegetarians under all circumstances. For example, from the perspective of liberating animals from exploitation, little objection can be seen to consuming animals that have died a natural death, assuming this were something we would want or would have much opportunity to do. Somewhat more realistic is the option of consuming eggs from hens that are permitted to live a quality of life worth living—that is, one in which they have freedom to roam about, to dust bathe, socialize, and engage in the variety of natural chicken behavior. Such chickens would be fed well, housed in conditions that protect them from bad weather and predators, and allowed to live out their natural life spans even after they no longer produce eggs. Unfortunately, though such systems have been experimented with in some places (e.g., in Britain, where living conditions are sometimes as good as described here except for not being allowed to live out their natural life span), eggs from farms with such conditions are not widely available for most urban and suburban consumers. The point remains that under appropriate conditions it would be consistent with liberating animals to consume some animal foods. Nonetheless, given the realities of the highly exploitive intensive farming systems in use today in the United States (and elsewhere), vegetarianism is a moral requirement.

In the case of animal experimentation, Sapontzis draws similar conclusions. There are certainly conceivable circumstances in which using animals as research subjects would be justified, as there are such circumstances for using human beings. The thrust of Sapontzis's position on animal experimentation is that the same kinds of principles should apply to both the use of animal and human research subjects. Generally speaking, three conditions can justify research with either humans or animals: (a) the subjects have given their free, understanding consent; (b) a guardian has determined (for those unable to consent) that participation in the experiment is either innocuous or likely to be beneficial to the subjects; or (c) the research is the only way to obtain a clear and present, massive, desperately needed good that greatly outweighs the sacrifice of the subjects, where the sacrifice is minimized and fairly distributed among those who stand to benefit from the research (236).

It is commonly thought that the consent condition (a) is inapplicable to animals, as they surely cannot give or withhold consent from something they cannot understand. But Sapontzis argues to the contrary that animals can in a perfectly straightforward way give and withhold consent. The struggle of animals to escape and the need to incapacitate and restrain them reveal that the subjects do not give their consent. Of course, they may not understand the experiment, but neither must a human subject who contemplates participation. The consent requirement is intended to protect subjects from unwanted interference, whether or not they understand the experiment.

Objections to Sapontzis's View

As we have seen, Sapontzis avoids theory building and bases his analysis on the convergence of ideas from different moral outlooks that he believes are represented in commonsensical, intuitive moral judgments. Some might regard such avoidance of theory as a strength, but others view it as leaving the arguments on shaky, uncertain ground (see Frey 1983). While many philosophers hold that intuitive judgments are important data for any moral theory, those who do typically hold that one role of moral theory is to help us to refine our intuitions—to eliminate those that merely express bias, to decide which ones to retain when tensions emerge, and so forth (Regan 1983, 135). Other moral theorists question the value of appeals to intuition altogether, because they may express prejudice, tend to moral conservatism, and make ethics ineradicably subjective (Singer 1974). Clearly there is a fundamental methodological debate in moral philosophy about the role of intuitions in sound moral thinking—a debate we will not be able to settle here.

Summing up the difficulty of assessing Sapontzis's view without this context, Frey says, "To eschew theory in favor of moral intuitions and 'everyday morality' does not positively advance the case for animal liberation in the absence of the relevant, methodological discussion" (Frey 1983). Frey's point is a bit overstated. As we have seen, many of the points Sapontzis makes (such as his clear understanding of the central meaning of animal liberation, the important distinction between ordinary and auxiliary principles, his challenge to traditional notions of the importance of reason in morality, and his novel assessment of what is important in the marginal-case argument and of the possibility of animal virtue) provide useful and refreshing perspectives from which to view many of the debates concerning the moral status of animals.

Bernard Rollin

Telos and Rights.   The idea that modern scientific evidence must be consulted in assessing human relations and obligations to animals is evident in the works we have considered, but the impact of science may be even more far-reaching than has been indicated so far, according to both Bernard Rollin and James Rachels. Both have argued that an understanding of modern science should change the way we look at ourselves, our relation to animals, and the very way in which ethics is conducted.

Like Sapontzis, Rollin does not attempt to defend a detailed moral theory but attempts instead to show that animals have the right to be dealt with or considered as moral objects by any person who has moral principles, regardless of what those moral principles may be (1981, 47). Thus, in *Animal Rights and Human Morality* Rollin attempts to establish a "metaright" by arguing that any moral theory we apply to humans must also be applicable to animals. He argues that the usual bases for excluding animals, such as lack of rationality or lack of a soul, do not bear close scrutiny. His arguments here are very much in accordance with those of Regan, Singer, and Sapontzis, in that he argues that it is possession of interests that is crucial in determining who must be given moral standing. Having argued for this metaright, he develops an account of specific rights for animals based on their interests and their telos (nature). This account ties moral theory to the scientific investigation of animals in a most promising way.

According to Rollin, the interests of a being are determined by its telos. The notion of telos derives from Aristotle, but the term as used by Rollin does not carry Aristotle's connotation of a fixed and determinate function and nature; rather, Rollin's use of the term refers to the notion of that which is genetically determined, including physical as well as psychological needs and characteristics (39). Organisms generally have a drive to fulfill their telos and most basically to continue to live. Those beings that, in addition to having a telos, are also in some sense aware of their struggle to fulfill it should all be the objects of moral concern. Rollin speaks of such organisms as having interests, and it is the possession of interests that grounds their being objects of moral concern.

While giving animals' interests a central place, Rollin's view is importantly different from Regan's and Singer's in focusing centrally on *whatever* interests are present in an individual, regardless of how different they may be from human interests. While Rollin agrees that we can see that animals are morally considerable by reflecting on what makes our own lives valuable, he does not hold the elements of human cognition, such as rationality, to be paradigmatic of what makes a life valuable. Thus, Rollin's approach is closer to Sapontzis's formulation in avoiding a homocentric weighing of interests.

Furthermore, Rollin cautions that our assumptions about animals' interests must not be modeled on faulty comparisons with ourselves but must be determined empirically. We must not assume, for example, that because a sheep will eat shortly after surgery that this animal is not suffering pain and stress. Humans do not respond in this way, but such behavior is an adaptive response to stress in sheep. Ironically, scientists who experiment with animals notoriously fail to take seriously the implications of expanding scientific knowledge about animal suffering and animal needs. Rollin confronts scientists' inconsistencies, such as using animals as models in research on pain and anesthesia but questioning whether these animals feel any pain. His 1990 book, *The Unheeded Cry: Animal Consciousness, Pain, and Science*, confronts the scientific community with their failure to incorporate the extensive scientific evidence on pain and suffering in animals into their thinking about the ethics of animal research.

What specific rights do animals have? To determine this, it is necessary to consider their telos. An animal has a right to the kind of life that it's nature dictates. Because the notion of telos as used by Rollin is grounded in such sciences as ethology, neurophysiology, and sociobiology, the specific rights of specific animals must be delineated in light of what we find out about animals from these sciences and must be open to change as new information is obtained.[16] In general, however, we can say that social animals have the right to live with their conspecifics, birds have the right to fly freely, solitary animals have a right to their territory, and so on.

Objections to Rollin's View.   A fundamental problem that surfaces is the question of what constitutes human nature. Rollin remarks that "animal nature is simpler than human, and though we may despair of knowing man's nature, animal nature seems in principle more accessible" (55). But if we cannot know human nature, then we cannot know what specific rights humans have, since, according to Rollin, specific rights are based on one's nature. And if we cannot know this, then we cannot know how to resolve apparent conflicts between humans and other animals, since we cannot know even whether we are dealing with a human right or a human transgression. For example, if hunting were a fundamental aspect of human telos, then would this imply that humans ought to have even a prima facie right to hunt? Rollin clearly does not think that hunting or meat eating are natural for humans. But even if they were, Rollin would no doubt counter that the right to life of the animal is more basic, and the moral nature of humans requires us to thwart some of our desires to respect the interests of others: "We make moral choices according to principles of right and wrong and need not operate simply by instinct in our eating behavior. We can shape our natures according to right and wrong, and, in any case, do not require meat either to live or to live well" (63).

The lack of an account of human telos presents one sort of problem in resolving conflicts between humans and other animals, but even where telos is known, it is not clear how conflicts should be resolved: "If a flea is mildly debilitating to [a] dog why ought we kill it? Is the life of a rabbit worth more than the lives of three frogs? Ultimately, it appears that these cases must be decided dialectically, on a case-to-case basis" (61).

Rollin does not offer rules for deciding under what circumstances human interests outweigh the interests of other animals, or how to determine which of various sorts of interests and harms ought to trump others. Since conflicts between humans and other animals over issues such as meat eating, experimentation, hunting, and trapping are at the heart of the animal rights controversy, this lack of a means for determining the answers to questions of conflict appears to detract from Rollin's position.

A feature of Rollin's account not yet touched on may form the basis of a reply, however. Rollin discusses the "gestalt shift" phenomenon, in which we come to see the same objects or facts in an entirely new light. Coming to see that animals matter morally, caring about them, and empathizing with them may form the basis for creative solutions to moral conflict situations. After all, given that we care about our children, most of us do not need to have rigid rules of conflict resolution in order to determine how to treat them in various situations. While Rollin's account appears lacking in the traditional realm of ethical theory it may fare better within the newer feminist approaches, such as the ethic of caring discussed by Carol Gilligan.

While Rollin's account is incomplete, it is nevertheless important in showing that the rights of animals can be established from a number of different moral perspectives, and that specific rights can be generated from a scientific understanding of the interests of animals, rather than from homocentric projections of human interests. In addition, Rollin's first book, *Animal Rights and Human Morality*, is important for another reason. There he provides a much-needed advance over earlier treatments of such issues as animal research. For example, his careful discussion of the widely varying ways in which animals are used in science (and how the issues about their usage are potentially varied as well), the role of legislation and possibilities of reform, and the problem for reformers posed by the desensitization toward animals that occurs as a normal part of scientific education has all contributed to a richer, more complex understanding of the issues facing proponents of animal rights in this country.

James Rachels

Evolution and Animal Rights.   In *Created from Animals: The Moral Implications of Darwinism* (1990) James Rachels offers a challenge to the standard way in which philosophers think about ethics, as well as a new and important moral principle which deserves serious consideration. Like Rollin, Rachels thinks that what science, particularly evolutionary theory, shows us about our relation to animals must be taken seriously in moral theory. He sees in the work of

Darwin a fundamental challenge to the view that humans are categorically different from other animals and argues that this provides the basis for a fundamental challenge to traditional morality. Philosophers generally maintain that it is a mistake to attempt to derive moral conclusions or "ought" statements from factual or "is" statements. The impossibility of passing from "is" to "ought" statements is referred to as the "is-ought" gap, and those who attempt to cross this gap are guilty of the "naturalistic fallacy." Rachels argues that even if one cannot deduce moral conclusions from factual premises, traditional morality is tied to fundamental assumptions that are no longer tenable in light of evolutionary theory. In avoiding the naturalistic fallacy, philosophers have overlooked these crucial assumptions as well as the Darwinistic challenge to them.

In particular, traditional morality is based on the assumption that species boundaries mark essential differences, and that different species are arranged in a hierarchical manner, with Homo sapiens at the top of the scale. But modern evolutionary theory views species in a nonhierarchical manner and the notion of species itself as an arbitrary and pragmatic boundary. As Darwin put it, "I look at the term species, as one arbitrarily given, for the sake of convenience, to a set of individuals closely resembling each other, and that it does not essentially differ from the term variety, which is given to less distinct and more fluctuating forms. The term variety, again, in comparison with mere individual differences, is also applied arbitrarily, and for mere convenience' sake."[17]

But an arbitrary boundary laid down for the sake of convenience cannot support the categorical differences in moral worth and moral treatment enshrined in traditional morality. As we have seen, other philosophers have charged that discrimination on the basis of species is morally arbitrary, since species differences cannot be reliably tied to genuinely morally relevant differences. Rachels goes further, pointing out that the species boundary marks no real boundary at all, making the likelihood of its being correlated with morally significant boundaries virtually nil.

Nevertheless, defenders of speciesism argue that most humans, in possessing rationality and autonomy, are different from most other animals in morally relevant ways. This position is usually rounded out by adding that, because humans are normally rational, even those humans who lack this characteristic should be treated with respect. Animals are not normally rational and are not deserving of respect. Rachels suggests that the idea of basing the treatment of individuals on what is "normal" for their species is a carryover from pre-Darwinian thinking about species, and should be abandoned. Darwinian biology gives primacy to individuals in all their diversity over the old notion of species. Rachels suggests that we ought to do the same, adopting what he calls "moral individualism"—the view that how an individual may be treated is determined not by group memberships but by consideration of her own particular characteristics. Given that humans and animals are not simply different but that there is a complex pattern of similarities and differences, morality should respect this complexity. Insofar as two individuals (regardless of their species) are similar, they should be treated similarly, while to the extent that they are different, they should be treated differently.

Rachels points out that moral individualism is more plausible in many respects than speciesism. For example, chimpanzees do not normally read, write, or discuss morality. But if one appeared who did, the fact that normal chimps do not would be no rational basis for excluding this reading chimp from attending college classes—and for electing instead to perform invasive research on her.

We treat nonhumans differently from humans in a variety of ways. Rachels asks, Can the presence or absence of a single characteristic such as rationality or autonomy be relevant to all such differences in treatment? He argues that a difference between individuals that justifies one sort of difference in treatment might be completely irrelevant to justifying another difference in treatment. Intelligence and rationality are relevant to such issues as whether to admit someone to law school. If one student is admitted and another rejected, then board scores and college grades are relevant in justifying this. In another context, however, one's degree of intelligence and rationality would be irrelevant. A doctor who gave one patient a shot of penicillin, while putting another patient's arm in a cast, would need to justify this in terms of differences in their ailments, not in terms of differences in their intelligence and rationality. This leads Rachels to formulate this principle: "Whether a difference between individuals justifies a difference in treatment depends on the kind of treatment that is in question. A difference that justifies one kind of difference in treatment need not justify another."[18] And further, "Our treatment of humans and other animals should be sensitive to the pattern of similarities and differences that exist between them. When there is a difference that justifies treating them differently, we may; but when there is no such difference, we may not" (1987, 197).

This principle provides a powerful challenge to the rationality and consistency of speciesism, for this is clearly a principle we recognize and apply within the boundaries of our own species. We immediately recognize that members of our own species who happen to be deficient in human rationality and intelligence should be treated differently only where these differences are relevant; we will not admit them to college or hold them responsible for their actions as we do normal adult humans. But such differences are not a reason for using them in invasive experiments or in other ways exploiting them. With regard to these treatments, it is other characteristics, such as ability to experience pain and pleasure, that are morally relevant.

Rachels's moral individualism provides a powerful answer to those who raise the perennial question, "But where do you draw the line? Must we avoid killing cockroaches?" In light of Rachels's analysis, it becomes clear that there is no one line to be drawn, unless we wish to be arbitrary. Instead there is a fabric of characteristics and treatments appropriate to those characteristics.

While Rachels's proposal is not part of a detailed moral theory, it nevertheless brings together in a simple principle an idea implicit in many arguments for animal rights: we saw its initial appearance in Singer's analogy between racism, sexism, and speciesism. A serious reconsideration of the relevance of the Darwinian revolution for morality is long overdue, and Rachels's book provides a powerful analysis that has implications not only for our view of animals but for the way in which philosophers approach moral questions generally.

Objections to Rachels's Views.   Serious questions remain to be answered regarding moral individualism, however. How finely tuned should such a morality be to the relevance of individual differences? The presumption of equality ("all men are created equal") is an injunction to ignore individual differences when it comes to the rights of human beings. Voting rights, rights of marriage and reproduction, and pursuit of career goals and public office are all cases where relevant differences between individuals' abilities could be cited, yet we would surely be loath to invoke individual differences as grounds for exclusion in such areas. While it is unlikely that Rachels would suggest that we change policy in this regard, his principle provides no clear grounds for deciding when individual differences that are undoubtedly relevant should nevertheless be ruled out of consideration.

Those who do not accept a Darwinian perspective, instead believing a religious perspective such as Christian creationism,[19] will not find Rachels's analysis convincing. For many people, we must answer the questions regarding the nature of animals and any obligations we may have toward them by looking to religious teachings rather than science. Of course, there is a good deal of controversy among those who do hold a creationist perspective about many aspects of the view. For example, there are questions about the extent of the incompatibility of creationism with evolutionary accounts, stemming from questions about how literally to take the biblical creation story. Although the weight of scholarly opinion is in agreement with Rachels's view here, the possible conflict between Rachels and creationists raises the more general question of the relationship between religion and animal rights.

Andrew Linzey

Christianity and the Rights of Animals.   Considering only the philosophers we have discussed so far, it may seem that the idea that animals have rights arises from a purely secular perspective and is incompatible with a religious, particularly Christian, perspective. Indeed, Peter Singer paints a very negative picture of the influence of Christianity on the treatment of animals (1990, 189–202). Nevertheless, a growing number of scholars and theologians have turned their attention to this issue in recent years, and their work gives a much different picture of the moral issues confronting Christians in this area.

A number of individuals have made significant contributions to thinking about Christianity and animal liberation. An important figure in this context is S. R. L. Clark, whose *The Moral Status of Animals* (1977) examined possible Christian views on the question of animals and morality. In 1986 Tom Regan organized a large conference at Essex University in Britain, bringing together theologians from many different religious traditions (Judaic, Christian, Muslim, Hindu, Buddhist, and Confucian) to discuss religious perspectives on the use of animals in science. This conference gave rise to a volume of essays edited by Regan, *Animal Sacrifices* (1986). As these articles reveal, the theological issues concerning the place of animals and our obligations to them are far from settled and have only recently become a serious topic of debate.

Andrew Linzey, a theologian and biblical scholar, argues that the Christian tradition has, for the most part, failed to address seriously the questions of the theological significance of animals. As a result, rather than having clearly worked out answers, the Christian tradition provides ambiguous and sometimes inconsistent perspectives. Theologians have held that animals were made both for our use and at the same time for the glory of God. They have commended vegetarianism and also justified meat eating. They have spoken of reverence for life and also justified some barbarism toward animals. As Linzey puts it, the thinking, or at least the vast bulk of it, has yet to be done.[20]

Linzey points out the oversimplifcations and mistakes that some writers have made in taking the Christian tradition to be indifferent to the plight of animals. Consider, for example, the idea that man has dominion over the creation. Genesis is often read to suggest that human beings may do whatever they wish with animals. Yet, as Linzey argues, the power of humans is not absolute but dependent on God's order, which humans are commanded to look after and preserve (26). Linzey points out that absolute dominion is incompatible with both the overall dependency of man on God and with specific prohibitions, such as God's directive to vegetarianism: "'I give you all plant that bear seed everywhere on earth, and every tree bearing fruit which yields seed: they shall be yours for food'" (26).

But, says Linzey, if dominion does not mean absolute power, then the question Christians must answer is, "How, morally speaking, should we exercise our power over animals?" Linzey argues that the answer can only be sought in terms of the model of Jesus Christ. According to Linzey, the model of lordship the life of Christ gives believers, then, is not one of despotism but one of service and stewardship. Thus, while Jews and Christians have been right, according to Linzey, to point to man's God-given power over the nonhuman, they have been wrong in interpreting what this power means.

Linzey explains the popularity of the view that humans have absolute dominion over animals as stemming from the influence of Saint Thomas Aquinas, who was profoundly influenced by Aristotle and Saint Augustine, who gave preeminence to man's rationality. Rationality, according to Aquinas, is the key to spiritual status, and thus animals, who lack rationality, also lack souls. The valuing of immaterial souls and the devaluing of the physical world and animals are all a part of the Greek, particularly the Aristotelian, tradition—a tradition built on hierarchical value in which those lower on the hierarchy are not only less valuable but may be used by those who are higher. Linzey argues that hierarchy is Aquinas's Greek distortion of the biblical notion of monarchy. Just as Christ, viewed as a monarch, expresses his lordship through sacrifice and service, so Christians should view their role in relation to animals.

Linzey sees in Christianity not only the value of animal life but a place for the notion of animal rights. He speaks of "theos-rights" to indicate the origin of rights in God and to "effectively champion the inherent goodness of what God has given . . . in the strongest moral language available" (72). He argues that animals have the right to be free from wanton injury, which would include such things as hunting, bullfighting, and use of performing animals in entertainment: "Every act of making animals suffer harm, pain or deprivation for our pleasure or entertainment is a practical sign of our ungenerosity to God. It shows that we have not begun even in a minimal way to grasp divine benevolence" (105). He champions vegetarianism for Christians as a way of living free of violence and "making peace with creation" (51).

Criticisms of Linzey's Views.   As Linzey himself makes clear, however, much in the Christian tradition and in the Bible appears to go against animal rights. The Catholic tradition, in particular, has remained firm in denying that Christians have any obligations toward animals. For every Saint Francis there are such Church leaders as Pope Pius IX, who refused to allow a Society for the Prevention of Cruelty to Animals to be established in Rome, on the grounds that to do so would suggest that people have duties to animals (Singer 1990, 196). Little appears to have changed since this mid-nineteenth-century ruling. And for every passage in the Bible exhorting care for animals, there are others suggesting indifference. Linzey has made an important contribution, however, in showing that the issue is far from cut and dry.

Mary Midgely

Why Animals Matter.   In *Animals and Why They Matter* (1983) Mary Midgley explores the question of animal rights in relation to established concepts and ways of thinking, rather than attempting to build a moral theory on new ground. Though both Sapontzis and Linzey approach matters in a similar fashion, Midgley offers a somewhat different perspective than those we have discussed. While clearly in sympathy with the view that conventional accounts of morality grant too meager a place to animals, Midgley believes that a proper understanding of their place cannot be achieved without a much more fundamental critique of the very tools that conventional moral theories employ. Animals do matter, but why this is so is much more difficult to say than others have suggested.

Midgley points out that the very question of our relations with animals appears hard to take seriously or fit within our current ethical thinking. Arguments for taking animals seriously are often dismissed as "sentimental, emotive, childish, impractical, superstitious, insincere—somehow not solid."[21] Understanding the roadblocks to serious and careful thinking about our relationships to animals is indispensable to progress in this area.

Midgley asks why animals matter not only because of the interest of the question itself but to challenge predominant views (usually tacit) of the very center of morality (64). Should morality center on concerns with justice, rights, and equality as utilitarians, rights theorists, and contractarians all would have it? Midgely does not think so, and *Animals and Why They Matter* is an extended consideration of what she argues are the limitations and oversimplifications in much modern discussion. Her position is not that we should say that animals do not have rights. It is just that morality is much wider than the framework of these concepts, and we need further concepts to work with.

Not only the rights framework, but the rationalist perspective within which it is couched requires rethinking, according to Midgely. All the philosophers we have previously discussed in this chapter are united in rejecting rationalist arguments against animal consciousness, as well as the exclusive emphasis on rational thought as the source of all value. Midgely does not dispute these arguments but sees more complexity and ambivalence in rationalism, claiming that "even 17th Century rationalism does not furnish us with a clear and unanimous licence to poison all the pigeons in the park" (47). The German rationalist philosopher Gottfried Leibniz, for example, stressed the continuity between intellect and other forms of consciousness, and between nonconscious and conscious life. He saw animals as life forms differing from people only in degree and was reputed to take care not to harm even a tiny worm or a fly. Rather than restricting consciousness to human beings, then, a countervailing force in rationalism is to see reason at work everywhere (46). Midgely further challenges the very separation of reason and emotion in rationalism, arguing that these aspects of the mind are complex and intertwined: "Sensitivity requires rationality to complete it, and vice versa. There is no siding on which emotions can be shunted so as not to impinge upon thought" (43).

Midgely next turns to the central concepts of rights and justice that have emerged within the rationalist framework. The word *rights*, in particular, Midgely argues is "really desperate" (61). It was in trouble long before animals were added to its worries. The word has clear, descriptive legal uses, but it also has unclear moral uses. The ambiguity in the term expresses, in part, the imperfectly understood connection between law and morality. The very obscurity of the concept makes it effective in campaigns for change, and Midgely suggests that eighteenth-century revolutionaries exploited these ambiguities to good effect. But rights talk is an essentially destructive tool that can be used like a lever to remove particular obstacles. It can be used to draw attention to problems but not to solve them. For, Midgely argues, "In its moral sense, it oscillates uncontrollably between applications which are too wide to resolve conflicts ('the right to life, liberty and the pursuit of happiness') and ones which are too narrow to be plausible ('the basic human right to stay at home on Bank Holiday'). As many people have already suggested, its various uses have diverged too far to be usefully reunited" (63).

Midgely sees similar problems with the concept of equality, which she sees, along with the concept of natural rights, as having "no built-in limits," being essentially tools for widening concern. As such, these concepts require supplementation by more detailed and discriminating ideas. At the same time, equality is in practice an "in-group" concept—a tool for rectifying injustices within a group, not for widening that group. This is because, from a political point of view, it is too difficult both to defend equality within a particular group and to seek to extend the boundaries of that group. Accordingly, the illuminated circle of individuals who are to be treated equally are always surrounded by the "outer darkness" of those who are ignored (68). The Greeks argued egalitarianism in a society that kept slaves and regarded women with disdain. Jean-Jacques Rousseau, who championed the rights of man, denied entirely the rights of women.

Turning to utilitarianism, Midgely once again sees problems of oversimplification. She questions utilitarianism's strict impartiality, particularly the idea that preference for our own species is entirely unjustified. Midgely appeals to the empirical evidence about our own as well as other species to argue that attachment to particular individuals and groups is unavoidable and widespread. While such partialism is the source of much cruelty and suffering, it is also the wellspring of our caring about others (102). The species boundary itself is not a trivial but an important one. As such, the analogy often drawn with racism is not entirely appropriate. Indeed, Midgely sees the concept of "racism" itself to be inadequate, since it combines too many disparate ideas, such as the triviality of the distinction between races, group selfishness, and perpetuation of an existing power hierarchy (100). The work that the concept of speciesism can do, then, is (like rights and equality) the destructive work of clearing away arguments for dismissing concern for animals. As such, the concept is useful, but once again, only in a preliminary way.

While maintaining the moral significance of the species boundary, Midgely also insists that it is morally relevant that we do live in a mixed community and not in species isolation as we develop bonds of sympathy with animals. For example, Midgely points out that wherever there are horses, there are some people who actually prefer them to humans. The very domestication and exploitation of animals is aided by bonds of trust and understanding (especially in the case of large animals, such as horses or elephants). It is extremely unlikely that we are always mistaken in identifying the feelings and thoughts of animals: "How odd it would be if those who, over many centuries, have depended on working with animals, turned out to have been relying on a sentimental and pointless error in doing so, an error which could be corrected at a stroke by metaphysicians who may never have encountered those animals at all" (115).

Midgely never offers a direct answer to the question she sees as central: Why do animals matter? Nevertheless, these last remarks about our sympathy and bonds with animals appear to be an important piece of the puzzle. In fact, if we think about it, we do care about animals. Complete dismissal of their welfare is extremely difficult to maintain, and those who attempt to maintain it will have to explain away the inconsistency of their own occasional lapses into concern. Given the interconnectedness between emotions and intellect, this cannot simply be dismissed as emotion and sentimentality.

Criticisms of Midgley's Views.   It is ironic that Midgely's central criticism of concepts such as rights, equality, and speciesism is that they are destructive rather than constructive, for Midgely's book is itself essentially destructive rather than constructive, offering no alternative to these concepts nor any clear picture of what directions to go in to begin to build better frameworks. Some of her remarks, especially about the interconnectedness of reason and emotion, are suggestive of feminist frameworks, but they are not well enough developed to determine what might be made of them.

Nevertheless, criticism can be extremely valuable, if it is well taken. Are the concepts of rights and equality essentially destructive? It is not clear that this is so; nor is it clear that the ambiguities cannot be eliminated with further theoretical work. As philosopher Karl Popper pointed out, it is up to us to define our terms clearly, rather than to complain passively about what is unclear. Is it a conceptual difficulty with the notion of equality that there are always individuals left out of consideration, or is this simply the limitation of some of those who have used the concept? Surely this is not a limitation of all uses, since Singer's use does not appear to leave any sentient being out in the dark. Furthermore, as we have seen, Tom Regan has developed a detailed theory of rights and has offered positive principles of conflict resolution. Such specific theory building cannot be tossed aside simply because historically the term has been used in broad, conflicting and ambiguous ways. Rather, an effective criticism along the lines suggested by Midgley would have to involve determining that these theories leave out someone who ought to be included within the scope of morality.

In the final analysis, Midgley alerts us to the fact that the very terms in which the philosophies of animal rights are articulated carry with them traditions that may ultimately provide unsatisfactory frameworks for those who care about animals. In the absence of clear alternatives to such frameworks, however, we are entitled to an argument once offered by Lyndon Johnson: "I'm the only president you've got."

Conclusion

Certainly the theoretical positions of the philosophers we have examined diverge in many significant ways, such as the divergence between the consequentialist approach of Singer and the rights-based theory of Regan. It is reasonable to view this diversity as a strength in the animal rights movement: after all, the divergences in theoretical frameworks represent a variety of positions seriously entertained by moral philosophers today. The challenge to traditional ways of thinking about animals is not simply the product of the replacement of one ethical theory by another. Perhaps this fact itself adds some support to the contention of these philosophers that the exclusion of animals from the scope of moral concern is arbitrary—owing partly to flawed assumptions about the differences between animals and humans and partly to the tendency to place ourselves at the center of the universe.

Thus we have seen a new philosophical perspective on our relations with nonhuman animals converging from diverse theoretical perspectives. In the end, the philosophers we have examined here agree not only in the overall conclusions they draw but in many of the arguments for those conclusions. When taken together, these arguments pose a fundamental challenge to traditional morality and its assumption of the superiority of humans and the primacy of human interests, and this is a challenge both to professional philosophers and to those who uncritically live their lives by the tenets of traditional morality. This challenge can be summarized as follows.

(1) The traditional exclusion of animals from the sphere of serious moral concern is based not on a carefully reasoned analysis but at least partially on outdated, factually incorrect assumptions about animals. Traditional morality assumes categorical and fundamental boundaries between species; it assumes that animals are cognitively and emotively deficient in various ways (e.g., irrational, unfeeling, unconscious). These assumptions are unsupportable in light of the evidence of modern science, including evolutionary theory, psychology, ethology, and neurophysiology.

(2) Once the factually incorrect assumptions about animals are removed, arguments for excluding animals from moral concern based on these assumptions collapse.

(3) The most straightforward and plausible way of amending these theories involves extending moral concern to animals.

(4) Genuine moral concern for animals implies a genuine regard for their interests. However we settle the issues that arise in difficult cases of conflict of interest (and for a vast amount of our use of animals, no such conflict exists), we cannot ethically pursue our interests by routinely sacrificing the interests of other animals.

(5) While not all of the morally relevant interests of humans or animals constitute rights, the seriousness with which we must regard

many of the interests of animals is reflected in the view that these constitute moral rights, such as the rights to life and liberty.

(6) The extension of serious moral concern to animals implies a radical reassessment of many of the things humans do to animals, including raising them in factory farms for food, using them in laboratories, hunting them, trapping them and using them for entertainment. In short, to have their interests and rights respected, animals must be liberated from human exploitation.

Chapter Seven

Other Voices: Environmentalism, Ecofeminism, and Animal Liberation

The animal rights movement is one of a number of liberation movements: the feminist movement, the civil rights movement, the gay/lesbian rights movement, and movements for the liberation of third world peoples. The environmental movement, while not a "liberation" movement, is an important contemporary movement whose fate is tied in with animal liberation. Those who argue for the rights of animals argue that speciesism is analogous to racism and sexism. Seeing the analogy leaves the question of the connection among these oppressions unanswered, however. Are all these oppressions part of a common fabric, such that working to end them all is a realistic and consistent goal? Or are the goals of animal liberation unrelated to—or even in some respects at odds with—these movements?

The connections of animal liberation to these other movements is a matter not only of theoretical interest but also of great practical import. One common objection to animal liberation is that those who devote their time to it are suffering from badly misplaced priorities. Animal rights activists are often asked, How can you worry about the suffering of animals when there is so much human suffering? When children are starving and homelessness is on the rise? When the environment is being destroyed? When women's rights are being eroded? These objections assume that working for the liberation of animals is irrelevant to these other issues, or even detracts from them. But if the oppressions have common sources, different questions arise: Is it possible to be a feminist, or an environmentalist, without also being an animal liberationist?

Environmentalism and Animal Liberation

Environmentalists and animal liberationists would seem to be the most natural of allies. A healthy environment is essential for the well being not only of humans but of all animals. Without habitat, the wild animals whose rights the animal liberationists would defend will cease to exist. Similarly, individual animals are crucial parts of the environment and must be valued and preserved by environmentalists. Often animal rights organizations include concern for the environment in their literature;[1] unfortunately, however, despite these useful liaisons, there are complexities and conflicts that cannot be ignored.

Before we can address these conflicts, though, we must consider a definitional issue. One of the first difficulties in understanding the relationship between environmentalism and animal liberation is defining what is meant by environmentalism. Today nearly everyone, including George Bush and McDonald's restaurants, wants to be considered an environmentalist. Nevertheless, some self-proclaimed environmentalists are as much in conflict with genuine environmentalists as they are with animal liberationists.

Conservationism.   For many years the predominant view labeled "environmentalism" was the "conservation of natural resources" view, according to which the environment is an important resource for humans and ought to be used wisely, so as not to be used up or destroyed. Thus, if all the wild rivers were dammed, future generations of human beings would not have the pleasure of visiting wild rivers. If all the elk or bears were shot, future generations of hunters would be deprived of the pleasure of hunting them. And extinction of flora is undesirable because of the potential medicinal uses to which various plants might have been put. This view has been historically instrumental in arguments to establish national parks and to regulate and limit hunting.

Although conservationism has clearly contributed to the preservation of wilderness areas in the United States, this view is not a genuine environmental ethic, for the conservation of natural resources view does not attribute any inherent value to the environment at all, seeing it as merely of instrumental value for humans.[2] Thus, conservationism is really just a variant of humanism—one that happens to regard the environment as particularly desirable for the furtherance of human goals. Just as it is not possible to regard other humans or animals with genuine respect while treating them as merely instrumentally valuable, so this is not possible in the case of the environment. Thus, conservationists are willing to exploit and in some cases destroy the environment in order to further human goals. For example, fish and wildlife managers routinely defoliate areas in order to promote the growth of browse for deer at the expense of other species. They do this in order to promote "maximum sustainable yield" of deer for hunters (Baker 1985). This sort of exploitation is no more consistent with a genuine ethic of the environment than it is with animal liberation.

We need not include conservationism when we discuss the compatibility of environmentalism and animal liberation, since conservationism is itself opposed to true environmentalism. Those views we will include all agree that the environment has an inherent value, independent of human needs and interests. Even granting this basic agreement, though, there still remains a diversity of environmentalist views, but within this diversity it is possible to find two differing approaches: individualism and holism.

Individualistic Moral Extensionism: Rights for Trees, Insects, and Oysters?   One common objection to animal liberation is the "vegetable" or "cockroach" objection. According to this objection, if we agree to grant rights to animals, then we ought to extend our concern to all of them, including insects. Furthermore, we ought to extend concern to plants and trees as well. This objection is often offered to show the impossibility of the animal rights position. After all, you have to eat something. It can also be taken as a proposal to extend moral consideration to living things generally. This view shares with animal liberation the idea that the moral categories already in place for humans should be extended to include a wider range of beings. As a result, both views are sometimes classified as versions of "moral extensionism" (Callicott 1980).

According to defenders of animal liberation, the fact that animals are conscious and can and do take an interest in their lives entitles them to moral consideration. While various approaches may differ somewhat in which mental characteristics (ability to feel pleasure and pain, having interests, being a subject of a life, etc.) are important, all agree that the presence of such mental states confers value on animals. There are two kinds of challenge to this claim. One is that sentience is not a morally distinguishing characteristic—that it is simply not relevant to determining moral considerability. The second challenge is that sentience is not a necessary condition of moral considerability, even if it is a sufficient one. In other words, even if sentience is a morally distinguishing characteristic, other characteristics can also confer moral status on an individual.

Kenneth Goodpaster, for example, has posed these challenges, arguing that sentience is irrelevant and arbitrary as a criterion of moral considerability. Just as animal liberationists such as Singer have argued that rationality is irrelevant and human-centered, so sentience is equally arbitrary, according to Goodpaster. And just as those who take human rationality as their criterion are speciesists, so those who take sentience as their criterion are "vertebrate chauvinists." Goodpaster argues that sentience is not an end in itself but has evolved as a means to further the goal of survival. Therefore, because sentience is ancillary to life, the capacity to live rather than the capacity to experience pleasure and pain should be the criterion of moral considerability. And even though one cannot cause trees or plants to suffer, one can harm them in other ways, and thus we should morally consider these individuals in deciding what to do.[3]

Goodpaster's arguments fail to show that sentience is morally irrelevant. First, the analogy to what animal liberationists say about rationality is not persuasive. Neither Singer nor any other animal liberation proponent has argued that the presence or absence of rationality is morally irrelevant. Clearly, there are morally relevant differences between individuals who are rational and those who are not. A rational agent can be harmed in ways that an individual lacking rationality cannot be—most directly by being denied opportunities to exercise that rationality. For example, rational individuals can be harmed by being denied educational opportunities, while individuals lacking rationality cannot. Singer argues that rationality is not a necessary condition for moral considerability, which is quite different from arguing that it is irrelevant.

Second, it is difficult to see why the assumption that sentience evolved as a means to further survival should make sentience morally irrelevant. In general, the argument "A evolved in order to further B, therefore A is morally irrelevant and B is morally relevant" is very weak. According to some biologists, such as Richard Dawkins, all organisms can be said to have evolved as "survival machines" for the preservation of the genes. It hardly follows from this that only genes matter morally.

The claim that sentience is not a necessary condition for moral considerability appears much more plausible, however. Some people find it quite intuitive that endangered species, stretches of the Colorado River, old growth redwood trees, and the Mona Lisa should be regarded as having value. And for the most part, animal rights proponents have not denied this.[4] The focus of animal rights arguments has been to show that animals who are sentient ought to be given the sort of morally serious consideration that human beings are given, not to argue that animals are the only individuals other than humans who should count. Animal rights proponents such as Regan leave open the task of arguing for the moral considerability of the environment and other sorts of individuals.

In light of these last reflections, however, Goodpaster's proposal that moral considerability ought to be extended to all living things appears too narrow. For this proposal would exclude stretches of the Colorado River as well as the Mona Lisa, while including bacteria and tapeworms. While we might decide to include tapeworms as morally considerable, it is far from obvious that they should be included while the Colorado River is excluded. Clearly those in search of an environmental ethic need a broader criterion than life in order to value endangered species (as species, as categories, are not alive) and ecosystems.

Even more fundamentally, the suggestion that all living individuals be included in the moral sphere on the same footing ignores important differences among individuals and produces a welter of conflicts. How do we decide whose rights we should respect? Does the extension of respect to all life mean that the life of a moth should be given the same consideration as the life of a chimpanzee or human being? And what, precisely, does it mean to respect the life of a tapeworm or bacterium? It cannot mean that these individuals must not be killed, for their lives often pose a serious threat to humans and other animals. Furthermore, given the reproductive strategies of such organisms (i.e., production of vast numbers of offspring with few survivors), the vast majority of them are doomed to death. Increasing the numbers of rights holders to include oysters, tapeworms, and germs waters down the notion of rights so much as to make it utterly meaningless. (This is a fundamental problem with the Albert Schweitzer "reverence for life" view, and it is no wonder it is popular with animal researchers, for once an organism such as a fly or moth, whose killing is unavoidable, has been given the same status as a dog or a chimpanzee, the way has been paved for killing the latter. The only wrongful killing is "unnecessary" killing, where necessity is in the eye of the beholder.)

Evidently there are limits on reasonable extensions of the notion of individual rights. Developing an environmental ethic appears to require more than a simple expanding of the circle of morally considerable beings.

Holism and Deep Ecology.   In the face of these difficulties, deep ecologists—such as Arne Naess, George Sessions, Bill Devall, Michael Tobias, and J. Baird Callicott—have suggested that the system of thinking in terms of individuals and rights is itself at fault. We find ourselves with hopeless conflicts because we think of individuals as separate from the ecological systems of which they are a part. Instead, deep ecologists argue for the interconnectedness of all living and even nonliving systems and challenge ethical systems that ignore this interconnectedness. It is this questioning of the fundamental assumptions of Western ethics and culture, and the holistic alternative offered to it, that leads proponents to call this approach "deep."

What is an individual animal, and what is its value? David Brower has said that the California condor is more than just the flesh and sinews of the bird: it is flight, air currents, cliffs, and sky. The bird and the vast evolutionary forces that molded wings and feathers are inseparable, and to take the bird from its environment is to destroy it. This is more than mere poetry, according to deep ecologists, who argue that the interconnectedness of all things is a scientifically established principle of ecology.

The science of ecology reveals the interdependence of all organisms within ecosystems. The plants and animals we observe behave as they do and have the characteristics they have as the result of eons of evolutionary pressures, and they are adapted to their current environments down to the minutest details. Thus, if we wish to understand animals and their value, we should think holistically and understand them in their role in the whole biotic community. If the condor is nothing without the wilderness, then we cannot talk about the value of the condor's life without considering the wilderness too. According to deep ecologists, the most basic value is that of the biotic community as a whole: the flourishing of ecosystems.

Deep ecologists argue that their "ecocentric" or "biocentric" perspective finally transcends the homocentrism of moral extensionism. The conflicts we encountered with the extensionist approach can now be resolved, with the symbiosis and harmony of ecosystems as both model and goal. Because the moral imperative of deep ecology is to do what will contribute to the flourishing of ecosystems, our treatment of individuals must be decided on this basis. Germs, oysters, and tapeworms all have their place in the biotic community, and all contribute to its flourishing. Their death, too, is to be valued, because it is necessary for this flourishing.

Is valuing whole ecosystems compatible with animal liberation? Most deep ecologists do not think so, and the sources of conflict appear to reflect quite fundamental differences of worldview regarding not only animals but nature and the role of humans and animals in it. Animal liberationists see animals as individuals whose lives must be respected just as we respect the lives of other human beings. The rules of human society forbid killing other humans under most circumstances, and these rules should thus forbid the killing of our nonhuman sentient kin as well. Many liberationists envision a future "peaceful kingdom," a kind of Garden of Eden that can be brought about if only humans would cease their violent dominion over animals and nature. Deep ecologists agree that humans ought to cease to dominate animals and nature, but they have a different vision of nature.

In nature the laws of the human social realm, including the right not to be killed, are inappropriate. Rather, humans should come to accept and live within the laws of ecology, and one among these laws is the need for the death of individual animals, through predation, starvation, and disease. Humans should learn to live as citizens of the environmental community, to accept these deaths, and even to participate in them when they will promote the health and diversity of ecosystems. Thus, while animal liberationists would extend the morality of human society to include animals, deep ecologists would extend the principles of ecology to apply to humans. Deep ecologists challenge what they take to be a homocentric bias within animal liberation, both in the attempt to extend human society's standards to the animal realm and in the emphasis placed on sentient over nonsentient individuals. Like Goodpaster, the deep ecologists ask for a more "egalitarian" system, but, unlike him, they offer the good of the biotic community as a whole as a metric for treatment of individuals.

These differences in worldview translate into quite concrete conflicts between deep ecologists and animal liberationists, in at least four areas. First, animal liberationists oppose hunting, trapping, and fishing, whereas deep ecologists see such activities in some cases as legitimate. Aldo Leopold, an early visionary of deep ecology, found hunting to be a spiritual experience, and many contemporary deep ecologists share this perspective. In fact, the hunting and gathering societies of North American Indians are the ecological ideal of many deep ecologists, such as Paul Shephard.[5]

Animal liberationist objections to human hunting activities have led many deep ecologists to insist that consistency should require them to object to predation among animals as well (Callicott 1980). Conversely, environmentalists regard predation as a positive good, which keeps ecosystems in balance and assures the health of prey species. Caribou herds appear to need wolves, for example, in order to maintain their vigor.[6] Given the necessity of predation for the maintenance of many of the species animal liberationists seek to defend, this would appear to be an unwelcome consequence of the animal liberation position.

In fact, animal liberationists have not taken positions against animal predation, nor do their arguments against hunting require them to do so. The difference between human and animal predation can be summarized in a single word: necessity. Mountain lions cannot survive on a vegetarian diet, but modern humans can and frequently do. To maintain that the animal liberation position implies that one must oppose all predation, even when necessary for the survival of both prey and predator species, is somewhat akin to maintaining that those who believe in the right to life for humans hold a position that does not permit them to ever accept death. But to value and respect a life is not the same as to hold onto it under all circumstances.

This answer also explains why animal liberationists object to hunting while they do not condemn the historical practices of American Indians and other indigenous peoples. Historical circumstances change. Those who leave the city for a weekend of hunting are pursuing killing for pleasure—something quite different from the model of the American Indians, who killed animals out of necessity and could thus honestly respect and thank those they killed. But consider the absurdity of claiming, "I do not need to kill you for my life. I kill you for the pleasure of it, for the experience. But I respect you."

Defenders of trapping have nevertheless felt that the issue of Native American trapping gives them some support. The argument is sometimes made that because trapping is part of aboriginal culture, the issue must involve not just concern for animal suffering but also concern for the integrity of that culture. To demand an end to trapping while ignoring the close relation that Native American cultures traditionally have with their environments, and the spiritual nature of that relation, is at best to see only one side of the equation and at worst to commit a form of cultural genocide. The charge, then, is that animal rights advocates are in the paradoxical position of participating in the victimization of one oppressed group (Native Americans) in their efforts to end the oppression of another (animals). The environmental group Greenpeace, which had begun an anti-fur campaign in 1984, was convinced to drop the campaign a year later because of the native trapping issue. As a result, Greenpeace lost much support within the animal rights community.

The native trapping issue is complex, but a number of points deserve consideration in sorting it out. First, by fur industry estimates only a very small percentage of U.S. trappers are Native American, probably somewhere around 5 percent, though in Canada the percentage is likely higher (estimates range from 29 percent to 51 percent, but the Canadian Ministry of Natural Resources points out that there is no solid basis for any of these estimates), so the issue of trapping is not limited to or even primarily an issue of conflict between animal rights and native cultural traditions. Nor do all Native Americans practice traditional ways. In this regard it is useful to distinguish commercial from subsistence trapping.

Second, Native Americans are not all of one mind on this issue. Paul Hollingsworth, an Ojibwa artist and founder of Native/Animal Brotherhood, argues that the international fur industry and the Canadian government (which supports it) are using native people for their own ends without real concern for the survival of those native peoples. Instead, he regards the historical introduction of commercial trapping as part of the process of confining native people to reservations and of destroying their traditional culture. On the other hand, David Monture of Indigenous Survival International maintains that viewing historical Native Americans as simply the slaves of the fur trade is to distort the active role Native Americans took in fighting to have a part of that trade.[7]

Third, the argument that objection to the cruelty involved in trapping is unwarranted interference in native cultures seems to imply that there is an obligation of nonnative cultures to assure a market for the products of trapping, for the primary focus of the anti-fur campaign is on consumer choice. But why would it be reasonable to argue that moral objections to a product are unwarranted interferences when other reasons for declining markets are not? Would it be unwarranted interference in native trapping if consumers stopped buying furs because they were no longer fashionable—if cloth coats are "in" this year or because climate changes made them unbearably hot to wear? It is hard to see that one culture is acting to destroy another if it simply fails to supply a market for the latter's products, unless the reasons to do so are the intentional boycott of that culture's products because they are produced by that culture or people (as when the new Nazi government called for a boycott of Jewish businesses in April 1933).

Another area of conflict between animal liberationists and deep ecologists, also related to the killing of animals, arises over the issue of endangered species. Callicott has pointed out that many endangered species are not sentient, as they are plants or invertebrates. From an animal liberationist perspective, endangered species have no special status as the result of being endangered. Thus, if an endangered species, such as a wildflower, is threatened by the grazing of deer or rabbits, deep ecologists will advocate preserving the wildflower, even if this means killing deer or rabbits. Obviously, animal liberationists will oppose this. Animal protection societies and environmentalists have come into conflict in actual cases over this issue; for example, in the 1970s and 1980s the San Francisco SPCA objected to the shooting of deer on Angel Island as a means of protecting the native fauna there (Lutts 1990, 199–200).

The final area of conflict between deep ecology and animal rights arises because animal liberationists do not regard wild animals as having greater intrinsic value than domestic animals. Most deep ecologists, however, regard the intrusion of domestic animals into natural ecosystems as destructive and contrary to an environmental ethic. John Muir referred to domestic sheep, for example, as "hooved locusts." Environmentalists consider the time and energy devoted to helping domestic animals to be misplaced, and they value wild animals, whether plentiful or rare, more highly than domestic animals. Animal protection societies have attempted to block the shooting of species such as donkeys and goats where their overgrazing has threatened to damage the ecology of an area. Generally, they advocate more costly and time-consuming solutions to these problems (such as relocation) rather than simply ignoring the environmental problems created.

Despite the appearance of conflict, however, deep ecologists and animal liberationists are clearly united in their desire to eliminate the concentrations of vast numbers of domestic cattle, chickens, sheep, and pigs from the earth. Animal liberationists would remove them primarily because of the profound suffering and exploitation to which they are subjected, while environmentalists would remove them because of the profound environmental damage they do. As John Robbins has argued, raising these animals produces vast amounts of waste, pollutes streams with phosphate, and wastes millions of acres of land that could be opened up for wilderness and used to cultivate food for humans (Robbins 1987, pt. 3).

The real point of contention between deep ecologists and animal liberationists appears to be focused more on means than on ultimate ends; both seek elimination or vast reductions in the numbers of domestic animals. Animal liberationists, given their respect for the lives of these animals, could not countenance mass shootings but would insist on a gradual phasing out. But can deep ecologists be genuinely egalitarian in their thinking on this point when it comes to that most destructive of animals, human beings? There can be no doubt that humans are destroying ecosystems at a phenomenal rate and that vast reductions in our numbers would be a considerable help in alleviating this destruction. A consistent application of deep ecological principles clearly implies that the life of an endangered wildflower is worth more than the life of a child, but few are the deep ecologists who would earn the title "environmental fascist" by recommending mass killings in order to "cull" excess human beings. Thus, there appears to be an implicit double standard for the deep ecologist, to the extent that she or he proposes to countenance the killing of some environmentally destructive animals for the sake of ecological health, while allowing for less draconian methods of achieving balance in the case of humans.

This double standard regarding the killing of humans as opposed to other sorts of animals lies at the heart of the disagreement between deep ecologists and animal liberationists. To the extent that this difference concerns means for solving environmental problems (killing as opposed to birth control, relocation, etc.), there is little reason to think that it could not be resolved. To the extent that deep ecologists propose hunting and gathering societies as ideal models for future human societies, these conflicts may be irreconcilable.

Many deep ecologists do regard hunter/gatherer cultures, especially Native American cultures, as models of the ecoholistic perspective they would like to see come into being. As Callicott has pointed out, it appears that some American Indian cultures had an ecosystemic land ethic with many similarities to Aldo Leopold's land ethic. The Ojibwa, for example, represented the plants and animals of their environment as engaged in social and economic intercourse with one another and with human beings. Consistent with this view, the Ojibwa behaved with restraint and respect toward animals, plants, and the environment generally. Native Americans' spiritual beliefs also connected them with the earth, rather than providing a model of domination and separation from nature (Callicott 1980, 14).

There can be no doubt that we can learn a tremendous amount from Native American traditions. Nevertheless, the suggestion that we return to life-styles and attitudes like those of Native Americans is not one that most of us can meaningfully follow, since we and our ancestors were not participants in them to begin with. If we are to find a more respectful and less destructive way of living, we must first look back to the roots of our own dominionistic thinking—to the religious, scientific, and social traditions that got us into the ecological mess we are in today. Without understanding the roots of our own oppressive society, it is unlikely that we can genuinely transcend it. To this purpose, we turn to feminist theory and historiography.

Feminism and Animal Liberation

Animal liberation is today and historically always has been a movement predominantly of women. Currently, women constitute 70 percent of animal rights activists,[8] and many scholars interested in animal issues are women. Historically, the number of feminists and suffragists who were also vegetarians and antivivisectionists is legion.[9]

Feminist scholarship reveals the underlying structure of male domination of women in patriarchy and the world view that reinforces this structure. Increasing numbers of feminists have come to see this structure and worldview as simultaneously subjugating not only women but animals and nature as well.[10] Many feminists argue that these oppressions spring from the same sources and are mutually reinforcing. If these scholars are correct, then feminists, animal liberationists, and environmentalists are all chipping away at the same rock of oppression, and it is not possible to eliminate any one of these oppressions without removing them all.

Carol Adams has argued that there is a clear connection—both ancient and modern—between male domination and meat eating. She points out that gender inequality is built into the species inequality that meat eating proclaims, since for most cultures men obtain the meat. Where meat is a valuable commodity, those who control this commodity achieve power. Thus, if men were hunters, the control of this economic resource was in their hands (Adams 1990, 34). This analysis is supported by anthropological observation, which reveals that women's status is inversely related to the importance of meat in nontechnological societies. Adams quotes Roger Lewin and Richard Leaky's interpretation of the role of meat in power relations: "The equation is simple: the more important meat is in their life, the greater relative dominance will the men command. . . . When meat becomes an important element within a more closely organized economic system so that there exist rules for its distribution, then men already begin to swing the levers of power. . . . Women's social standing is roughly equal to men's only when society itself is not formalized around roles for distributing meat" (35).

Peggy Sanday's survey of more than 100 nontechnological cultures found a correlation between plant-based economies and women's power and animal based economies and male power. Economies based on meat are characterized by patrilineality, worship of male gods, and the sexual segregation of work activities, with women doing more and less valued work than men. Plant-based economies are much more likely to be egalitarian.

The association between meat and power—specifically male power—has remained strong throughout history. As Adams makes clear, people with power have always eaten meat. The aristocracy of Europe consumed large courses of meat while the laborer consumed complex carbohydrates. There is also an historical and ideological connection between consumption of animals and Western colonialism that few have noticed. Adams points out that colonialist white supremacists believed that their own heavily meat-based diet was the appropriate food for the "more advanced" white race. "Brain-workers" required lean meat as their main meal, but the "savage" and "lower" classes of society could live exclusively on coarser foods, according to George Beard, a nineteenth-century doctor. How is it that most cultures of the world can live well with little animal protein? Because, according to Beard, they are "little removed from the common animal stock from which they are derived. . . . Secondly, savages who feed on poor food are poor savages, and intellectually far inferior to the beef-eaters of any race." As Adams argues, this explanation divided the world into intellectually superior meat eaters and inferior plant eaters, playing a role in the ideology of oppression that enabled the English to justify conquering other cultures: "The rice-eating Hindoo and Chinese and the potato-eating Irish peasant are kept in subjection by the well-fed English" (30–31).

Adams suggests that racism is perpetuated each time meat is thought to be the best protein source. The emphasis on the nutritional strengths of animal protein distorts the dietary history of most cultures in which complete protein dishes were made of vegetables and grains. Information about these dishes is overwhelmed by an ongoing cultural and political commitment to meat eating (32).

Cookbooks, advertising, and popular culture generally reinforce the notion that meat eating is virile and that men need meat. Meat is commonly reserved for soldiers during war, and it is believed that working men need meat for strength. The relationship between the consumption of animals and male domination cannot, however, be understood as merely an economic inequality, such as might have occurred if men had controlled the procurement and distribution of some other commodity. Rather, we must understand the important parallels between what is done to animals in order to turn them into the consumables labeled "meat" and what is done to women when they are used as sexual objects in pornography, when they are raped, when they are dominated. Women already subconsciously acknowledge this connection when, being stared at by men, they say, "I felt like a piece of meat." To be consumed, animals must first be reduced from subjects to things (through killing); then they must be fragmented (through slaughter and butchering); finally, they are consumed. This violence provides the paradigm for the objectification, fragmentation, and consumption of women. Women are objectified and consumed through the visual images of pornography and through literal sexual violence. French brothels in which women are forced to serve 80 to 120 "customers" a night are called *maisons d'abattage* ("houses of slaughter"), and the bondage equipment of pornography—chains, cattle prods, nooses, dog collars, and ropes—are devices for the domination of animals.

The feminist literature discussing rape makes liberal use of metaphors of butchery and consumption, as Adams suggests: "Rape, too, is implemental violence in which the penis is the implement of violation. You are held down by a male body as the fork holds a piece of meat so that the knife may cut into it. In addition, just as the slaughterhouse treats animals and its workers as inert, unthinking, unfeeling objects, so too in rape are women treated as inert objects. . . . To feel like a piece of meat is to be treated like an inert object when one is (or was) in fact a living, feeling being" (54).

Violence of the sort required for consuming animals can be made acceptable in a "civilized" world only if it is cloaked in acceptable ideology and linguistically disguised through the use of euphemism and metaphor. If animals are not subjects, if they are not conscious or rational or feeling, we may do with them what we wish. Thus, within patriarchy animals are identified as inferior, irrational "beasts," and their inferiority can then be invoked as the justification for human domination of them. Any residual connections to violence can be masked through euphemistic expressions: the dead bodies of animals are "meat" and their blood is "drippings"; one eats hamburgers, steaks, hot dogs, sausages, veal, and so forth rather than formerly living beings (cows or pigs). Once this mechanism of ideological distancing is in place, it can be extended to apply to groups of human beings. As historian Keith Thomas has argued, infants, youth, the poor, blacks, Irish, insane people, and women were considered beastlike: "The ethic of human domination [of animals] removed animals from the sphere of human concern. But it also legitimized the ill-treatment of those humans who were in a supposedly animal condition."[11]

In her powerful 1988 book, *The Dreaded Comparison*, Marjorie Spiegel reveals how easily it followed from the concept that humans are evolutionarily better than animals that whites could be evolutionarily superior to blacks. The rationalizations for the subjugation of blacks and animals are the same, and even the methods and devices used to shackle, punish, and dominate are the same. And both blacks, as "savages," and animals were regarded as closer to nature—indeed, of being resuced from their primitive state. Both were viewed as beneficiaries of white domination.[12]

What, precisely, is the ideology underlying the domination of animals? One of its most fundamental tenets is that man is intellectually superior: man is the rational animal, and this rationality emanates from a mind far different from anything possessed by an animal. The soul of man is nonphysical and otherworldly, and all that is physical, including both the earth and animals, is of a different and lower order. In some Judeo-Christian thought the spirit is separate from the body, and it is the spirit that is of real value. The material world, including the earth, is thus devalued. The earth is our vale of tears, to be transcended. Our possession of immortal souls makes us special, makes us valuable, makes us "above" the other animals. This superiority gives us dominion over the earth.

The connection between this view of animals and the oppression of women could not be more intimate, for in some strains of Judeo-Christian thought women are argued to be inferior on precisely the same grounds: they are closer to nature, less spiritual, less rational, and—like nature and animals—to be dominated by males. In the Judeo-Christian view women are often considered temptresses, leading males back to the physical, ultimately to the fall from grace: women and the earthy sensuality they represent are to be avoided. Indeed, the view that men are superior to both women and animals predates Christianity. Here is Aristotle: "For all animals there is an advantage in being under human control, as this secures their survival. And as regards the relationship between male and female, the former is naturally superior, the latter inferior, the former rules and the latter is subject" (Spiegel 1988, 66).

That the ideologies of domination of women and animals are intimately related, if not identical, is implicitly acknowledged in, for example, Mary Wollstonecraft's *Vindication of the Rights of Women* (1792) being immediately parodied with Thomas Taylor's *Vindication of the Rights of Brutes* (1792). The point behind the latter piece was, quite simply, that arguments for the rights of women can be regarded as absurd when it is seen that the same arguments would lead to rights for animals.

The popular and religious ideology of domination of women, animals, and nature gained further support from the emerging science of the seventeenth century. As Carolyn Merchant argues in *The Death of Nature* (1980), the modern mechanistic view of science provides a new kind of rationalization for domination. Descartes, as we have noted, suggested that animals, lacking souls, lacked thought and feeling. Dissecting an animal—laying open a dog and nailing it to the side of a building in order to observe the circulation of the blood—is no different from laying bare the inner workings of a clock, and the screams of the dog are nothing but the noises of the mechanism as it is dismantled. And so Descartes's mechanism paved the way for the vivisection of animals and, ultimately, the vivisection of the earth. And that earth, once again, is viewed as female.

Francis Bacon tells us that we must put mother nature to the test: we must force answers from her, interrogate her. In fact, Bacon used the analogy of a witch inquisition to explain how the scientist manipulates nature in order to extract information: "For you have but to follow it and as it were hound nature in her wanderings, and you will be able when you like to lead and drive her afterward to the same place again" (Merchant 1980, 168). It is no accident that the great witchcraft trials raged during the time Europe was making the transition to a mechanistic worldview. According to Merchant, "The metaphor of the earth as a nurturing mother was gradually to vanish as a dominant image as the scientific revolution proceeded to mechanize and rationalize the world. The second image, nature as disorder, called forth an important modern idea, that of power over nature. Two new ideas, those of mechanism and of the domination and mastery of nature, became core concepts of the modern world. . . . As Western culture became increasingly mechanized in the 1600s, the female earth and virgin earth were subdued by the machine" (2).

It is interesting to note that women not only were immediately victimized within the mechanistic worldview but also challenged it. For example, Margaret Cavendish, the duchess of Newcastle, and Anne Finch challenged Descartes's view of animals, and, as Josephine Donovan has argued, their critiques constitute an early feminist resistance to a process that inevitably meant the destruction of women (Donovan 1990, 366). Furthermore, women became the primary activists in the nineteenth-century antivivisection movement, perceiving a relation between vivisected animals and their own fate in the hands of sexologists who anatomized women's sensuality into subspecies of deviance. In her study of the nineteenth-century English antivivisection movement, Coral Lansbury argues that women activists identified with the vivisected dog: "Every dog or cat strapped down for the vivisector's knife reminded them of their own condition." Elizabeth Blackwell, a pioneering woman doctor, saw ovarectomies and other gynecological surgery as "an extension of vivisection." For suffragists, "the image of the vivisected dog blurred and became one with the militant suffragette being force fed in Brixton Prison" (Lansbury 1985, 24, 82, 89).

A second, little-remarked-on feature of the nineteenth-century suffragist movement was that many of its leaders were not only antivivisectionists but moral vegetarians. As Carol Adams has noted, the importance of vegetarianism in the early feminist movement has been silenced by the dominant culture, just as the violence of meat eating and the arguments of vegetarians were silenced at the time as they are silenced today. Adams's analysis reveals that vegetarianism and feminism often appear together in the novels of women writers but that feminist literary critics and historians have left the meaning of this unexplored. Writers such as Iris Murdoch (*The Good Apprentice*), Isabel Colgate (*The Shooting Party*), Margaret Drabble (*The Ice Age*), and Mary Shelley (*Frankenstein*) all use vegetarianism in symbolically powerful ways. Vegetarianism often serves to declare women characters' break with male domination, while meat eating symbolizes continued domination. This important feature of feminism deserves much more attention than it has to date.

Ecofeminism: Transcending the Logic of Domination

Whether the domination of women, nature, and animals can be traced ultimately to meat-based cultures, it is clear that in the last three centuries Western culture has maintained an ideology that rationalizes and perpetuates both the devaluation and domination of all three. Ecofeminists, who have become convinced that these dominations are all manifestations of an underlying, single patriarchal system, call for a critique of patriarchy and a recognition of the common roots of oppression. According to ecofeminists such as Karen Warren these oppressions reinforce one another and are part of the same logic of domination. The hierarchy which is put into place when men are placed above women, animals, and nature gives rise to a moral structure in which valuing one type of individual means the devaluing of others. The spirit is valued, and thus the flesh is devalued; reason is valued, and thus emotion is devalued. This hierarchical structure is one suited for domination, and for the perpetuation of conflicts.

The rules of this logic, as Warren has described them, include the assumption that "if X is morally superior to Y, then X is morally justified in subordinating Y."[13] Thus, questions focusing on conflict, such as, "If you could save a child or a dog, but not both, which would you choose?," are used as a test for determining relative positions in the hierarchy. The outcome of these decisions is then used to rationalize the exploitation of those lower in the hierarchy. As we saw in our discussion of Sapontzis, there is a fallacy involved in using extraordinary situations in which hard choices must be made (lifeboats, burning buildings) as a basis for determining how we should treat individuals in ordinary situations where no difficult choices are presented. Still, this fallacy lies at the heart of the logic of domination.

The recent evolution of feminism can in part be understood in relation to this critique of hierarchical thinking within patriarchy. Liberal feminists, like animal liberationists, have sought to find an equal footing within the hierarchical structure provided by patriarchal ideology. Thus, both are part of the broad category of "moral extensionists" discussed earlier. Radical feminists have called for a critique of patriarchy, focusing primarily on the domination of women. Ecofeminists insist that the critique of patriarchy must be extended to include nature and that feminism needs an ecological perspective.

Ecofeminism takes as methodologically important the ecological principle that everything is related. Just as we cannot "fix" a part of an ecosystem without considering the effects on all the rest, so we cannot mend the oppression of women without addressing the other oppressions that are the pillars of patriarchy. Thus, we cannot end patriarchal domination simply by focusing on the male denigration of women, or by elevating women to a higher point in the hierarchy. The transformation from radical feminism to ecofeminism focuses primarily on this point: all forms of domination are related, and thus ecofeminism must include an analysis of racism, classism, speciesism, heterosexism, and the exploitation of the environment.

It is a further tenet of ecofeminism that solutions to ecological problems must include a feminist perspective. The ecological principle of the interconnection among forms of domination applies equally here: the oppression of nature cannot be eliminated without addressing and eliminating the oppression of women. Without a feminist perspective, deep ecologists may perpetuate sexism in the service of ecology—for example, through a reductionistic Malthusianism and the consequent proposal that human population must be forcibly controlled. Ecofeminists, on the other hand, will point to reproductive freedom for women as a means to achieve population reduction while simultaneously relieving a major source of women's oppression.[14]

The ecofeminist perspective may provide a key to resolving the conflicts between animal liberationists and deep ecologists examined earlier, for just as feminist analysis exposes the sexism inherent in draconian proposals for population control, it can also challenge the necessity of such measures as mass shootings, hunting, and trapping when applied to animals.

More generally, ecofeminists challenge the necessity of the hierarchical framework that poses such questions as, "Do you value individuals more, or the whole systems of which they are a part?" "Do you want to save endangered species, or protect jobs?" "If you were on a lifeboat with an endangered gorilla and a human being, and there wasn't enough room for all of you, which one would you toss out?" "Do you want us to do research on this baboon, or would you prefer us to do it on your child?" From an ecofeminist perspective, there are two kinds of problems with these questions. First, such questions assume hierarchy and conflict. They assume that to value ecosystems is to devalue individuals, and that the dichotomies of individual and whole, human and nature are real and normatively significant. Indeed, posing these questions in the abstract serves the function of rhetorically reinforcing hierarchy, demanding that we decide "who will count more."

Second, such questions presuppose a certain way of doing ethics—namely, that reason (a favored pole in the reason/emotion dualism) will provide a universally correct answer, based on a hierarchical determination of values and through the application of universally valid rules. Carol Gilligan discovered, in her discussions with women, a rather different approach, in which particularity, feeling, and relationships play a predominant role: "The moral imperative that emerges repeatedly in interviews with women is an injunction to care, a responsibility to discern and alleviate the real and recognizable trouble of this world . . . the reconstruction of the dilemma in its contextual particularity allows the understanding of cause and consequence which engages the compassion and tolerance repeatedly noted to distinguish the moral judgments of women."[15]

The deep ecologists' holistic vision, in its striving for a genuine egalitarianism, is very well suited to a feminist ethics of caring that seeks to dissolve conflicts through mediation or consensual decision making. As Marti Kheel has put it, "If we allow for an element of feeling in our interactions with nature, the positions represented by these camps (individualism/deep ecology) dissolve into different points on a circle. No point may, thus, be said to be more important than any other. . . . A vision of nature that perceives value both in the individual and in the whole of which it is a part is a vision that entails a reclaiming of the term holism from those for whom it signifies a new form of hierarchy. It invites us to see value not as a commodity to be assigned by isolated rational analysis, but rather as a living dynamic that is constantly in flux" (1985, 140).

The feminist ethics that emerges from Gilligan's studies and recent feminist ethical theory stresses the importance of eliminating conflicts, rather than sustaining them.[16] This is not to say that we do not ever encounter true conflicts but rather that knowing how to solve them involves knowing particularities of the situation, considering relations among those affected and ourselves, and attempting to serve the interests of all to the extent that this is possible. If we examine the conflicts between animal liberation and deep ecology in light of this approach, we can see that there is no reason to suppose that such conflicts are unresolvable. If deer are browsing on endangered wildflowers, then the deer should be relocated. But more importantly, we should look for ways to avert such conflicts to begin with. If we set aside enough habitat, we need not come to the point where we must save the last few remaining members of a species. If we leave predators in the wild, we will not need to hunt the excess numbers of deer that arise in their absence.

The ecofeminist critique challenges both the deep ecologists and animal liberationists to examine their ideologies and consider their participation in hierarchical thinking and the logic of domination to which it gives rise. For example, if hunting and meat eating are oppressive with respect to animals and women, then deep ecologists should consider whether they can reconcile these practices with their commitment to bioegalitarianism. If whole ecosystems are valued over the individuals that inhabit them, once again hierarchical thinking has won out over genuine egalitarianism.

Conversely, ecofeminism suggests that animal liberationists should examine their commitment to individuals over ecosystems and recognize that both human and animal life cannot be fully lived or understood independent of the ecosystems on which they are dependent. Animal liberationists should recognize that commitment to saving wilderness is an essential part of the program of animal liberation, for without habitat there will be no place for animals, once liberated, to live.

Furthermore, to the extent that animal rights theorists reject emotion and empathy and favor reason as a foundation for ethics, they participate in the very ideology that has made the oppression of animals possible. As Donovan has pointed out, animal rights theorists have been anxious to dissociate themselves from any emotional appeals on behalf of animals and to place animal rights on an entirely logical, dispassionate footing. This has been an important project, given that serious concern for animals has been dismissed historically as sentimentality. But empathy toward animals ought also to be positively acknowledged as a moral virtue and not dismissed as morally irrelevant.[17]

Conclusion

In light of feminist—particularly ecofeminist—analysis, the oppressions of speciesism, racism, sexism, and environmental destruction are all aspects of a single worldview and methodology: each is part of a structure that cannot be dismantled without eliminating all of its manifestations. Thus, not only is the movement for animal liberation compatible with these other movements, but it is of a piece with them. To some extent, the conflicts that have appeared between these movements have occurred because of misunderstandings and disagreements over strategy and are not genuine inconsistencies. This conclusion has important implications for the political dimensions of the animal rights movement.

Ecofeminism is both an important and a radical critique of the very categories in which our society thinks about ethical, political, and interpersonal relationships. The changes necessary to transform society along the lines of an ecofeminist politic are dramatic and will take time if they are ever to come at all. As a result, the ecofeminist approach may not be ideal in attempting to bring about some of the immediate changes in animal treatment that the animal rights movement seeks. If these changes are to be reflected in our legal system, for example, then they will be articulated in the vocabulary of rights and justice. Those who work to transform people's views and treatment of animals will, by pragmatic necessity, have need of the rights vocabulary and framework, even as they work to transcend its limitations.

It may also turn out that the rights framework continues to play a useful role in moral thinking, even if ecofeminist approaches are adopted, for while the nonhierarchical approach of ecofeminism appropriately counsels the elimination of conflict, there may nevertheless remain genuine conflicts after our best attempts to dissolve them. In those cases we may require recourse to principles of justice, such as those articulated within the rights framework. What ecofeminists may offer by way of alternative resolution remains to be seen and will no doubt repay our attention, but it would be premature to give up traditional moral categories without being convinced there is a satisfactory substitute.

Chapter Eight

Whither Animal Rights?

John Stuart Mill remarked that great social movements must go through three stages: ridicule, discussion, and adoption. This is a wonderfully optimistic and simple view. Of course, other possibilities exist, both more complex and less hopeful. A social movement may achieve some degree of influence but then face intense opposition from those whose interests oppose the movement, preventing it from reaching its goals. To a certain extent, this is the current situation of the labor union movement in the United States. A movement may even be pushed back to the stage of ridicule and finally wind up as a mere historical episode, as occurred with the temperance movement. Closer to home is the example of the nineteenth-century antivivisection movement, which was initially quite strong but ultimately lost its battle and strengthened the political power of its opposition in the process.

The animal rights movement is now at a critical crossroads. It has gained a large measure of national recognition and has clearly had an impact in some areas, such as the sagging fur industry and product testing. This has aroused intense opposition from industries with vested economic interests in the status quo. These vested interests are extremely powerful; they can outspend the movement in media campaigns by enormous factors, as we have seen. If the movement is to survive these assaults and achieve its goals, it needs both inner solidarity based on a clear understanding of its foundations and goals as well as some strong alliances.

As the movement attains wider appeal it is important to recognize that not just any sort of growth is progress. Millions of Americans now identify themselves to some extent as proponents of "animal rights," and on many fronts the American public is becoming suspicious of the good intentions of the corporate entities poised to crush the movement. The very commercialization that has watered down the environmental movement, however, has allowed George Bush to call himself "the environmental president" and made international Earth Day into a corporate sales opportunity should stand as a warning to the animal rights movement.

A number of challenges face the movement in its second decade. Among these are three that we will discuss here: developing a clear sense of what constitutes genuine progress toward the goal of animal rights; crucial decisions about the form that activism on behalf of animals should take; and, finally, which forms of animal exploitation should be emphasized by activists in trying to achieve change.

Reform or Abolition?

Tom Regan and Gary Francione have argued that the movement will have to face the question squarely of whether it will be a *rights* movement, working exclusively to put an end to the institutions that exploit animals, or whether it will also focus energy on reform, working within the confines of existing structures of exploitation. Their position is that the animal rights movement must focus exclusively on abolition, withdrawing from reformist work that only perpetuates conditions of exploitation. They argue that animal rights must not be watered down in an attempt to reach a broad base of people; animal rights carries with it a commitment to ending exploitive institutions, be they exploitive of nonhumans or humans. If the movement is genuinely to progress, animal rights proponents must recognize that animal rights and animal welfare are not the same.[1]

How this issue is resolved will determine the answer to some very crucial political questions, such as the alliances the movement will make with other social movements. Most immediately, will the animal rights and animal welfare movements work together for gradual reforms in the treatment of animals, or will the animal rights movement seek alliances with other liberation movements, such as the women's rights movement, the gay/lesbian rights movement, (some elements of) the environmental movement, and those working to empower minorities? This may appear to embody a false dilemma: Cannot the animal rights movement forge alliances with the humane movement *as well as* the various human liberation movements? While this is possible to some extent, there are fundamental difficulties.

As we have argued, animal rights is an idea conceptually distinct from the notion of welfare implicit in the humane movement. To respect the rights of animals is not to provide them with larger cages or to slaughter them less painfully; rather, it is to empty the cages and to cease slaughtering them. On the other hand, the humane movement seeks to improve the conditions of animals while continuing to use them. Its primary goal is to minimize avoidable pain and suffering of animals. This humane-use ethic does not require fundamental change in industries that exploit animals (human or otherwise) while the ethic of animal rights clearly does.

The animal rights movement is and must remain distinct from the humane movement. As Regan and Francione have argued, within the welfarist framework animals are regarded as property, and only humans are rightsholders. Within this framework the interests of humans are given a much more serious weighting, and a presumption in favor of exploitation is created. Thus, the moral framework established by the philosophy of animal welfare guarantees that nonhuman animals will almost always lose when their interests are balanced against the claims of human rights.

Although the ultimate goals of the animal rights movement are clearly different than those of the humane movement, many within the movement see the possibility—or even the necessity—of achieving those goals by gradual and reformist means. They work for such things as improvements in the conditions of laboratory animals, more humane methods of slaughter and humane transport laws. A visible and effective animal rights organization, Farm Animal Reform Movement, for instance, devotes itself both to abolition and reform. Its argument is that people must be educated one step at a time. Many cannot be convinced to give up consuming animals overnight, but they can be convinced to work for more humane conditions for farm animals. Similarly, antivivisectionist goals cannot be achieved immediately, but improvements in the Laboratory Animal Welfare Act and other such legislation will, according to some, gradually lead to abolition.

As Regan and Francione have argued, however, there is scant evidence that reforms of the institutions of exploitation will lead to abolition. Instead, reforms may actually prolong the existence of such institutions by making them appear more respectable. It is currently common for animal researchers to cite the Federal Animal Welfare Act in arguing that their use of animals is humane. As Regan, Francione, and many others have observed, the Institutional Animal Care and Use Committees mandated by the 1985 amendments to the Federal Animal Welfare Act generally operate as a rubber stamp, which is hardly surprising given that the membership of these committees are typically selected because they are favorably disposed toward research. Yet that these review committees exist allows researchers to claim that protocols are all carefully reviewed to assure that no "unnecessary" suffering occurs in laboratories.[2]

The same sorts of points can be made regarding other institutions. The existence of humane slaughter laws may lead people mistakenly to think that no suffering occurs in the process that provides them with meat. Regan and Francione argue that to reform or clean up an institution of exploitation helps fortify it against criticism and very likely prolongs its existence. Furthermore, they point out that working for abolition rather than reform of exploitive institutions can also be done gradually, so one is not forced to choose between gradualism and abolition. For example, people can be encouraged to give up eating veal as a step toward vegetarianism. This sort of campaign has, in fact, been much more effective than efforts to improve the conditions of veal calves. Whereas no law has yet been successfully passed to enlarge the size of veal-calf crates or improve their conditions of life in the United States (though legislation has repeatedly been introduced), the "Boycott Veal" campaign has contributed to a significantly reduced market for veal. According to the Humane Farming Association, of the 27 major veal-calf operations that existed in California just a decade ago, only three are left. Similar sorts of gradualist abolition campaigns apply to animal research, as Regan and Francione have argued. Working to eliminate product testing on animals or wound laboratories is both gradualist and abolitionist. These institutions can be eliminated one at a time.

Furthermore, there is no reason that animal rights and humane groups cannot work together on such campaigns. This already occurs and is very effective. HSUS has mounted a very effective "Shame of Fur" campaign that calls for an end to the ranching and trapping of fur-bearing animals; this campaign complements those of IDA, ARM, PETA, Friends of Animals, Lynx, and other animal rights organizations. Effective and important cooperation has been achieved on a wide range of issues, and the diversity of strategies and images provided by animal rights and animal welfare groups is also highly effective. As Regan put it, "many hands on many oars" is more effective than a single, monolithic strategy. Humane organizations are less likely than animal rights groups to engage in direct actions such as demonstrations and civil disobedience, but their billboards, educational materials, and legislative work can often complement the tactics of animal rights groups. So it is important to distinguish goals from tactics: gradualism is an approach that can be used to achieve either abolition or reform.

Regan and Francione present a powerful challenge to the direction the animal rights movement is taking. Central to this challenge is the sound suggestion that activists retain a clear sense of the movement's ultimate goal. And the recognition that one can work in a gradualist manner toward abolition of exploitation is reassuring. Still, there are certain problems with the position Regan and Francione advocate. First, if working for reform of exploitive institutions is not consistent with working for animal rights, then animal rights groups will not join forces when welfare groups take on reform campaigns, which is likely to spark resentment from humane organizations. Furthermore, welfarists may argue that animal rights groups are sacrificing attainable welfare goals now for the sake of hypothetical abolitionist goals later. The "purism" (or "fundamentalism," as it has been called by some) of animal rights proponents who refuse to work on reform campaigns can be expected to produce some splitting of efforts and some bad feeling, both between humane and rights groups and within the animal rights movement itself.

Many staunch proponents of animal rights have worked very hard on reform-oriented campaigns and see these efforts as part of their work for animal rights. Such people assume, of course, that reform measures do in fact lead to worthwhile improvements in the lives of the animals affected and will lead to more significant improvements later. But Regan and Francione have charged that such an approach is questionable in the case of many reforms. If the reforms are viewed as a means to attaining more meaningful changes later, then, they argue, working for reform can likewise be viewed as sacrificing the rights of animals now in the hope of eliminating exploitation later. Clearly the issue here turns on the difficult question of what works: Do reforms help end or help perpetuate exploitation of animals?

Whatever the outcome of that debate, it would be quite incredible to claim that no reformist measures can lead to significant improvements in the lives of exploited animals. Consider, for example, "downed" cows and pigs that cannot walk because of injury or illness. These animals are nevertheless prodded and in many cases hoisted with chains on and off of trucks and may lie without food or water for days at auctions and slaughterhouses. Their suffering is of the worst sort. To work to change the law so that it is no longer legal to sell and buy such downed animals would remove the incentive to keep these animals alive. No one who has seen what these animals go through could argue that this would make no real difference, and yet this appears to be a reform rather than an abolitionist measure—it would regulate the way animals to be slaughtered may be treated without questioning the fact of slaughter itself. Similarly, eliminating the use of battery cages in laying-hen operations, prohibiting debeaking, and requiring that all animals be provided with regular food and water during transport are all measures that would clearly reduce the amount of animal suffering. Should animal rights organizations refuse to work on such campaigns, at the risk of failing to help make these animals' lives at least somewhat more bearable?

This is a difficult choice. Regan and Francione argue that to work on reformist campaigns is to "offer one's support to measures one knows will exploit some animals *today* in the name of benefiting other animals (the ones who, reformists suppose, will *not* be exploited) in the future." And this is "blatantly inconsistent with respecting the moral inviolability of those animals who are exploited today." The problem with this argument is that it ignores the fact that one may not be able to prevent the violation of some who are exploited today. To try to at least ameliorate their suffering need not be an implicit endorsement of that exploitation. Is working to stop the practice of selling and buying downed animals an endorsement of the slaughterhouses, farms, and auctions that do so? Cannot one be a harsh critic of such enterprises while attempting to modify their operators' behavior? One sense in which reform measures clearly do not support exploitive institutions is by eating into their profits. That reforms are so strenuously resisted by the institutions that exploit animals is evidence that such measures are perceived as economically damaging.

A further problem with the proposal that the movement focus purely on abolitionist causes is that the line between abolition and reform may not itself be entirely clear. For example, is working to end pound seizure an abolitionist or a reform campaign? According to Regan, ending pound seizure is an example of an abolitionist goal. This seems sensible, since one is ending the sale of animals from a certain source, or ending the use of "random-source" animals entirely, and that seems abolitionist. Unless ending pound seizure actually reduces the numbers of cats and dogs used in laboratories, however, the effort will only force researchers to shift to exploiting a different population of animals. As such it is really a reform, not an abolitionist, campaign, and it is just the sort of reform that might easily lead to strengthening the institution of animal research in the long run. After all, the image of one's own dear pet being taken and sold to a laboratory is a highly effective catalyst for stirring emotion against animal research. When all animals in research are the faceless "purpose-bred" variety, the general public will have one less reason to care about the suffering of laboratory animals. A similar thing can be said about ending the use of favored species (such as dogs and cats) in animal research generally. Because the public identifies most with these species, this is the sort of change that may lead to greater acceptance of vivisection.

The issue of implicit support for animal research in the case of pound seizure has been a central source of contention. Should arguments against use of pound animals remain focused on just these animals? Is discussing the inferiority of research using random-source animals as compared with research using purpose-bred animals implicit support of the latter research? Do arguments against pound seizure that appeal to the betrayal of the true purpose of animal shelters as safe refuge for lost and abandoned animals sell out the cause of animal rights unless they include a mention of a more general opposition to animal experimentation?

The problem of distinguishing abolition from reform is most obvious in cases of gradual or piecemeal abolition. Advocating that people give up eating all veal appears to be abolitionist, but on Regan and Francione's principles either this is indistinguishable from advocating that people become vegans or it accepts the permissibility of eating some *other* animals: there appears to be no middle ground. The recent reduction in veal consumption provides a good example of this problem: while these days Americans eat less veal and less "red meat," they eat more chicken and fish. Surely the animal rights advocate does not want to support or endorse exploiting chickens and fish in the place of veal calves. Furthermore, without coupling the fight to eliminate veal with a campaign to eliminate dairy farms (veal calves are the male offspring of dairy cows), these calves will come into existence and will ultimately be killed. Thus, the net effect of a "no-veal" campaign carried out in isolation will be a reform in the way in which male calves are treated, not an abolition of their exploitation.

It is arguable that some gradualist abolition campaigns are difficult to distinguish from reform campaigns and are plagued with similar problems. One sort of reply to these objections suggested to us by Tom Regan is to argue that the pound seizure and no-veal campaigns really are abolitionist, even if they do not result in a net decrease in the use of animals or animal suffering, for they focus on particular sets of animals and insist that these animals can no longer be used. If animal exploiters then shift to another group, this is not within the control of those who are fighting for abolition. It is not possible to judge whether an approach is abolitionist, then, based on its consequences. One must look at the intent.

Even a campaign to eliminate the use of downed animals could be looked at as abolitionist in this light: the campaign identifies a certain group of animals (those that cannot walk) and fights to eliminate their use. Still, the use of the downed animals is not really eliminated; they are not then turned over to loving homes to be healed of their wounds but would be slated to be killed sooner rather than later owing to their injuries. Their bodies ultimately wind up being consumed—perhaps as dog food or chicken food. Similarly, pound animals saved from research do not have their rights respected, except in the cases where they are subsequently adopted; the overwhelming majority of animals in shelters in this country are killed, and this remains true whether or not the shelter sells to research facilities. Thus, it is at best unclear whether these are abolitionist or reform campaigns, and this reinforces the point that the line between these two is unclear.

Some gradualist abolitionist campaigns do appear untouched by this objection, however: these include campaigns to stop the Draize and LD50 and other product tests, to end commercial whaling and slaughter of seals, to end commerce in fur, and to end the use of animals in entertainment. These campaigns do not involve the likelihood of a shift to exploitation of other groups of animals.

Regan and Francione raise an important challenge but one reliant on a distinction between reform and abolition that is harder to make in practical cases than it at first appears, which somewhat dulls the critical force of the distinction. Despite this difficulty, the overall message they convey is quite important: "As Gandhi knew, a progressive movement's means create its ends." If the movement's goal is an end to all forms of exploitation, this should be the focus of its campaigns, and it should not water down its public stance to achieve a broader appeal. Animal rights will become a meaningless notion (as "environmentalism" threatens to be) if any gesture of concern for animals translates into "animal rights."

As Regan and Francione argue, opponents of animal rights can challenge the honesty of animal rights activists posing as reformists.

For example, Patrick Concannon of the Cornell Veterinary School has stated that animal rights advocates who support welfarist reforms "are not bound by any moral requirement to be truthful about their ultimate goals and intentions" (Regan and Francione 1992, 4). Of course, this charge can only honestly be laid at the feet of those who seek more than reform but do not openly avow so. Someone can certainly maintain that both respect for rights in the long run and reforms in the short run are desirable. Proponents of animal rights should indeed feel bound to truthfulness about their goals and not shrink from stating them for fear of sounding "too extreme." The more frequently the principles of animal rights are enunciated, the less extreme and threatening they will sound. This same issue can be raised for gradualist abolition campaigns. Those who defend the fur industry like to point out that next the animal rights movement will do away with leather and meat eating. Such fallacious arguments should not distract us from our objections to fur, but, while pointing out that the issue at hand is fur and not leather, animal rights activists ought not to shy away from the broader principle attributed to them.

Animal Liberation and Human Liberation

Speciesism is as indefensible as racism and sexism. This comparison has helped make the case for liberating animals clear to many people. More than just a rhetorical device, the comparison with other liberation causes expresses something central to the logic of the case for animal rights. Ecofeminism articulates a critique of patriarchal society emphasizing that such oppressions are not just analogous to but actually arise from a common source. These points suggest that the natural political allies of the animal rights movement are feminists, civil rights activists, and all those who fight for the rights of oppressed peoples—a point argued by Regan and Francione. To deny the relevance and importance of other cases of exploitation is to deny the foundation on which the argument for animal rights rests. Advocates of animal rights cannot remain indifferent to these other forms of exploitation and oppression.

The connectedness of all varieties of exploitation is conceptually clear, yet the situation is not so simple politically. Organizations believe they must focus their efforts to be effective, and some will not unreasonably choose to focus even more narrowly than others. But recognizing the interconnectedness of oppression presents a challenge to animal rights activists in a number of ways. Should they take stands on other issues such as the government-initiated murders of thousands of people in Central America or homelessness in the United States? Will this detract from their efforts and alienate potential supporters? Is failure to do so consistent with a recognition of the interconnectedness of oppression?

The issue becomes even more difficult when we note that controversial and divisive issues will inevitably arise when positions on other issues are considered. Should animal organizations take positions on abortion and the death penalty? Which position should be taken: after all, "pro-lifers" maintain that abortion is the violation of the right to life of the fetus, while "pro-choicers" maintain that a woman's right to choose is paramount. Both maintain that without protection a morally significant individual would be violated. It is not at all obvious what position on abortion follows from an animal rights perspective, for a fetus may well turn out to be a morally considerable individual, especially a developmentally advanced fetus with ability to feel pain. Moral claims for the rights of fetuses do not automatically translate into legal restrictions on a woman's right to choose an abortion, however, since the woman's right to self-determination is also a fundamental right. It is not hard to see the attractiveness of a narrow focus that maintains that an organization should stick entirely to activities related to its stated purpose.

Another pragmatic concern of animal rights organizations is that many within other liberation movements do not as yet recognize the legitimacy of animal rights or welcome the comparisons, though these comparisons are compelling (see Spiegel 1988). Despite that somewhere around three-quarters of the animal rights activists are women, feminists (with some exceptions) do not by and large acknowledge the connection or make animal rights a part of their agenda. In the case of African-Americans and Native Americans, the situation is even less hopeful. For example, part of the agenda of Native American rights involves rights to hunt, trap, and fish, even in environmentally sensitive areas. These rights of native peoples to carry on their lifestyle appear to present conflicts with animal rights. Are these conflicts merely apparent or are they real? Is the fabric of oppression all of one piece, as Regan has argued, so that the fundamental interests of all those oppressed are in harmony? The direction of the movement depends very much on how these questions are answered.

Another way of putting the question is, How much of the world must change for the goal of animal rights to be achieved? Is it possible to leave the fundamental social, political, and economic structures as they are, simply modifying them so that they no longer involve the exploitation of animals? Is it possible, as Alex Pacheco describes it, to simply market compassion and leave everything else the same? The idea is quite simple: consumers demand products that are not tested on animals, so companies stop testing. Consumers no longer want furs, so trapping and ranching of fur bearing animals ceases. People no longer want hamburgers, so McDonald's offers them soyburgers. Enlightened, compassionate shoppers recognize there is no need for exploitation and demand nonexploitive alternatives, which are then provided. But is the fact that the products of animal exploitation are often unnecessary or even in some cases harmful to consumers enough to motivate their elimination?

Clearly there are many cases where focus on the needs and interests of consumers would require drastic changes, but where the corporate structure is quite unwilling to change. Southern California suffers from severe air pollution from the burning of fossil fuels, especially from automobiles. In the San Bernardino Valley, for example, the risk of cancer for women is much greater than it is in other regions of the country. It would be in the public interest to provide mass-transit systems and automobiles using alternative fuels. But the oil and automobile industries do not see this as profitable. It is more profitable to spend money on advertising to continue to convince the public that their real interests lie in owning a new car.

Thus, the long-term success of "marketing compassion" depends on who has the most money to spend—those who wish to see an end to exploitation or those who have a vested interest in continuing with the status quo. Abolishing institutional animal exploitation requires a much more thoroughgoing critique of these institutions and their motivations; it requires educating people about the nature of the corporate powers that stand to gain from the myriad forms of exploitation they currently practice, affecting humans, nonhumans, and the environment.

The animal rights movement ought to unflinchingly stick by its principles. These principles require a commitment to ending exploitation in all its forms, not merely to reforming it. The implications for the alliances the movement ought to form are clear. Educating feminists and gay/lesbian rights activists and those fighting for the rights of third world peoples, the homeless, and the environment about the oppression of animals ought to be a high priority for the movement. Those who already understand exploitation and are concerned to stop it are most likely to understand and become committed to animal rights. Of course, those in the humane movement who are already concerned about animals are also good prospects for education. While the American Medical Association and other foes of animal rights are at work to drive a wedge between the humane groups (characterized as moderate and reasonable) and animal rights activists (characterized as dangerous terrorists), the animal rights movement must unmask this propaganda and present the moral case for animal rights to all those who profess concern for animals.

Campaigns: What Should Be Central?

Throughout its history, animal rights activism has placed a heavy emphasis on antivivisectionism. The rise of the movement in the 1970s and 1980s began with the successful protests against experiments sponsored by the Museum of Natural History in New York, the powerful revelations and prosecution in the Silver Spring monkeys case, and the emergence of World Day for Laboratory Animals protests in 1983 as the first and most visible actions of the movement. Theoretically, events similar in scale to World Day were to focus on farm animals, but neither The Great American Meat-Out nor World Farm Animals Day have had the support or recognition of the antivivisection campaigns. The only campaign closely rivaling antivivisection in scale or energy is the anti-fur campaign.

The question naturally arises whether antivivisectionism should continue to occupy such a central position in the movement. There are both issues of principle and strategy to consider in relation to this emphasis. As a matter of principle, it would seem plausible that to some extent the more animals an institution exploits and the more seriously it exploits them, the more attention and protest that institution ought to receive. By any measure, the vast majority of exploited animals are those raised on factory farms. While there may be as many as 100 million animals used in laboratories in the United States each year, this figure pales beside the nearly six billion animals Americans eat annually. Nor is the suffering in laboratories worse than in factory farms. Thus, there is a straightforward argument for putting much more effort in this direction: this is where the suffering is.

From a strategic perspective, farm-animal suffering is a suffering in the power of ordinary people to affect in their daily lives—simply by ceasing to consume these animals. Furthermore, the case for exploiting animals for food is more easily refuted than the case for scientific research with animals. With the rise of health-conscious avoidance of many animal products, the existence of millions of vegetarians in the United States and elsewhere, and the strong evidence that consumption of animals is environmentally disastrous and a waste of food in a world with many hungry people, there can hardly be much controversy as to whether it is necessary or wise to use animals in this way. Thus, there is very little room for mounting "us vs. them" campaigns against a movement intent on eliminating the eating of animals.

This is not to suggest that this battle is more easily won. Clearly bringing about change here faces formidable obstacles also. Agribusiness constitutes one of the most powerful forces in our economy, and the availability of tremendous financial resources to fight the movement cannot be ignored. And there is also an important difference between being opposed to laboratory uses of animals and being opposed to agricultural uses of animals: the latter implies a much greater change in Americans' life-style. After all, serious moral objections to factory farming seem to imply refraining from contributing to the demand for its products, and that is a choice that most of us face three times a day. Bringing about change here is not simply a matter of participating in demonstrations, writing letters, or lobbying for legislation but most fundamentally a matter of changing oneself. While that is a source of enormous gratification for most animal rights advocates, it also makes achieving real progress for animals very difficult. Progress here will be slow and hard won.

This is also not to suggest that the movement should curtail its campaign against vivisection. Rather, the issue is whether the same sort of energy could and should be put into highly visible national campaigns on behalf of farm animals supported by the major animal rights organizations, which are able to lead the movement's direction. Within smaller, more local organizations the question of where to focus campaigns also needs to be thoughtfully discussed. It is vital that the movement not fall into a "calendar activism" mentality, turning from one campaign to another as the designated days or weeks (World Week for Laboratory Animals, Meat-Out, Fur-Free Friday, etc.) roll around. If the movement is not to lose its momentum, it must be clear in its philosophy and goals and focused in its efforts.

The calendar activism problem is exemplified particularly well by the 1992 experience with World Week for Laboratory Animals. Initially, the protests were planned for a day, but in the late 1980s they grew into a week of activities. Movement leaders should be asking themselves how long the World Week protest strategy can be effective. The 1992 World Week protests were virtually ignored by the media throughout the United States. Spreading events throughout the week forces activists (most of whom work for a living) to choose among the various events, making turnout at any one event light. Even where civil disobedience was threatened, as it was during a protest at Cedar's Sinai in Los Angeles, the media no longer finds World Week a newsworthy event. In the absence of startling new revelations concerning particular laboratories (e.g., the sorts of abuses documented regarding Thomas Gennarelli's Head Injury Lab or the Edward Taub case), the media do not find the protests worth covering.

Of course, the influence of powerful organizations (such as the AMA) on just how the media covers, or fails to cover, animal rights protests should not be overlooked; to wield such influence is an explicit part of their strategy. But even if such pressure has been applied, it is clear that World Week is losing momentum. How to respond to this lack of attention on the part of the media is a serious question the movement will have to face. A natural response is simply to continue to "up the ante" with more and more provocative actions (more civil disobedience, etc.). Whether this is either an effective or an ethical response is a serious question, to which we now turn.

Tactics: The Moral High Road

Movements that strive for moral reforms must clearly demonstrate their moral strength and consistency. Their success depends on appealing to the wider community's sense of justice, which is a rather delicate affair that can easily backfire if one does not understand the moral values of the community one is trying to change. Additionally, the honesty and good faith of reformers is crucial if such appeals are to have an impact. The foes of animal rights seem to understand these issues: the tactic of associating animal usage (no matter how exploitive) with freedom of choice and painting animal rights activists as "violent terrorists" are both appeals to just such mainstream values.

Mohandas Gandhi and Martin Luther King, Jr., both understood the importance of this moral high ground in bringing about their remarkable achievements. Nonviolence, an absolute commitment to truth, and an appeal to the highest moral principles were hallmarks of their approaches. If the animal rights movement is to achieve its goals, it must strive to live by the same high standards. After all, what makes this movement worthy of public attention and participation is its claim that morally we have fallen short in failing to include animals within the scope of our moral community. To achieve the moral high ground, however, we must clearly understand what it is. Commitment to nonviolence sounds straightforward, but it requires clear answers to nontrivial questions. For example, what counts as violence? Is verbal harassment (e.g., shouting at persons wearing furs) a form of violence? (It is not an adequate reply here to point out that the person being harassed has caused more suffering and violence; two wrongs do not make a right.) Is any damage to property a form of violence—or should we make distinctions between forms of property damage (destroying equipment, "monkey wrenching," burning down buildings where animal exploitation occurs)? Are there any circumstances (self defense, defense of another) where violence is justified? Under what circumstances is civil disobedience justified? If those in the movement do not have carefully considered answers to these questions, they are likely to carry out indefensible actions that provide the opposition with a potent weapon of criticism. This is the most fundamental reason that philosophy—specifically ethical analysis—is fundamental to the movement and that simplistic approaches ("marketing compassion") are inadequate and even dangerous.

Many of these questions arise in thinking about the use of civil disobedience. Civil disobedience is an attempt to persuade the community through extralegal means to recognize the injustice of the status quo, and thus is usually performed openly in public. The presence of strong moral motivations and violation of law both tend to excite passions and can thus help promote discussion of an important issue. This form of direct action has become increasingly popular within the animal rights movement, and it is not difficult to see why. To those who see a serious injustice and are committed to bringing about change, results come frustratingly slowly, if at all. The temptation to engage in forms of activism that seem like they will accelerate progress is very strong.

Additionally, there can be little doubt that consideration of what form activism should take is seriously affected by the prospect of reaching many more people through the electronic media. One can

Animal Emancipation member arrested for practicing civil disobedience during the 1990 World Week for Laboratory Animals protest at the University of California at Santa Barbara. *Courtesy Animal Emancipation*

spend weeks on an event that informs a few hundred people of one's message, while a carefully planned activity that receives media coverage in a major urban area can reach hundreds of thousands of people in just a few minutes. But such media coverage—especially television, with its reliance on images—calls for increasingly sensational events to cover, especially as activism on behalf of animals has become more common. Activists who contemplate what form their action should take can hardly fail to notice that a six-hour demonstration with posters and chanting outside a fur salon is a lot less likely to make the six o'clock news than a five-minute sit-in inside that blocks access to the racks and results in arrests. Certainly it is arguable that civil disobedience is justifiable in some cases. The law treats animals as property, and proponents of animal rights have good reason to think that laws allowing animals to be exploited are immoral. But it does not follow from this that any and all civil disobedience in the name of animals is justified. How, then, can we make reasonable decisions about the justifiability of proposed civil disobedience? In what follows, we rely heavily on the useful suggestions made by Robert T. Hall.[3]

Civil disobedience clearly poses a difficult moral problem. Such activity occurs when someone violates a law (or a regulation or policy) for a moral reason. Not all legal violations motivated by moral conscience can be rejected out of hand as immoral, but neither does their origin in conscience automatically assure us that they are morally acceptable. To assess civil disobedience we must weigh competing claims. On the one hand is the claim that valid law and respect for other people has for us; on the other are the particular moral commitments that motivate civil disobedients—for example, the assertion of moral rights or the protection of vital interests of others. In weighing these things, three considerations seem most important in coming to a conclusion that any particular act of disobedience is justified:

(a) the moral reasons favoring disobedience must outweigh the moral considerations in favor of obedience,

(b) the agent must acknowledge and maintain his or her general moral obligation to obey the law and must view his or her disobedience as transcending this prima facie duty (civil disobedience is thus distinguished from rebellion and revolution), and

(c) the agent must acknowledge and maintain his or her general moral obligation to respect the interests of others and must view his or her disobedience as transcending this prima facie duty (civil disobedience is thus distinguished from crime).

That these duties are prima facie has two important implications. First, an action for which one has a prima facie duty is an action one has a valid moral reason to perform, but this reason may not necessarily be conclusive: in some circumstances it may be overridden by competing values. Second, even when a prima facie duty is overridden by other values it still has some moral importance in how we conduct ourselves.

The import of the latter point is that even if one's moral duty to break the law outweighs the duty to obey it, the residual effect of the duty to obey the law ought to have some influence on the way the action is carried out, making it as far as possible compatible with obligations that have been overridden. The civil disobedient recognizes that, though the duties to obey the law and to respect other people's interests may have been overridden in a certain situation, these duties nonetheless exercise some influence over the nature of her action. In most cases the residual influence of the overridden duty is manifested by the act of civil disobedience's possessing such characteristics as (a) exhausting legal remedies prior to undertaking an illegal act; (b) the agent's willing submission to arrest and punishment; (c) the agent's knowledge of the social and legal implications of his or her act; (d) use of the least violent means possible; (e) effective publicity of the morality of the act; and (f) the appropriateness of the action to its own purpose. Sometimes discussions of civil disobedience lay great emphasis on the presence of such conditions as the submission to arrest and punishment, even going so far as to define civil disobedience in such terms. Although the reason for such emphasis is easy to see, it is nonetheless a mistake to think that any of these characteristics is a necessary condition of an act of civil disobedience's being morally acceptable; rather, these are the most typical ways in which agents show their respect for law and other people while violating the law to make their point. It is possible in a given situation that one or more of these characteristics will be omitted and an act still be justified.

Placing oneself between an animal and the barrel of a loaded gun at an event such as the annual Hegins, Pennsylvania, pigeon shoot is a justifiable case of civil disobedience in light of these criteria. For many years activists have tried to stop these brutal events, during which thousands of pigeons are shot for "fun." Activists had come to the shoots and protested, had written to newspapers and petitioned government agencies—all to no avail. They finally decided to take more aggressive steps and physically prevent the shooting. Obviously all legal means to save these animals were exhausted: the action was the only one appropriate, as anything else would allow the animals to be killed. The action was well publicized and used the least violent means possible—endangering only those undertaking the civil disobedience. And the participants clearly submitted themselves for arrest and imprisonment (members of

PETA remained in jail for over a week after the 1991 action at the Hegins shoot).

In contrast, chaining oneself to a rack in a fur salon and demanding that the store stop selling furs is not as clearly justifiable in light of the above criteria; it is unclear that the act is necessary to prevent animal suffering and that other available legal means have been exhausted. The fact that such an act is nonviolent and may be counted on to draw media attention to an issue is not enough to justify it.

The fire that leveled the animal research facility under construction at the University of California at Davis was allegedly set by the Animal Liberation Front. Whoever set the fire clearly violated a number of fundamental principles justifying disobedience. The act was not necessary to save any animal lives; it was not the least violent course of action (it could have killed or seriously injured someone had they been inside the building); it was not clearly appropriate to the ends sought or effective in achieving them; and those who performed the action were not willing to submit themselves to arrest or imprisonment.

The actions of the Animal Liberation Front raise particularly difficult questions, because they have often been quite effective in revealing cases of animal abuse and in removing animals from hopelessly abusive situations. Without the ALF the movement would not have the tapes of the University of Pennsylvania Head Injury Clinic, for example. Furthermore, it seems likely that the threat of ALF raids has been a deterrent to animal research in some cases. On the other hand, the kinds of activities engaged in by the ALF could also undermine progress for the animal rights movement. As we have seen, ALF raids provide a rich source of material for those who wish to discredit the movement by labeling activists as violent terrorists bent on interfering with medical progress. There is a real risk that the more radical tactics of break-ins could turn the public away from the movement, especially when these involve property destruction or threaten individuals. These concerns, of course, apply not solely to ALF raids but also to forms of activism that the public perceives as too radical. As one fur industry representative told us, "We don't have to do anything these days, we're just watching the animal activists undo themselves."

Ultimately, however, the justifiability of ALF raids cannot be determined solely by looking to see whether these raids are effective in advancing the movement. In addition, we must ask whether such raids constitute a morally justifiable response to animal exploitation. What to think of such raids given the civil disobedience criteria we have outlined is more difficult than may at first appear. Perhaps the clearest purpose of these raids is simply to rescue exploited and endangered animals, and as such might profitably be viewed as conscientious resistance to evil rather than an attempt to engage the public's sense of justice through extralegal means. If we take this position then we would not ask whether the acts satisfy the criteria of civil disobedience but whether the evil being addressed is outweighed by the manner of addressing it. It follows from the view that animals are rightsholders whose lives must be respected that laws treating animals as property are fundamentally unjust. Violating such laws in the least violent ways in order to defend the lives of animals is morally permissible, just as the Underground Railroad was a moral response to the unjust laws enslaving blacks. Thus, rescuing an animal who is destined for mutilation in a laboratory is not prima facie wrong. This does not, of course, justify various other actions the ALF has taken credit for, such as the destruction of property and the defacing of buildings.

But ALF raids also seem to be intended as contributions to the debate concerning society's future relations with animals, as part of the attempt to convince people to rethink their views. Why else would ALF raiders sometimes refrain from taking animals (as in the University of Pennsylvania raid) and risk discovery by making contacts with the press to publicize their actions? If so, then it would seem appropriate to consider ALF raids as a form of civil disobedience. While we might immediately point out that they do not clearly satisfy all the criteria—for instance, raiders do not submit to arrest and prosecution—we need to recall that these criteria do not each serve as necessary conditions of an action's justifiability. Such things as the nature of the message conveyed by spokespeople and the limited nature of the action (e.g., refraining from damaging property) may well symbolize the raiders' respect for law and other people in place of these traditional signs.

In the end, moral reservations about the justifiability of such raids may arise primarily for a utilitarian reason: though it is likely that in many cases there were no legal remedies left to save the lives of the rescued animals, that so few can be saved in this way raises the question of whether such raids help advance or interfere with work toward the structural changes needed to ameliorate the situation of such animals. If they can help advance the cause (as we believe the break-in at Gennarelli's lab did), then there is a strong case for them. If the opposition succeeds in controlling the public image of the movement (and characterizes it negatively as "terrorist" and "violent") as a result of such break-ins (whether or not they do involve violence), then such raids seem counterproductive to the advancement of animals' interests.

Some claim that such raids are not only morally permissible but also obligatory. Even given the animal rights position, this claim is questionable. There is no physical possibility of rescuing more than a tiny fraction of the animals currently in laboratories and factory farms in this way, and it is infeasible for most activists to be involved in such activities. Animal rights activism is simply not broadly enough accepted to make widespread liberation feasible. (It required a widespread opposition to slavery throughout the free states and Canada to make the Underground Railroad viable.) Because we cannot be morally obligated to do what it is not physically possible to do, animal rightists cannot be morally obligated to liberate animals. Nonetheless, those who do choose to engage in such activities may well consider themselves to be doing only what morality demands. What is supererogatory may appear to the agent as nothing heroic or saintly at all, but under the guise of duty.

We cite these examples in the hopes not of resolving the issue of the conditions that justify conscientious lawbreaking but of showing the importance of informed discussion of such issues within the movement, prior to action. The moral justifiability of such acts must be the first consideration; their potential for publicity comes as a lesser consideration.

A somewhat different set of issues face animal rights advocates with respect to some of the tactics and rhetoric employed even within legal demonstrations. One concerns the temptation to vilify individuals opposed to the movement. Demonstrations at individuals' houses, posters showing pictures and telephone numbers of researchers who use animals, and the like all manifest this approach. While it is very tempting to paint your opposition (regardless of which side you are on) as evil and lacking in scruples, it is not at all clear that this strategy makes sense given the philosophies of animal rights. After all, animal rights advocates make an institutional critique rather than one based on the cruel character of abusive individuals. Of course, there are cruel actions and cruel individuals, and animal rights advocates can point this out just as anyone else can. But making that the focus of activism can be a distraction from the animal rights message: the changes animal rights advocates call for are structural changes to institutions, and thus it is important not to misconstrue the nature of institutional violence. It is by sanctioning the manipulation of animals for human ends with little or no concern for animal well-being or feeling that institutions enable researchers, farmers, and others to exploit them with a clear conscience. Focusing attention on the individuals rather than the nature of the institutions that enables them to behave as they do may distract from this central issue.

Focusing on individuals may in fact be more than a distraction: it seems to fall right into the hands of those who defend the practices in factory farming, fur ranches, rodeos, and laboratories. After the ALF raid at the University of California at Riverside, an ALF spokesperson stated that the experiments being conducted were cruel. The response was predictable: the university defended the good character of the scientists, pointing out that the agency that accredits laboratories had recently given the university a clean bill of health.[4] The underlying message was that the behavior within the laboratory was well within standards accepted by the community, and that does seem to be an appropriate defense against charges that behavior is aberrant. This is not to say that individuals functioning within a context of institutional violence bear no responsibility for their participation, but only that a clear focus on the real culprit—institutionally sanctioned violence—is crucial.

Beyond the question of the sort of publicity it creates, the tactic of personal attack raises deeper questions about the means to achieving the ends of animal rights. A clear understanding of the extent of animal suffering at the hands of human beings can certainly create anger and even rage, but how should this anger most effectively be channeled? Is it possible to bring about compassion through negative confrontation? A person intimidated into storing her fur coat by the taunts of activists may be turned into an active opponent of animal rights. Even activists' language needs to be considered. Are violent slogans (such as "waging war on vivisection") consistent with the ultimate goals of animal rights?

Tactics: The Arguments

Vivisection is a moral issue: if it were not, humans would be used as experimental subjects.

—Dr. Nedim Buyukmihci

The theme of taking the moral high ground applies not only to actions, but to the arguments used by the movement to promote its ends. One frequently hears the suggestion that sympathy for antivivisectionism or vegetarianism be cast primarily or even solely in terms of human interests—for example, that vivisection leads to bad medicine and eating animals leads to heart disease and cancer. There is nothing wrong with pointing out the human costs of exploiting animals: this is part of an integrated appreciation of the change animal rights philosophies call for. As Jon Wynne-Tyson wisely put it in *Food for a Future* (1975), "Although this book deals with the social, historical, economic, nutritional and health aspects of a more humane eating pattern, it also attempts to examine diet in the context of a philosophy for life that meets the standards of today."[5] But if the proposal is that people will only be convinced by self-interested arguments and that the moral arguments should be neglected or downplayed, the approach is morally flawed.

First, neglecting the moral grounds for animal rights is simply dishonest, since the core of the real issue for proponents is the rights of animals, not the interests of one species (Homo sapiens). Second, it perpetuates speciesism, precisely by placing the debate in terms of human interest, and is thus one-sided. And, third, such an approach fails to respect properly its audience, precisely by assuming that those being addressed (unlike the speaker) have no real interest in morality and are merely self-interested and utterly speciesistic.

Neglecting the moral arguments is also unlikely to produce the desired results. Consider the issue of vivisection. Placing the entire weight of the argument against vivisection on grounds that animal research is not applicable to human health can never lead to the abolition of vivisection. If, for instance, a convincing case could be made that animal research has not led to any improvements in human health (we do not think this case can be made, but we use it for speculation), researchers could still argue for pursuing animal research on the grounds that it is interesting in its own right. In other words, whether or not animal psychology and physiology is applicable to humans, it is interesting to know about animals. Whether or not animal research leads to cures for human diseases, it may well tell us more about animal behavior and physiology and lead to cures for animal diseases. Knowledge is, after all, a fundamental value, and freedom of inquiry is important.

It is only a moral argument, to the effect that the rights of animals constitute a more significant value than the freedom of inquiry of scientists, which can counter such a defense of animal research, just as it is only a moral argument that limits the uses of human research subjects where such uses might actually be quite productive. After all, we do not reject the Nazi experiments on unwilling concentration camp victims as a model for procuring future experimental subjects solely because the Nazi experiments were scientifically unsound.

Furthermore, the history of the antivivisection movement offers a lesson here. The biomedical community was very effective in defeating the arguments of those challenging the scientific validity of animal research during the nineteenth century. Independent of questions about the scientific merits of animal research today, the sheer political power of the biomedical establishment makes it unlikely that arguments for the scientific worthlessness of animal research can succeed. To understand why, it is important to take into account the sociology of scientific institutions. As philosopher and historian of science Thomas Kuhn has pointed out, science is not an institution open to criticisms from outside the community of recognized scientists. The worldviews (or paradigms) within which scientists operate are seldom successfully challenged, unless serious and systematic failure forces scientists into a crisis. Even then, such criticisms must come from within the recognized community of experts, and who counts as an expert is very narrowly circumscribed (Kuhn 1970). Thus, finding medical doctors who disagree with the use of animals in research is not likely to make any impression on the biomedical community, even if it does make an impression on the general public. Many physicians schooled before the new experimental medicine that advances in bacteriology brought in the late nineteenth century could be found to support the antivivisectionist cause, but they carried little influence within the developing science itself, and ultimately they were left behind as relics of an outdated medical education (Turner 1980, 98).

It is very unlikely that the scientific validity of animal research can be successfully challenged by the animal rights movement. While it is important for nonscientists to engage in critical assessment of scientific institutions—for instance, to point out cases of scientific failure and fraud and to promote alternatives—the "vivisection is fraud" campaign is unlikely to succeed. Specific research proposals may be successfully challenged for concrete reasons, but if vivisection is to be rejected as a scientific method on scientific grounds, this will happen in response to crisis from within the halls of science.

But there is a further reason to think that scientific arguments against vivisection will fail. Other animals are in fact very much like us; chimpanzees are remarkably like us, sharing 98 percent of our genes, for example. Similarity is something animal rights proponents are happy to emphasize in other contexts. For example, in John McArdle's famous paradox for the researcher, he asks, "Why do you do research on animals?" The researcher replies, "Because they are like us." Asks McArdle, "How can this be morally justified?" The researcher replies, "Because they are *not* like us."

This paradox is a double-edged sword, however. Our connectedness to animals makes it impossible to claim that animal research will always be misleading and irrelevant to the case of human beings. The question, fundamentally, is not whether vivisection is good or bad science, any more than the question whether to use human prisoners or orphans is good or bad science. The question is whether it is morally justifiable.

In the final analysis, the animal rights movement is a movement for social change based on issues of justice and our moral duties to others. While social utility is not irrelevant in these matters, it is not the central focus in this liberation movement or in others. The reason for desegregating schools, giving women the right to vote, and demanding an end to apartheid is fundamentally that these things are owed to these individuals as a matter of justice. If it could be shown that women are less contented as a result of their liberation, this would not justify taking away their rights. If it could have been shown that elimination of slavery would have resulted in the complete economic collapse of the South, it would still have been necessary to free the slaves. What issues of social utility have to teach us is that we must intelligently and compassionately administer justice; these considerations can never be a ground for overriding the rights of others.

Despite the many analogies that can be made to other social movements and the many lessons activists can learn from them, the animal rights movement is unique: animals cannot join in the struggle for their rights as the subjects of other movements can. Has there ever been a case where one group has altruistically worked for and won liberation for another, entirely helpless group? If this movement succeeds, it will be a remarkable accomplishment against incredible odds. These odds notwithstanding, the animal rights movement has been remarkably successful in mobilizing people to think and care about animals' interests for the first time in their lives. Thousands have become vegetarians or vegans and have changed their personal life-style to reflect their new philosophy. As we have seen, however, the advances the movement seeks are not going to come rapidly, as these imply significant institutional as well as personal change, and there are those with a vested interest in resisting this change. In the outcome of this struggle, future historians may read something not only of the hearts of those who comprise this movement but of humanity's capacity for compassionate change as well.

Notes and References

After first mention, references are hereafter cited in the text.

1. Why Animal Rights?

1. *New York Times*, 24 June 1865.
2. *San Bernardino Sun*, 12 May 1991.
3. David Hume, *An Inquiry Concerning Morals* (1751; Indianapolis: Bobbs-Merrill, 1957).
4. For more detailed and fuller accounts of the problems of factory farming, see Peter Singer, *Animal Liberation*, 2d ed. (New York: Avon Books, 1990), chap. 3, as well as Jim Mason and Peter Singer, *Animal Factories* (New York: Crown Publishers, 1980).
5. *The Animals' Agenda*, December 1989, 16.
6. Stuart Ellins, "A Question of Balance."
7. Daniel S. Moretti, *Animal Rights and the Law* (London: Oceana Press, 1984), 52–55.
8. *The Animals' Voice* 2, no. 6 (1989): 21–22.
9. *The Animals' Agenda*, July–August 1986, 29.
10. PETA (People for the Ethical Treatment of Animals), "Ranch-Raised Fur: Captive Cruelty," in *Facts for Activists*.
11. Office of Technology Assessment, U.S. Congress, *Alternatives to Animal Use in Research, Testing, and Education* (New York: Marcel Dekker, 1988), 43.
12 Andrew Rowan, *Of Mice, Models, and Men: A Critical Evaluation of Animal Research* (Albany: State University of New York Press, 1984), 39.
13. Dallas Pratt, *Alternatives to Pain in Experiments on Animals* (New York: Argus Archives, 1980).
14. Bernard Rollin, *Animal Rights and Human Morality* (Buffalo, N. Y.: Prometheus Books, 1981), 98.

15. In recent years the number of animals used in dissection and classroom experimentation has been decreasing, since the National Science Teachers Association has come out in favor of more ethical and pedagogically effective alternatives. Furthermore, students have gained some rights to refuse dissection, especially at the elementary and high school levels, and young people are asserting these rights more and more frequently.

16. Burlington, N.C., *Times-News*, 23 October 1990.

17. *The Animals' Agenda*, June 1987, 29.

18. Harry F. Harlow, *Learning to Love*, 2d ed. (New York: Aronson, 1974).

19. Singer 1990; Rollin 1981; Rowan 1984; Michael Allen Fox, *The Case for Animal Experimentation* (Berkeley: University of California Press, 1986).

20. Bernard Rollin, *The Unheeded Cry: Animal Consciousness, Pain, and Science* (Oxford: Oxford University Press, 1990).

2. Historical Roots

1. The earliest societies in England and America, such as the RSPCA and the ASPCA, identified themselves as societies for the prevention of cruelty to animals, and so it would be equally appropriate to refer to the humane movement as the "anti-cruelty movement." The term *humane* caught on around the turn of the century and is used here because it is the more commonly used term today.

2. Daniel Dombrowski, *The Philosophy of Vegetarianism* (Amherst: University of Massachusetts Press, 1984).

3. Keith Thomas, *Man and the Natural World* (New York: Pantheon, 1983); Dix Harwood, *Love for Animals and How it Developed in Great Britain* (New York: Columbia University Press, 1928).

4. Jeremy Bentham, *An Introduction to the Principles of Morals and Legislation* (1823; New York: Hafner Publishing, 1948).

5. As James Turner points out, the vegetarians among the humane movement were considered extremists who took logic beyond all practicality. Consider the case of Louis Gompertz, one of the founders and the second honorary secretary of the SPCA in England. Despite his efficient and active service, he was drummed out of the society as less than the ideal leader, for besides the fact that he was probably considered a liability given the prevalence of anti-Semitism (he was a practicing Jew), as a vegetarian he was considered somewhat unbalanced, a fanatic, and Turner clearly shares the opinion. See his *Reckoning with the Beast: Animals, Pain, and Humanity in the Victorian Mind* (Baltimore: Johns Hopkins University Press, 1980), 42.

6. Richard Ryder, *Animal Revolution: Changing Attitudes towards Speciesism* (Oxford: Basil Blackwell, 1989), 96–97.

7. Mohandas Gandhi, *An Autobiography: The Story of My Experiments with Truth*, trans. Mahadev Desai (1927–29; Boston: Beacon Press, 1957), 48.

8. *Who Was Who in America.* Historical Volume 1607–1896, rev. ed. (Chicago: Marquis–Who's Who, 1967), 150.

9. Sidney Coleman, *Humane Society Leaders in America* (Albany, N.Y.: American Humane Association, 1924), 71–75.

10. Roswell C. McCrea, *The Humane Movement: A Descriptive Survey* (New York: Columbia University Press, 1910); William Schultz, *The Humane Movement in the United States, 1910–1922* (New York: Columbia University Press, 1924; rpt., New York: AMS Press, 1968).

11. This variety of youthful cruelties is depicted in the second engraving of William Hogarth's 1751 *Four Stages of Cruelty.* For discussion of Hogarth's engravings in relation to the concepts of cruelty and animal rights, see Lawrence Finsen, "'His heart exposed to prying eyes, to pity has no claim': Reflections on Hogarth and the Nature of Cruelty," *Between the Species* 2 (1986): 12–18.

12. Peter French, *Antivivisection and Medical Science in Victorian Society* (Princeton, N.J.: Princeton University Press, 1975), 20–33.

13. Coral Lansbury, *The Old Brown Dog: Women, Workers, and Vivisection in Edwardian England* (Madison: University of Wisconsin Press, 1985), 10–12.

14. Thomas Kuhn, *The Structure of Scientific Revolutions*, 2d ed. (Chicago: University of Chicago Press, 1970).

15. Even though vaccination predates germ theory: it was used 100 years earlier by Lady Montague, who learned of it in Turkey, and was advanced by Edward Jenner's experiments (on a small boy) showing that one could be immunized against smallpox by using cowpox.

16. John Duffy, *The Sanitarians: A History of Public Health* (Urbana: University of Illinois Press, 1990), 195.

17. Susan Sperling, *Animal Liberators: Research and Morality* (Berkeley: University of California Press, 1988), 54–55.

18. Thomas McKeown, *The Role of Medicine: Dream, Mirage, or Nemesis?* (Princeton, N.J.: Princeton University Press, 1979).

19. Percy Frankland and Mrs. Percy Frankland, *Microorganisms in Water: Their Significance, Identification and Removal, Together with an Account of the Bacteriological Methods Employed in Their Investigation* (London: Longman's Green, 1894), 152–54.

20. William Williams Keen, *Animal Experimentation and Medical Progress* (Boston: Houghton Mifflin, 1914), 247–48

21. The term *cattle* has historically been extended far beyond bovines, to refer more generally to any kind of livestock. The term, interestingly enough, is derived from the same root as is *chattel*, or property, and the term was even used in Harriet Beecher Stowe's *Uncle Tom's Cabin* to refer to slaves (*The Compact Edition of the Oxford English Dictionary* [Oxford: Oxford University Press, 1971]).

22. Emily Stewart Leavitt and Diane Halverson, "The Evolution of Anti-Cruelty Laws in the United States," in *Animals and Their Legal Rights* (Washington, D.C.: Animal Welfare Institute, 1978), 11–12.

23. In fact, Angell employed some rather innovative educational strategies, indicative of the kind of influence that these early humane leaders exerted. He reports that he persuaded the city of Boston to loan him, *at city expense*, 17 uniformed policemen, who went door to door throughout the city canvassing for members for the newly formed MSPCA. They signed up 1,200 of the 1,600 initial members. Later, these policemen delivered a free copy of the first edition of *Our Dumb Animals* to over 30,000 households in the city, and this model was followed in many other towns and cities (George Angell, *Autobiographical Sketches and Personal Reflections* [Boston: American Humane Education Society, 1892], 13–14). See also Coleman 1924; Gerald Carson, *Men, Beasts, and Gods: A History of Cruelty and Kindness to Animals* (New York: Charles Scribner's Sons, 1972).

24. The story of women's involvement in the humane movement brings one rapidly face to face with the sexism of the times. Sidney Coleman reports that women could not sit on the boards of directors of charitable societies, nor could they serve as officers (1924, 177). Caroline White was invited to form a "women's branch" of the Pennsylvania SPCA. As this was a women's organization, she was permitted to serve as president (Coleman 1924, 146). She also founded the American Antivivisection Society (at the urging of Frances Power Cobbe) in 1883, but "considerable difficulty was experienced in finding a gentleman who would act as president" (1924, 205).

25. Such accounts of witnesses of outrageous brutalities being motivated at the time to form societies are legion. The San Francisco SPCA "is said to owe its origin to the squealing of a pig." Apparently, the pig had escaped and was being handled brutally by its captors, bringing the society's founder, J. S. Hutchinson, into the street in response to the squeals (Coleman 1924, 155).

26. Francis Rowley, *The Humane Idea: A Brief History of Man's Attitude toward the Other Animals, and of the Development of the Humane Spirit into Organized Societies* (Boston: American Humane Education Society, 1912), 39–42.

27. This editorial is of interest because it exemplifies that public expressions of concern did exist even prior to formation of the ASPCA and that this concern was not, as is commonly thought, solely directed to pets and work animals but extended at least for some to laboratory and food animals.

28. Saul Benison, Clifford Barger, and Elin Wolfe, *Walter B. Cannon: The Life and Times of a Young Scientist* (Cambridge: Harvard University Press, 1987), 171.

29. William Gary Roberts, "Man before Beast: The Response of Organized Medicine to the American Antivivisection Movement," B.A. thesis, Harvard University, 1979.

30. One important lesson for the current political scene from the example of the early humane leaders' conservatism concerns the implications of linguistic choices. Today the term *animal rights* is fast replacing the earlier phrase *animal welfare*. Old bastions of the humane movement, such as the ASPCA, have adopted the new terminology (in the ASPCA's case, even producing a presumably definitive guidebook to animal rights). But while the terminological change may represent the recognition that the deeper challenges of the animal rights movement are gaining serious attention in the public consciousness, the real test of whether one holds an animal rights position lies elsewhere than in the choice of terminology. Earlier in the century, for example, Francis Rowley used the term in a number of places: "We wait till the time of the revival of learning before we begin again to hear, save here and there, any voice that clearly intimates that animals have rights that man is bound to respect" (1912, 27). We always have to ask what is meant by a commitment to rights—whether in speaking of animals' rights we are assuming a priority of human interests and thus rights that only affect the manner of usage, or rights that might limit the very fact of usage.

31. Emily Stewart Leavitt, "Humane Slaughter Laws," in *Animals and Their Legal Rights* (Washington, D.C.: Animal Welfare Institute, 1978), 36–45.

32. David Macauley, "Political Animals: A Study of the Emerging Animal Rights Movement in the United States," *Between the Species* 4 (1987–88): 55–68.

33. John Robbins, *Diet for a New America* (Walpole, N.H.: Stillpoint Publishing, 1987), 170–220.

34. See Philip Windeatt, *The Hunt and Anti-hunt* (London: Pluto Press, 1982).

35. Helen Jones, "Autobiographical Notes," *Between the Species* 4, no. 1 (1988): 71–74.

36. Cole Phinizy, "The Lost Pets That Stray to the Labs," *Sports Illustrated*, 29 November 1965, 38; Rowan 1984, 56.

37. The latest additions to the act (1985) have called for such changes as on-site committees to review proposed research, on the model of the institutional review boards that are mandated to review research with human subjects (L. Finsen, "Institutional Animal Care and Use Committees: A New Set of Clothes for the Emperor?" *Journal of Medicine and Philosophy* 13 [1988]: 145–58). The most recent controversy involved an attempt by the USDA to promulgate a set of rules to administer the Laboratory Animal Welfare Act that many in the animal rights movement saw as an attempt to gut what little force the act had by allowing local research institutions to set their own standards for care of animals.

38. Henry Spira, "Fighting to Win," in *In Defense of Animals*, ed. Peter Singer (New York: Harper & Row, 1985), 199.

39. As Richard Ryder has pointed out, this action provides an excellent

model for cooperation among animal organizations: Greenpeace generated the headline publicity, IFAW had mobilized its supporters to bombard the prime minister with letters, and the RSPCA negotiated with the government directly.

40. Alex Pacheco, "The Choice of a Lifetime," *Between the Species* 6, no. 1 (1990): 36–39.

41. *The Animals' Agenda*, July–August 1984, 8.

42. *The Animals' Agenda*, May 1985, 1, 8–11.

43. *The Animals' Agenda*, September 1985, 10.

3. Organizations, Tactics, and Politics

1. Interview with Alex Hershaft, June 1990.

2. Ingrid Newkirk, "One Person's Efforts," *Between the Species* 1 (1985): 45–47.

3. *Animal Rights Reporter*, March 1989, 12.

4. *Animal Rights Reporter*, November 1988, 4.

5. Dana Forbes, "Where Animals Come First: Black Beauty Ranch," *The Animals' Agenda*, September 1989, 26.

6. Cleveland Amory, *The Cat and the Curmudgeon* (Boston: Little, Brown & Co., 1990), 222.

7. Christopher Anderson, "Court Favours Mice, Rats, Birds," *Nature* 355 (16 January 1992): 191.

8. Los Angeles *Daily News*, 9 November 1985.

9. *The Animals' Agenda*, June 1991, 37.

10. *Against All Odds: Animal Liberation, 1972–1986* (London: Arc Print, 1986), 9.

11. *PETA News*, November–December 1989, 17.

12. Cole McFarland, "Portrait of a 'Terrorist,'" *The Animals' Voice* 3, no. 1 (1990): 41.

13. Los Angeles *Daily News*, 9 November 1985.

14. *The Animals' Voice* 3, no. 1 (1990): 11.

15. Ingrid Newkirk, *Free the Animals!* (Chicago: Noble Press, 1992), 336.

16. *Philadelphia Daily News*, 15 January 1990, 3.

17. *Philadelphia City Paper,* 19 January 1990.

18. For example, James M. Jasper and Dorothy Nelkin, *The Animal Rights Crusade: The Growth of a Moral Protest* (New York: The Free Press, 1992).

4. Issues and Campaigns of the 1980s

1. Dena Jones-Jolma, "The Fight to Reform Trapping in Arizona," *The Animals' Agenda*, March–April 1993, 23.

2. *New York Times*, 19 November 1989.
3. Merritt Clifton, "Knocking Fur to the canvas," *The Animals' Agenda*, November 1990, 32.
4. Victoria Moran, "When the Fur Wearer Isn't the Fur Bearer," *The Animals' Agenda*, September 1989, 50–51.
5. *New York Times*, 2 April 1988.
6. *Wall Street Journal*, 3 January 1991.
7. *Newsweek*, 18 December 1989.
8. *U.S. News & World Report*, 1989.
9. *New York Times*, 26 February 1991.
10. *Savvy Woman*, February 1989, 15–16; *Successful Farming*, February 1989, 15.
11. *The Animals' Voice* 2, no. 1 (1989): 22.
12. *The Animals' Voice* 4, no. 2 (1991): 58.
13. *New Scientist*, 4 August 1990, 64.
14. Summit for the Animals, comp., *Declaration of the Rights of Animals: Adopted and Proclaimed at the March for the Animals, the Tenth Day of June, 1990, in Washington, D.C.*, 1990.
15. *The Animals' Voice* 3, no. 5 (1990): 13.
16. Mary Ann Violin, "Mobilization for Animals: Pushing at the Boundaries of the Possible," *The Animals' Agenda*, September–October 1982, 1, 8–11.
17. Bernard Unti, "Using Animals in the Classroom," *The Animals' Agenda*, July–August 1986, 10.
18. Bill DeRosa, "Moving Forward Against Dissection," *The Animals' Agenda*, September–October 1988, 42.
19. *Sacramento Bee*, 4 April 1989.
20. Carol Grunewald, "Are Companies Doing Enough to Stop Toxicity Testing on Animals?" *The Animals' Agenda*, September 1986, 17–18.
21. *The Animals' Agenda*, March 1988, 31.
22. *The Animals' Agenda*, April 1987, 25.
23. *The Animals' Agenda*, January–February 1989, 30.
24. *The Animals' Agenda*, July–August 1987, 8.
25. *The Animals' Agenda*, March 1990, 41.
26. *The Animals' Agenda*, October 1989, 40–42.
27. *Journal of the American Veterinary Medical Association*, December 1968.
28. Michael Giannelli, "The Decline and Fall of Pound Seizure," *The Animals' Agenda*, July–August 1986, 13.
29. John McArdle, "Lies by the Pound," *The Animals' Agenda*, October 1986, 34.
30. *The Animals' Agenda*, January–February 1989, 28.
31. *The Animals' Agenda*, January–February 1989, July–August 1990, October 1990, December 1990.

32. Edward Duvin, "Getting Out of the Killing Business," *The Animals' Voice* 5, no. 2 (1992): 19.

33. Marcia King, "Throwaway Animals," *The Animals' Agenda*, 11 May 1991, 12–20.

5. *The Opposition*

1. Patricia Hausman, *Jack Sprat's Legacy: The Science and Politics of Fat and Cholesterol* (New York: Richard Mauk Publishers, 1981), 28.

2. P. Imperato and G. Mitchell, *Acceptable Risks* (New York: Viking, 1985), 9–24.

3. *Lancet* 2 (1959): 56.

4. Ron Baker, *The American Hunting Myth* (New York: Vantage Press, 1985), 34–35.

5. Ralph Lutts, *The Nature Fakers: Wildlife Science and Sentiment* (Golden, Colo.: Fulcrum, 1990), 21.

6. Luke Dommer, "Who Pays the Tab for Wildlife Conservation?" *The Animals' Voice* 4, no. 1 (1991): 47.

7. Wayne Pacelle, "Wildlife Mismanagement," *The Animals' Agenda*, September 1991, 14–15.

8. National Rifle Association, "NRA Member Guide: NRA Positions on Hunting," *American Hunter*, March 1991, 12.

9. Wayne Pacelle, "Saviours or Sellouts?" *The Animals' Agenda*, July–August 1988, 8.

10. "The 'Animal Rights' War on Medicine, *Reader's Digest*, June 1990, 73.

11 *Scientific American*, June 1990, 18.

12. Lizanne S. Hughes, "Portraits of a Partnership for Life: The Remarkable Story of Research, Animals, and Man" (Ciba-Geigy Pharmaceuticals, 1991), 12.

13. Phil Maggitti, "The Opposition in Motion," *The Animals' Agenda*, June 1990, 17.

14. *New York Times*, 5 October 1990.

15. *Los Angeles Times*, 9 February 1991.

16. Eric Fleck, "The Great Veal Controversy: Activists Need the Facts," *Nation's Restaurant News*, 11 February 1989, F9.

17. Patrice Greanville, "Furrier Voices," *The Animals' Agenda*, December 1987, 35.

18. *The Animals' Voice* 2, no. 6 (1989): 32.

19. *Congressional Quarterly*, 21 July 1990, 2301.

20. Gary Francione, "Hunting Hunters," *The Animals' Voice* 2, no. 6 (1989): 48.

21. *Los Angeles Times*, 8 August 1990; PETA News, November 1990.

22. *The Animals' Voice* 6, no. 1 (1993): 45.

23. Tom Regan, "Misplaced Trust," *The Animals' Voice* 3, no. 1 (1990): 23.

24. Crescenzo Vellucci, "The Enemies Within," *The Animals' Voice* 4, no. 2 (1991): 49.

25. *The Animals' Voice* 3, no. 4 (1990): 56.

26. *The Animals' Voice* 4, no. 2 (1991): 52.

27. *Los Angeles Times*, 10 May 1993.

6. Philosophies of Animal Rights

1. Singer writes in *Animal Liberation* that while studying at Oxford he met Richard Keshen, another graduate student and a vegetarian. Keshen introduced him to other vegetarians, including Stanley and Rosalind Godlovitch. Rosalind was a particularly important influence, as she had "worked out her ethical position in considerable detail." Singer's first article about animal issues was a review of a book the Godlovitches had edited (along with John Harris), *Animals, Men, and Morals*.

2. Donald Griffin, *Animal Thinking* (Cambridge: Harvard University Pres, 1984).

3. Act utilitarianism is contrasted with "rule utilitarianism," which maintains that we should evaluate the utility of general rules of conduct rather than directly evaluate specific actions. According to rule utilitarians, in some cases it would produce better consequences overall to follow a rule (e.g., not to kill except in certain clearly defined kinds of cases, such as self-defense) even when following it in some situations would not lead to the alternative that produces the highest degree of utility.

4. Some authors maintain that Singer's important contribution is precisely in the area other than his utilitarianism. See Helmut Kaplan, *Philosophie Des Vegetarismus: Kritische Würdigung und Weiterführung von Peter Singers Ansatz* (The Philosophy of Vegetarianism: Critical Assessment and Continuation of Peter Singer's Beginning) (Frankfurt am Main: Peter Lang, 1988).

5. *Los Angeles Times*, 19 August 1988.

6. Critics of hunting have pointed out that such justifications are often based on erroneous data, and in fact, habitat and species preservation are not best accomplished by allowing hunting. See Baker 1985; and Robert Loftin, "The Morality of Hunting," *Environmental Ethics* 6 (1984): 246–49.

7. Michael Lockwood, "Singer on Killing and Preference for Life," *Inquiry* 22 (Summer 1979): 157–70.

8. Kai Nielsen, "Against Moral Conservatism," *Ethics* 82 (April 1972): 117.

9. Tom Regan and Peter Singer, "The Dog in the Lifeboat: An Exchange," *New York Review of Books*, 25 April 1985, 56–57.

10. R. G. Frey, *Rights, Killing, and Suffering* (Oxford: Basil Blackwell, 1983), 197–203.

11. Tom Regan, *The Case for Animal Rights* (Berkeley: University of California Press, 1983), 26.

12. Susan Finsen, "Sinking the Research Lifeboat," *Journal of Medicine and Philosophy* 13 (1988).

13. Kantianism offers a moral perspective emphasizing acting according to principles founded in reason rather than evaluating the value of consequences (as does utilitarianism). For Kant, the most basic moral principle is called the categorical imperative, which (in at least one formulation) states that we should act so as to treat all rational beings as ends in themselves and not as mere means to our own ends. See Immanuel Kant, *Grounding of the Metaphysics of Morals*, trans. James Ellington (Indianapolis: Hacket Publishing Co., 1981).

14. This conclusion also accords with the one we drew with regard to application of Regan's worse-off principle. There, we concluded that because the worse-off principle was intended to apply to extraordinary situations, it could not be applied to an institution such as animal research.

15. S. F. Sapontzis, *Morals, Reason, and Animals* (Philadelphia: Temple University Press, 1987), 77.

16. Rollin is not suggesting that we bridge the "is-ought" gap in this case. His argument for the relevance of science does not mean that what rights anyone has—human or otherwise—can be considered to be a scientific question pure and simple but rather a question with a scientific component.

17. Charles Darwin, *Origin of Species* (New York: P. F. Collier & Sons, 1859), 88.

18. James Rachels, "Darwin, Species, and Morality," *The Monist* 70 (1987): 106.

19. While there are many religious alternatives to Darwinian evolutionary theory of the origins of species, we discuss the Christian perspective here on the assumption that it is the most common alternative readers will be likely to hold.

20. Andrew Linzey, *Christianity and the Rights of Animals* (London: SPCA, 1987), 23.

21. Mary Midgley, *Animals and Why They Matter* (Athens: University of Georgia Press, 1983), 9.

7. Environmentalism, Ecofeminism, and Animal Liberation

1. PETA and Trans-Species Unlimited carry this message, and John Robbins's EarthSave is devoted to both environmental and animal issues. Michael W. Fox of HSUS has long expressed concerns for the environment as well as animals, and this appears to be the current direction of HSUS. *The Animals' Agenda* acquired the subtitle "International Magazine of Animal

Rights and Ecology" in the late 1980s, and as of the early 1990s this had changed to "Helping Animals and the Earth," in each case as a result of editorial staff changes.

2. J. Baird Callicott, "Animal Liberation: A Triangular Affair," *Environmental Ethics* 2 (1980): 311–38; Tom Regan, "The Nature and Possibility of an Environmental Ethic," in *All That Dwell Therein* (Berkeley: University of California Press, 1982), 184–205.

3. J. Baird Callicott, "The Search for an Environmental Ethic," in *Matters of Life and Death*, ed. Tom Regan (New York: Random House, 1986), 401.

4. But see S. F. Sapontzis in *Morals, Reason, and Animals*, chap. 14, for a dissenting voice.

5. Paul Shephard, *The Tender Carnivore and the Sacred Game* (New York: Scribners, 1973).

6. Farley Mowat, *Never Cry Wolf* (Boston: Little, Brown & Co., 1963).

7. *The Animals' Agenda*, December 1988, 9; December 1989, 17.

8. In the nineteenth century women could not serve as officers of organizations. Today, there are numerous women in top positions in animal rights organizations, though casual observation suggests that men may still fill more positions at the top than is representative of their numbers within the ranks of activists.

9. Josephine Donovan, "Animal Rights and Feminist Theory," *Signs* 15 (1990): 359.

10. See Carol Adams, *The Sexual Politics of Meat: A Feminist Vegetarian Critical Theory* (New York: Continuum, 1990); Susan Griffin, *Woman and Nature: The Roaring Inside Her* (New York: Harper & Row, 1978); Carolyn Merchant, *The Death of Nature: Women Ecology and the Scientific Revolution* (San Francisco: Harper & Row, 1980); and Marti Kheel, "The Liberation of Nature: A Circular Affair," *Environmental Ethics* 7 (1985): 135–50.

11. Keith Thomas, *Man and the Natural World* (New York: Pantheon, 1983), 44.

12. Marjorie Spiegel, *The Dreaded Comparison: Human and Animal Slavery*, 2d ed. (New York: Mirror Books, 1988), 18, 66, 72.

13. Karen J. Warren, "The Power and the Promise of Ecological Feminism," *Environmental Ethics* 12 (Summer 1990): 125–46.

14. George Bradford, *How Deep Is Deep Ecology?* (Ojai, Calif.: Times Change Press, 1989).

15. Carol Gilligan, *In a Different Voice: Psychological Theory and Women's Development* (Cambridge: Harvard University Press, 1982), 100.

16. Nel Noddings, *Caring: A Feminist Approach to Ethics and Moral Education* (Berkeley: University of California Press, 1984).

17. There are important exceptions to the deemphasis of empathy within the work of animal liberationist philosophies, including the work of Michael W. Fox (*Returning to Eden* and *One Earth, One Mind*) and S. F. Sapontzis (*Morals, Reason, and Animals*).

8. Whither Animal Rights?

1. Tom Regan and Gary Francione, "A Movement's Means Create Its Ends," *The Animals' Agenda*, January–February 1992, 40–43.

2. Lawrence Finsen, "Institutional Animal Care and Use Committees: A New Set of Clothes for the Emperor?" *Journal of Medicine and Philosophy* 13 (1988), 145–58.

3. Robert T. Hall, *The Morality of Civil Disobedience* (New York: Harper & Row, 1971).

4. *Los Angeles Times*, 24 April 1985.

5. Jon Wynne-Tyson, *Food for a Future: The Complete Case for Vegetarianism* (New York: Universe Books, 1975), preface.

Selected Bibliography

Adams, Carol J. *The Sexual Politics of Meat: A Feminist Vegetarian Critical Theory.* New York: Continuum, 1990. A fascinating historical and current analysis of the relationship between feminism and meat eating; maintains that the images and attitudes toward women and animals are importantly related. Argues that meat eaters unconsciously uphold a sexist and patriarchal culture. Places the work of major figures in the feminist canon within a tradition of challenging the sexual politics of meat.

Baker, Ron. *The American Hunting Myth.* New York: Vantage Press, 1985. Details how the hunter-dominated state and federal wildlife agencies are systematically destroying America's wildlife and natural lands. Explodes the myth that hunters are responsible for subsidizing parks and wilderness by showing that taxpayers are instead footing the bill for the special interests of hunters. A well-researched and revealing document.

Donovan, Josephine. "Animal Rights and Feminist Theory." *Signs* 15 (1990): 350–75. Excellent discussion of the intersection between feminist theory and animal rights and how animal rights theorists can benefit from an infusion of feminist theory.

Fox, Michael Allen. *The Case for Animal Experimentation.* Berkeley: University of California Press, 1986. A moderate defense of some animal research; an interesting document not only because it gives many of the arguments most often presented by researchers but also because its author renounced it shortly after it was published. Intended originally to be a definitive, empirically informed, and philosophically sophisticated defense of animal research, it presents much interesting material, detailed descriptions of research, and interviews with researchers, but does not quite manage to make its case. (To date, the only extended philosophical defense of animal research.)

Griffin, Donald R. *Animal Thinking.* Cambridge: Harvard University Press, 1984. Argues that animals think; provides evidence from ecology, neurology, and philosophy to support this contention and details the nature of animal consciousness. An informative and fascinating work.

Lansbury, Coral. *The Old Brown Dog: Women, Workers, and Vivisection in Edwardian England*. Madison: University of Wisconsin Press, 1985. Engrossing study of a historical episode and what it reveals about the relations between the antivivisection movement, the woman suffrage movement, and the trade union movement in Edwardian England; analyzes the social consciousness of the time vis-à-vis Victorian pornography and its use of cruelty and animal fantasies.

Linzey, Andrew. *Christianity and the Rights of Animals*. London: SPCA, 1987. Very useful for anyone who wants to look seriously into the relationship between Christianity and animal rights; makes a strong case for the rights of animals from within a biblical perspective and argues that the often repeated claims that Christianity justifies dominion over animals are mistaken.

Mason, Jim, and Peter Singer. *Animal Factories*. New York: Crown Publishers, 1980. Provides a detailed account of the conditions under which laying hens, broiler hens, pigs, cows, and veal calves are kept; the illnesses generated by these conditions; and the solutions, in the form of drugs and mutilations, provided by the industry. The environmental hazards created by factory-farm waste and the economic forces driving the industry (and driving small farmers out of the business) are also treated.

Merchant, Carolyn. *The Death of Nature: Women, Ecology, and the Scientific Revolution*. San Francisco: Harper & Row, 1980. Details how the scientific revolution of the sixteenth and seventeenth centuries displaced a world view based on cooperation between humans and nature and established a mechanistic view of nature sanctioning exploitation; gives a historical perspective to the roots of current attitudes toward both animals and nature and their exploitation in the name of science.

Midgley, Mary. *Animals and Why They Matter*. Athens: University of Georgia Press, 1983. A nontechnical narrative exploring how social-contract thinking from Hobbes on has shaped our moral and political ideas and the problems this has raised for those who are not "proper" contractors, such as women, animals, and aliens. Provides a critical assessment of the attempt to extend conventional moral categories such as rights to animals.

Rachels, James. *Created from Animals: The Moral Implications of Darwinism*. Oxford University Press, 1990. Argues that Darwin's revolution has powerful implications for our moral outlook and our view of ourselves in relation to animals. A careful historical treatment of Darwin's remarks on religion and morality, together with an insightful philosophical analysis of the interrelations among the scientific and moral perspective, make this an important historical and philosophical contribution. Concludes with a fresh, simple, and novel approach to the moral status question. Accessible and clear yet philosophically groundbreaking.

Regan, Tom. *The Case for Animal Rights.* Berkeley: University of California Press, 1983. A rigorous and thorough defense of the rights of animals; essential reading for anyone serious about the philosophical foundations of the notion of animal rights. The first part takes an extended look at the nature of animal minds, bringing the reader from an extended critique of Cartesian views denying animal consciousness to contemporary scientific perspectives detailing the complexity of animal awareness. The second half develops a theory of the value of animal lives, along with a defense of the rights of animals, detailed principles and carefully worked out applications of the theory to issues of vegetarianism, vivisection, hunting, and so forth.

_____. *The Struggle for Animal Rights.* Clarks Summit, Pa.: International Society for Animal Rights, 1987. In part an autobiography; also contains discussions of some important and sometimes neglected issues, such as the role of culture in the struggle for animals rights, the challenge of religion, and civil disobedience. Students' rights to refuse dissection, sealing, animal research, and pound seizure are further issues taken up in this accessible book on the movement as seen from the inside.

Regan, Tom, and Peter Singer. *Animal Rights and Human Obligations.* 2d ed. Englewood Cliffs, N.J.: Prentice-Hall, 1989. Provides a good overview of historical and contemporary writings for and against the idea of animal rights. Contains brief historical pieces by Aristotle, Descartes, Kant, Bentham, Darwin, Schweitzer, and others, as well as useful essays on the nature of animals. Concise defenses of animal rights by Regan and Rachels, and religious perspectives on animals by Andrew Linzey. Contains one of the rare defenses of factory farming and a good section on animals in science.

Robbins, John. *Diet for a New America.* Walpole, N.H.: Stillpoint Publishing, 1987. Brings together in one place the impact of meat eating on human health, animal suffering, the environment, and world hunger. Not only powerfully written but chock full of detailed information and good references to the literature in all these areas. Very likely this book has convinced more people to become vegetarians in recent years than any other single work other than Singer's *Animal Liberation.*

Rollin, Bernard. *Animal Rights and Human Morality.* Buffalo, N.Y.: Prometheus Books, 1981. A straightforward overview of several philosophical approaches, their implications, and their inconsistencies over the issue of the moral status of animals. Defends the view that animals have interests and that these interests must be given moral consideration, and then details some of the moral issues. Particularly good discussion of the complexity of animal research. A good introduction to the issues.

_____. *The Unheeded Cry: Animal Consciousness, Pain, and Science*. Oxford: Oxford University Press, 1990. Scientists have, until quite recently, denied the common-sense obvservation that animals feel pain and suffer. The history of this denial, its adverse effects on science, and the extensive evidence for the commonsensical view are the focus of this book, written so that nonscientists can clearly understand it, while scientists can benefit from its analysis.

Rowan, Andrew. *Of Mice, Models, and Men: A Critical Evaluation of Animal Research*. Albany: State University of New York Press, 1984. Somewhat dated, this book is an evenhanded summation of the various sorts of animal research and the history of controversy surrounding them. An excellent overview of the history of the pound seizure battle and data on many topics by a biochemist who has worked within the humane movement.

Ruesch, Hans. *Slaughter of the Innocent*. Bantam Books, 1978. Something of a classic in the movement. An impassioned attack on vivisection, relentlessly describes the agonies endured by animals in research and charges vivisectors with scientific fraud, malice, and madness. Many in the movement take this to be the ultimate hidden truth about animal reseach. The depictions of animal suffering are haunting, but the analysis of the motives and mindset of scientists is fairly incredible and surely not an accurate depiction of the majority of those involved in animal research.

Ryder, Richard. *Animal Revolution: Changing Attitudes towards Speciesism*. Oxford: Basil Blackwell, 1989. A good historical overview of the British animal rights movement, both in the nineteenth century and the twentieth, written by an important and knowledgeable participant in that movement's recent history.

Sapontzis, S. F. *Morals, Reason, and Animals*. Philadelphia: Temple University Press, 1987. This excellent, well-reasoned, and clear book deserves serious attention. Rather than arguing from a particular theoretical perspective, Sapontzis offers arguments for animal rights on the basis of consistent extensions of current accepted moral views. The moral (in)significance of reason and rationality and the role of reason for moral agents are insightfully discussed. Offers some of the clearest and best discussions anywhere of vexing objections to animal rights—for example, the issue of animal predation.

Singer, Peter. *Animal Liberation*. 2d ed. New York: Avon Books, 1990. One of the definitive books of the movement, presenting up-to-date and detailed descriptions of the institutions of animal exploitation and the suffering they cause and a clear statement of the utilitarian approach to animal liberation. Insightful comments about the state of the movement and its recent history are also included in this new edition. For many, the "bible" of the movement.

_____, ed. *In Defense of Animals*. New York: Harper & Row, 1985. In this short anthology Singer has brought together articles by philosophers, biologists, activists, and lobbyists for animal rights. A good place to read firsthand accounts of the stories that have become important landmarks of the movement, such as the Silver Spring monkeys and the campaigns against the Draize and LD50. Short and clear overview of Regan's philosophy (by Regan) and the issues of animal research, zoos, and factory farming. An excellent brief introduction to the movement and its issues.

Spiegel, Marjorie. *The Dreaded Comparison: Human and Animal Slavery.* New York: Mirror Books, 1988. Powerfully illustrates the similarities between the enslavement of blacks and the enslavement of animals. With a preface by Alice Walker, graphic photographs and illustrations, and revealing historical quotations and dynamic prose, this book is deeply disturbing. As Walker says, the book can be read in an hour but will take a lifetime to forget.

Thomas, Keith. *Man and the Natural World.* New York: Pantheon, 1983. Useful source for those who want to pursue the scholar's interest in the history of ideas (primarily English). Details the growth of humane sensibility and the idea of nature and our place in relation to it.

Vyvyan, John. *In Pity and in Anger: A Study of the Use of Animals in Science.* 1969. Marblehead, Mass.: Micah Publications, 1988. Both a fascinating history and an indictment of vivisection; portrays nineteenth-century vivisectors such as Claude Bernard and these vivisectors' opponents, such as Frances Power Cobbe and Anna Kingsford.

Index

301

The Authors

Susan Mills Finsen is associate professor of philosophy and chair of the Philosophy Department at California State University, San Bernardino. She has long been active in the animal rights movement and has published articles on animal rights for the *Journal of Medicine and Philosophy, Between the Species*, and Westview Press. She has also published articles on the philosophy of biology in *Philosophy of Science*. She received her Ph.D. in history and philosophy of science from Indiana University (1982).

Lawrence Finsen is professor of philosophy at the University of Redlands in California. For 1993 to 1994 he is serving in Tokyo as resident director of the California Private Universities and Colleges Exchange Program at Waseda University. His long involvement with animal rights has included arranging conferences of philosophers to discuss animal rights issues as well as participation in symposia on these topics. He has published articles and reviews on animal rights in *Between the Species*, the *Journal of Medicine and Philosophy*, and the *Los Angeles Times*. He received his Ph.D. in philosophy from the State University of New York at Buffalo in 1982.

The Finsens are co-founders of a regional grass-roots animal rights group, Californians for the Ethical Treatment of Animals. They live in Redlands, California, with their daughter, Thalia, and various other creatures.